BEN JONSON AND THE POLITICS
OF GENRE

While Ben Jonson's political visions have been well documented, this is the first study to consider how he threaded his views into the various literary genres in which he wrote. For Jonson, these genres were interactive and mutually affirming, necessary for negotiating the tempestuous politics of early modern society, and here some of the most renowned Jonson scholars provide a collection of essays that discuss his use of genre. They present new perspectives on many of Jonson's major works, from his epigrams and epistles through to his Roman tragedies and satirical plays like *Volpone*. Other topics examined include Jonson's diverse representations of monarchy, his ambiguous celebrations of European commonwealths, his sexual politics, and his engagement with the issues of republicanism. These essays represent the forefront of critical thinking on Ben Jonson, and offer a timely reassessment of the author's political life in Jacobean and Caroline Britain.

A. D. COUSINS is Professor of English at Macquarie University.

ALISON V. SCOTT is Lecturer in Literature at the University of Queensland.

BEN JONSON AND THE POLITICS OF GENRE

EDITED BY

A. D. COUSINS AND ALISON V. SCOTT

CAMBRIDGE
UNIVERSITY PRESS

CAMBRIDGE UNIVERSITY PRESS

Cambridge, New York, Melbourne, Madrid, Cape Town, Singapore, São Paulo, Delhi

CAMBRIDGE UNIVERSITY PRESS
The Edinburgh Building, Cambridge CB2 8RU, UK

Published in the United States of America by Cambridge University Press, New York

www.cambridge.org
Information on this title: www.cambridge.org/9780521513784

First published 2009

Printed in the United Kingdom at the University Press, Cambridge

A catalogue record for this publication is available from the British Library

ISBN 978-0-521-51378-4 hardback

for David and Matthew & for Valerie, Malcolm, and Andrew

Contents

Notes on contributors

TOM CAIN is Professor of Early Modern Literature at Newcastle University. He has edited Jonson's *Poetaster* for the Revels Plays, and has just finished an edition of *Sejanus* for the forthcoming Cambridge edition of *The Works of Ben Jonson*. He is currently working on a major new edition of the poems of Robert Herrick, funded by the Arts and Humanities Research Council, due to be published by Oxford University Press in 2010.

A. D. COUSINS is Professor of English at Macquarie University. His books include *Donne and the Resources of Kind* (2002) and *Shakespeare's Sonnets and Narrative Poems* (2000). He is co-editor of the forthcoming *Cambridge Companion to the Sonnet* and the author of many essays on early modern British literature and culture.

RICHARD DUTTON is Humanities Distinguished Professor of English at Ohio State University. He has published widely on early modern drama, with particular emphasis on censorship, authorship, and the works of Ben Jonson. He has also edited a number of dramatic texts, including a volume of Jacobean pageants, four plays by Middleton, and Jonson's *Epicene*. His piece in this volume largely grows out of work done while editing *Volpone* for the Cambridge Ben Jonson. He has recently been awarded a fellowship by the National Endowment for the Humanities to work on the revision of Shakespeare's plays for performance at the courts of Elizabeth I and James I and the impact of this on their surviving texts.

ROBERT C. EVANS is Professor of English at Auburn University Montgomery. He is the author of several books (and various essays) on Jonson. His current research interests include Renaissance women authors, pluralist literary theory, and modern American fiction.

EUGENE D. HILL is Professor of English at Mt Holyoke College. He has written *Edward, Lord Herbert of Cherbury* (1987) and numerous articles on Elizabethan tragedy. He is also co-editor of the *Garland Encyclopedia of Tudor England*.

MAREA MITCHELL is Associate Professor of English at Macquarie University (Australia). She has published on medieval and early modern studies, including *The Book of Margery Kempe*, Donne, Shakespeare, Weamys, Wroth, and romance, and is currently working on rewritings of Sidney's *Arcadia*.

JOHN ROE is Reader in English and related literature at the University of York (UK). His main literary interests are Shakespeare and Elizabethan poetry as well as Renaissance Italian literature. He has edited *Shakespeare: The Poems* (1992; revised and updated 2006) and has published *Shakespeare and Machiavelli* (2002). He is currently working on a short monograph on *Romeo and Juliet*.

ALISON V. SCOTT is Lecturer in Literature at the University of Queensland (Australia). She is the author of *Selfish Gifts: Gift Exchange and English Courtly Literature, 1580–1628* (2006) and articles relating to early modern literature and court culture. She is currently completing a monograph on *Languages of Luxury* in early modern England.

Acknowledgements

We would like to thank the following people for the many ways in which they have helped with the preparation of this book: Michael Ackland, Helen and Neil Cadzow, Jim and Maureen Cahillane, Mauro Di Nicola, Heather Dubrow, Arthur F. Kinney, Geoff and Penny Hiller, Manfred and Janet Mackenzie, and Dani and Tony Napton.

The emblem on the front cover of this book has been reproduced from George Wither's *Collection of Emblemes Ancient and Moderne* (1635) with the generous permission of the Huntington Library. We would also like to acknowledge the Department of English at Macquarie University for its financial support and Dr Geoff Payne for compiling the bibliography. Finally, our thanks to Stephen Tabor at the Huntington Library and Ambrose Chong at Macquarie University for kindly assisting us as we prepared this book for publication.

Introduction

A. D. Cousins and Alison V. Scott

There have been many discussions of Jonson's political vision – or visions – but this is the first book-length study of how Jonson deployed 'the resources of kind' in order to shape his political fictions. As with the counterpart to this volume, *Donne and the Resources of Kind*, our starting point is Bakhtin's insistence that each genre offers a window on the world: that each of the kinds makes available a perspective on the world, one which is inherited and variously renewed (or sometimes, of course, inherited but not renewed).[1] The questions arising from such a consideration necessarily include these. If genres each offer a perspective – which is to say, in effect, a confluence of perspectives – on the world, how does any given writer use what they make available? How are those perspectives enlarged or diminished, redirected or subverted, violated or endorsed? In this case, then, how does Jonson use genre to offer representations of the political – to refigure what he perceived as the political actualities of early Stuart society? Thus, correlatively, to what extent does he involve his readers in the remembering and remaking of genre, thereby drawing them into recognition of and putative acquiescence with his renderings of political concepts and relations?

Engaging with the Jonson canon by way of those and other such questions, this book at once complements current scholarship and reinterprets major Jonsonian texts. It offers a widely ranging overview of the Jonson canon but does not lay claim to completeness – a task that would necessitate a very much larger volume. Recent commentary on Jonson's works has tended to focus upon the politics of possessive authorship, addressing in particular questions of textual materiality and consumption that surround Jonson's production of the 1616 Folio.[2] In its reconsideration of the Folio as cultural artifact, however, that scholarship relies on a range of studies which investigate pervasive aspects of Jonson's work. Those include Jonson's classicism (Maus, 1984), his patronage relations (Evans, 1989), his laureate ambitions (Helgerson, 1983), his humanism (McCanles,

1992), and his realism (Haynes, 1992).[3] Such studies have focused enquiry into the relationships among Jonson's texts, their varied readers/audiences, and the forms of authority they seek, shape, and are shaped by which the present volume reconsiders and advances in relation to Jonson's politics of genre.

If there is anything upon which recent Jonson commentators agree it is that the relationships Jonson crafts with his reader/s are complex, deliberate, and political. Borrowing the notion of a 'theatre of poetry' from Martial, as Rosalind Miles points out, Jonson challenges his reader to become his 'ideal audience . . . and to share his standards and accept his assessments'.[4] Persistently engaged in the task of creating that ideal reader – most obviously in the *Epigrams* as A. D. Cousins' essay in this volume discusses, but also across the canon – Jonson's contrary attempts to assert authority over his text and image at the same time as he is forced to acknowledge his ultimate lack of authority over his subject have provided an abiding critical focus.[5] A 'Men-making' poet who was nevertheless unavoidably dependent upon the men (and women) that he 'made', Jonson employed the rhetoric of wisdom, virtue, and understanding to assert the value of his texts and, by implication, of his reader/s. Ideally, the value of text, subject, and reader correspond – the subject of a text lives up to the praise Jonson offers, his writing is revealed as truth, and his judicious reader understands this and never mistakes it for anything less noble. Nevertheless, Jonson's anxieties about that ideal and the points at which it might potentially break down permeate his work.

Apart from the *Epigrams'* famous appeal for understanding, then, which obviously implies a fear of and disgust for *misunderstanding*, Jonson expresses regret at having praised a 'worthless lord' in 'To My Muse', variously seeks the protection (from a rancorous and ignorant multitude) of wise and charitable critics in the prefaces to his drama, and asserts that his 'sound and nourishing' masques are not for those of 'airy tastes' in *Hymenai*. Picking up on those anxieties and directives, many recent studies of the Jonsonian canon – particularly material studies focusing on the politics of publication – have engaged with the twin ideas of authority and authorship to illuminate tensions in and among the texts and in relation to Jonson's self-presentation. Joseph Loewenstein's work is exemplary in that regard, perceiving the 1616 Folio as 'a groping move forward to later authorial property rights' while at the same time acknowledging that it is modelled on and authorized by 'the economics of patronage'.[6] Sara Van den Berg, meanwhile, advances what has become a customary association between the Folio's organization and the identity of the author. In her essay 'Ben Jonson and the Ideology of Authorship', she argues that the Folio represented an attempt by Jonson to 'reconcile the impersonal resources of genre and rhetorical mode with the personal resource of his own unique voice'; its frontispiece more an announcement of authorship than an advertisement for the contents of the book.[7]

Tackling those and related questions from a different perspective, meanwhile, critics such as Barbara Smith, Michael G. Brennan, Helen Ostovich, and Julie Sanders have recently investigated Jonson's textual authority in relation to gender politics; Sanders, in particular, broaches the problem of reconciling Jonson's antifeminist depictions of female communities (*Epicene*'s collegiates) in the drama with his 'feminocentric ventures into the masques'.[8] A recent article by Christopher Gaggero draws on Sanders' discussion to argue that Jonson's portrayal of women in fulfilling public roles in *Catiline* marks an attempt to mobilize the gender politics of civic humanism to challenge the positions of political absolutism.[9] Nevertheless, in terms of Jonson's gender politics, there is important ground yet to be covered. In her exploration of the politics of gender and genre in *A Celebration of Charis*, and the interconnectedness of its representation of the female with Jonson's praise of Mary Wroth, Marea Mitchell goes some way to addressing that gap here. Significantly, her chapter in this volume highlights important intersections between Jonson's politics of genre and the gender politics of his work, and suggests how Jonson's 'imagining of a female point-of-view ... illuminates the corners and shadows of seventeenth-century sexual conventions'.

Other critics have approached the politics of Jonson's works from a more specifically ideological perspective, focusing especially on his classicism.[10] For several commentators, Jonson's imitation of and allusions to classical authors are legitimizing tools, and fundamental within his self-presentation as discriminating author. In her fine study of *Ben Jonson and the Roman Frame of Mind*, then, Katharine Eisaman Maus influentially argues that Jonson inherits 'a set of moral and psychological assumptions [from the Roman moralists] that condition the way he construes ethical, social, and artistic issues'.[11] Pivotally, that inheritance shapes his critical perspective, his preference for particular literary genres, and his complex relationships with his audiences and readers. Similarly, Michael McCanles has asserted the centrality of the classical tradition of *vera nobilitas* – a set of arguments concerning 'the true foundations of aristocratic status' redeployed by Renaissance humanists to serve their own 'educational agenda' – in Jonson's work.[12] As both John Roe's chapter on Jonson's verse epistles and Robert C. Evans' chapter on his country house poems discuss, however, the politics of the gift provide a point of intersection between Jonson's poetics of ethics and the material world he seeks to transcend: Jonson's 'free labours' must finally seek payment.

Invoking classical authors enables Jonson, as Roe observes here, 'to establish the desired relationship between himself and his patron . . . a relationship of equals', but that relationship is always problematic because 'the world that exploits gift-giving, and wilfully disregards the relationship of mutual respect that Jonson is eager to promote' always threatens to obtrude. In an innovative reconsideration of *Volpone* (the culmination of a career-long interest in the play and a host of related publications), Richard Dutton reads the relationship between Volpone and Mosca in terms of those most difficult aspects and contradictions of the patronage relations Jonson was obliged to pursue, even after he had come to resent the patron in question.[13] Dutton argues that *Volpone* is unusual (for a 'comedy') in its directly political attack on Robert Cecil's 'perverse exploitation of religion . . . in pursuit of wealth and power'. In connecting the play's examination of metempsychosis with Donne's poem 'Metempsychosis, or the Progress of the Soul', Dutton's chapter brings Donne criticism to bear on the Pythagorean show of *Volpone*, and illuminates a specific and hitherto unexamined political context of Jonson's drama.

In his poetry, his drama, and his masques Jonson reflects on the difficulties and disjunctions of his relations with the patronage economy and, conversely, with the emerging literary marketplace. Rosalind Miles' study – *Ben Jonson: His Craft and Art* – is distinctive in stressing the dramatic qualities of Jonson's poetry and perceives a Jonson in constant dialogue with himself, playing out various roles in his poetry and utilizing interlocutors to test, affirm, and/or unravel particular views.[14] In his study of Jonson's rhetoric of discrimination, however, McCanles advances a complementary view that the *vera nobilitas* argument enables what he calls dialectic 'ethical perceptions' that make the 'praise of true nobility' possible for Jonson only when it is connected with an 'attack on those who do not possess it, who pretend to it, and who therefore pervert it'.[15] Intersecting with that idea, Robert C. Evans returns in his chapter to his earlier discussion of the inherent tensions of Jonson's poems for the Sidney circle to demonstrate how the idealistic praise of 'To Penshurst' and the political criticism of 'To Sir Robert Wroth' complement one another to promote the same ethical values and to present the same reflexive relationship between discriminating poet and subject.[16] '[T]he credibility of poet and of addressee stand or fall together', as McCanles eruditely remarks of Jonson's poetry;

as such, the poet's relationship with his addressee has been deemed key to his self-presentation as ethically discriminating.

McCanles' notion that Jonson's praise of true nobility is essentially enabled by his attacks on those who do not possess it suggests the complex dynamic of Jonson's pervasive didacticism. In his reading of Jonson's tragedies here, Tom Cain demonstrates that Jonson utilizes such an ethical dialectic in his dramatization of the dangers of political ambition and corruption in Roman history, while A. D. Cousins demonstrates how the *Epigrams* 'juxtapose vision with lie . . . the dystopian against the eutopian, the satiric against the epic' in order to set apart the virtuous understanders of Jonson's book from the ignorant misunderstanders of the same. Discussing stoic and humanist models of wisdom and virtue, both chapters implicitly challenge the new historicist construction of the relationship between Jonson's texts and royal authority.[17] Of course, Jonathan Goldberg's landmark study *James I and the Politics of Literature* (1983), which furthered Stephen Orgel's seminal work on the Jonsonian masque, famously asserted the alignment of Jonson's writing with James' kingship, discussing the one as reflexive of and dependent upon the authority of the other for legitimation.[18] In her reassessment of the politics of the Jonsonian masque in this volume, Alison Scott draws on that critical history to further Martin Butler's astute challenge to Orgel's and Goldberg's 'totalizing' treatments of the subject.[19] Where Butler asserts that Jonson's masques 'negotiated' variant political processes of power, acting as 'transactions that served to shift, manoeuvre and reshape the forms in which power circulated', Scott demonstrates the crucial role of classical notions of decorum in that negotiation.[20] Her chapter illuminates the politics of Jonson's interdependent defences – of his ethical integrity as a humanist writer, and of the significance of the 'royal form' he dominated for the majority of James' reign.[21]

As royal masque writer, even more than as laureate poet (Helgerson, *Self-Crowned Laureates*), Jonson's political position arguably grew in its complexity as James' reign advanced. In particular, as several recent critical readings have suggested, his audiences multiplied and diversified.[22] As a result, the Jonsonian masque was shaped by various and sometimes conflicting patronage networks, at the same time as his politics (the way he wrote for the king, *and* the royal family, *and* his courtly audience) was shaped by the limitations, and also by the freedoms of the genre. Critical enquiry into the ways in which Jonson adapted his work for different audiences and for different readers – within both patronage and sale economies – has led some critics to speak of many different Jonsons, an idea which several of the chapters here explore.[23] While the notion of multiple Jonsons deploying various political strategies in particular genres of writing and for particular audiences appears incongruous for a writer who expressed his horror of what Ian Donaldson has called 'the loose self', Maus' work suggests that such flexibility and pragmatism on Jonson's part does not necessarily sit in opposition to his longstanding ideal of the 'centred' or 'gathered' self.[24] In her reading, it is possible to 'see Jonson's work in different genres as a series of strategies for representing possible relationships between desire and its objects, between demand and supply', where the comedies manifest a desire to accumulate in a climate of scarcity, as opposed to the masques and celebratory poetry that depict a world of plenty, which risks satiety but which can also escape the competitive acquisitiveness of the comic world.[25]

James Loxley perceives the necessity of writing for multiple audiences as a task which puts Jonson politically at odds with himself and causes him to manifest a self-multiplication of the kind so often satirized in the comedies,[26] but Maus asserts a contrary view. She suggests that Jonson's emphasis on the virtues of his own poetic labours persists across genres, audiences, and politic designs allowing him 'to exempt himself both from the implausibilities of his ideal worlds, and from the reductiveness of his satiric ones'.[27] Richard Burt stresses a similar point when he notes that '[i]n order to "fit in" with one audience, Jonson willingly censored himself; yet the censored criticism emerged in another context'.[28] Dutton's reading of *Volpone* in his chapter suggests that the play represents one of those moments in which criticism censored elsewhere emerges in another context, while Eugene Hill's discussion of *Timber* illuminates how it might be understood as simultaneously censorious and censored in its approach to issues of politics. The contradictions implicit in that authorial flexibility and diverse literary production for different markets appear primary to the radical disjunctions in the perspectives on life, and particularly on what constitutes a virtuous life, that Jonson offers in the different genres of his writing. In considering how Jonson deploys genre to offer a confluence of perspectives on the world, then, the chapters in this volume bring together many related strands of Jonson criticism to advance our understanding of the author, his work, the politics of his writing, and the political contexts of its production in important ways.

The chapters themselves are diversely interactive. Discussing the politics of *Epigrams*, A. D. Cousins suggests that Jonson begins his collection with a sequence of political representations designed apparently to encompass rather than to subordinate those that follow – and which enable him to evoke, and notionally to overgo, the epigrams of Martial. Jonson feigns at the start of *Epigrams*, Cousins argues, that eutopian commonwealths and a eutopian political economy characterize the Jacobean state. The quintessence – not the totality – of James I's Britain can be discerned in an ideal community of national worthies (recurrently portrayed in stoic or neostoic terms), itself linked epistemically with an ideal community of understanders (who thus belong as well to the republic of letters), which is crowned by the elaborately mythologized presence and rule of the king. Political fabling and mythologizing, then, inaugurate *Epigrams*; the eutopian is feigned – with some wariness – in order that it may encompass its necessarily acknowledged and excoriated opposite. Eutopian and dystopian visions are also considered by Robert C. Evans in his chapter on Jonson's country house poems. Having engaged robustly with the extensive commentary on the politics of Jonson's *To Penshurst* and *To Sir Robert Wroth*, Evans proceeds to contrast the poems by highlighting especially the country-court dialectic informing the second. The emphatic eutopianism of the former he sets against the emphatic dystopianism of the latter as it boldly satirizes the court in favour of the community centred upon Wroth's country house. Evans' chapter invites us to reconsider Jonson's depictions of class and of hierarchy in the twin country house poems.

Religion is crucial, as Evans acknowledges, to Jonson's representations of class and of community; and so is myth, particularly of course in his imaging of the king. Cousins pays close attention to the myth-making, masque-like celebration of James in Jonson's fourth and fifth epigrams. Alison Scott, when discussing the masques themselves, explores 'the way in which Jonson draws attention in his masques to the paradoxical nature of the genre's political work (truthfully reflecting *and* truthfully praising James and his court), and then deliberately evokes classical ideas of *kairos* (timeliness) and decorum (seemliness) in order to forge a feasible reconciliation of those contraries', thereby effecting what David Lindley calls 'self-sufficient myth' through a process of courtly negotiation.[29]

Essential to that outcome, Scott argues, is this: 'Jonson rhetorically positions his audience/reader as Apollonian, in line with the ideals of the masque proper, rather than as Dionysian in terms of the disproportions and distortions of the antimasque, at the same time as he entertains them with Dionysian revels.' A Nietzschean perspective on the mythologizing politics of the genre as deployed by Jonson takes us beyond entrenched new historicist critique, illuminating the nuances of negotiation throughout the masques. 'The politics of the Jonsonian masque', Scott concludes, 'are . . . always at once engaged with Platonism and Sophism, the affirmation of immutable truth and the adaptation to contingent truth; and they thus invoke and construct a Ciceronian decorum that unites political utility with ethical discrimination and honesty'. Yet sexual politics, no less than those of the court, are represented in mythic terms by Jonson, and Marea Mitchell's chapter focuses on 'A Celebration of Charis in Ten Lyric Pieces'. There, she claims, 'Jonson . . . constructs a dialogue that allows not one but two women to speak, and also gives them the last word'. She continues:

'Charis' . . . redefines notions of female desire as an active rather than a negative virtue. Two women express their opinions concerning desirable features in men, and part of their power over the speaker lies in the fact that the hypothetical ability to say yes or no to the poetic lover seems to have a material force absent from so many other poetic and sonnet sequences.

Mitchell proposes that Jonson re-voices the (male) erotic lyric in order to deflate male-centred notions of romance. His doing so, she observes, would have interested an innovative writer of romance such as Mary Wroth, with whom the sequence has at times been associated. In fact, as Mitchell subsequently demonstrates, to consider Wroth's *Urania* in relation to 'Charis' is to appreciate the literary as well as the personal links between Jonson and his patron.

The politics of patronage – which is at once to say, of clientage and praise and counsel – are further considered by John Roe in his chapter on the verse epistles. Engaging with Jonson's desire to appear independent but also with his obligation to be variously deferential, Roe makes this point, which ties in with Cousins' account of how stoic discourse functions in *Epigrams*: 'When we consider the political aspect of Jonson's poems, particularly the epistles, then we need to take into account his extraordinary capacity for transforming the subject and enabling it to enlist different values all at once.' Roe adds, in a reading of *To Sir Robert Wroth* complementary to that by Evans: 'Jonson applies the stratagem . . . of gently urging his subject to undertake an appropriate conduct by depicting him as already doing it.' It is a remark which illuminates the political nuances of gift-giving in Jonson's verse: as occasion suits, Jonson enacts the role of humanist counsellor by offering a hypothetically persuasive gift of praise, that is to say, a hypothetically seductive likeness of a potential self. It illuminates, too, the politics of Jonson's dealing with female patrons, for it highlights one of the means by which Jonson attempts to bring sameness, on his terms, out of unavoidably emphasized social and gender differences.

How Jonson used the perspectives of comic or tragic drama to shape political fictions is discussed by Richard Dutton and by Tom Cain. The former examines the politics of patronage, of religious conflict, and of state affairs as represented in *Volpone*. Focusing in particular on the 'show of the metempsychosis of the soul of Pythagoras, performed for Volpone by Nano, Androgyno and Castrone early in the play', and on that 'show' in relation to Donne's poem *Metempsychosis*, Dutton explores the extent to which Jonson's beast-fable comedy offers an amused and bitter commentary on Robert Cecil and the aftermath of the Gunpowder Plot. Cecil benefited from the Plot, as English Catholics saw it, but they – Jonson's co-religionists at the time – of course did not. Like Roe, Dutton is interested by Jonson's being 'trapped in a world of patronage compromise'; and he sees *Volpone* as concerned with the politics of patronage yet as being preoccupied with a specific patron at once grandiose, widely dangerous to believers in the Old Faith, and intrusive into the creative process. Since, Dutton suggests, 'what is at issue in [Jonson's] play' is 'the perversion of a society's soul', *Volpone* pushes comedy to the border of tragedy.

And of Jonson's political fictions in his Roman tragedies, Tom Cain writes: 'These were not to be plays of great psychological complexity, nor would their protagonists be particularly heroic. Their profundity would lie in the questions they raised about the business of government and the dynamics of power, past and present.' He adds: 'Jonson's plays during this period show him moving towards a... political position... involving freedom of speech and limitation of the absolute powers of the monarch.' Moreover: More and Machiavelli, like Lipsius, Camden, Cotton, and other humanist historians, compared 'ancient and modern events' so that readers could 'more easily draw those practical lessons (*quella utilita*) which one should seek to obtain from the study of history'. In all three of his Roman plays Jonson was to attempt precisely that, dramatizing Rome in the crucial late republican and early imperial period, from 63 BC to AD 31, for the light it could shed on his own political and social milieu. In doing this, however, he did not turn to Rome, even in *Poetaster*, as a paragon to be imitated.

In the case of *Sejanus*, he argues for example, one can discern oblique commentary – in accord with current 'republican' thinking – both on the Cecils and on the aftermath of the Gunpowder Plot. Nevertheless, 'Jonson would have wished his audience to apply the lessons of his Roman history, not by identifying exclusive representations of contemporary political actors, but through a recognition of how the dynamics of power and ambition could be discerned in a range of contemporaries.' In his closing remarks he observes with reference to *Catiline*: 'This is a treatment of classical republicanism which must at least qualify the characterization of

Jonson as an ardent monarchist, an authoritarian in politics as in his attitude to his literary output.' His chapter intriguingly complements what Cousins and Scott suggest about Jonson's difficulties in constructing mythic personae for King James.

The difficulties of writing at all about politics are implied, Eugene D. Hill asserts, by Jonson's choice of epigraph for his *Timber, or Discoveries*. Locating the quotation from Persius' fourth satire in context – and in relation to Isaac Casaubon's commentary on that poem – Hill reflects:

Indeed the cue of the Persian tag directs us to an uncanvassed function of the *Discoveries*. Scholars have offered various possibilities: notes for a series of lectures on rhetoric, raw material for future verse compositions, for example. But what if, like Persius, Ben had in mind an assemblage of political commonplaces for political writing?

As he neatly points out, 'Kingship, adulation, virtue, decorum: the text positions its readers at the fruitful fraught intersection of the literary and the political.' Hill argues that in the *Discoveries*, then, 'Jonson was not only identifying with the great known masters of the past, but providing stuff for the unknown readers of the future who would find themselves inclined *rem populi tractare*.' They would be, presumably like Jonson himself, guided but not commanded.

Occasions demanded, and the perspectives of the kinds facilitated, that there be different Jonsons, politically speaking – or, perhaps one could better say, complementary and variously nuanced Jonsonian personae. The chapters of this book show, for example, that if there is an adulatory Jonson voicing the masques, that particular Jonson cannot be thought merely adulatory or univocal. True, the decorums of occasion and of genre fashion as they constrain him but, in being seen always already to do so, they draw attention not only to themselves but to the ways in which he negotiates and inflects them. Something similar can be observed in the rhetoric of the country house poems, where the Jonsonian speaker's hyperbolic praise lays bare its own genial excesses – and exclusion, especially in *To Sir Robert Wroth*, has much to tell. Against such fluidity within confinement one could set, as can be seen elsewhere in what follows, the 'republican' scrutiny of absolutism that pervades the Roman tragedies. The politics of genre in Jonson's hands are therefore those of a humanist scholar who seems to have been, certainly, pugnacious and stubborn yet also quite aware of wisdom's limitations when engaging with political actualities.

NOTES

1. *Donne and the Resources of Kind*, ed. A. D. Cousins and Damian Grace (Madison: Fairleigh Dickinson University Press, 2002). See, for example, Bakhtin's/Medvedev's *The Formal Method in Literary Scholarship: A Critical Introduction to Sociological Poetics*, trans. Albert J. Wehrle, rpt 1978 (Cambridge, MA: Harvard University Press, 1985), 133–5. See also Bakhtin's *Problems of Dostoevsky's Poetics*, ed. and trans. Caryl Emerson (Manchester University Press, 1984), 106 and 157, along with his *Speech Genres and Other Late Essays*, trans. Vern W. McGee, ed. Caryl Emerson and Michael Holquist, rpt 1986 (Austin: University of Texas Press, 1987), 78–81.
2. Joseph Loewenstein, *Ben Jonson and Possessive Authorship* (Cambridge University Press, 2002); Richard Dutton, *Ben Jonson: Authority: Criticism* (Basingstoke: Macmillan, 1996); Sara Van den Berg, 'Ben Jonson and the Ideology of Authorship', in *Ben Jonson's 1616 Folio*, ed. Jennifer Brady and W. H. Herendeen (Newark: University of Delaware Press; London/Toronto: Associated University Presses, 1991), 111–37; Bruce Boehrer, 'The Poet of Labour: Authorship and Property in the Work of Ben Jonson', *Philology Quarterly* 72 (1993): 289–312 and also *The Fury of Men's Gullet: Ben Jonson and the Digestive Canal* (Philadelphia: University of Pennsylvania Press, 1997), especially chapter three.
3. Katharine Eisaman Maus, *Ben Jonson and the Roman Frame of Mind* (Princeton University Press, 1984); Robert C. Evans, *Ben Jonson and the Poetics of Patronage* (Lewisburg: Bucknell University Press; London: Associated University Presses, 1989); Richard Helgerson, *Self-Crowned Laureates: Spenser, Jonson, Milton and the Literary System* (Berkeley: University of California Press, 1983); Michael McCanles, *Jonsonian Discriminations: The Humanist Poet and the Praise of True Nobility* (University of Toronto Press, 1992); Jonathan Haynes, *The Social Relations of Jonson's Theatre* (Cambridge University Press, 1992).
4. Rosalind Miles, *Ben Jonson: His Craft and Art* (London: Routledge, 1990), 173–4.
5. In Miles' view this has led critics to focus heavily on the personal voice in Jonson's work at the expense of investigating its dialogic qualities (*ibid.*, 172).
6. Joseph Loewenstein, 'The Script in the Marketplace', *Representations* 12 (1985): 101–14, 109.
7. Van den Berg, 'Ben Jonson and the Ideology of Authorship', 111.
8. See Barbara Smith's *The Women of Ben Jonson's Poetry: Female Representations in the Non-Dramatic Verse* (Aldershot: Scolar Press, 1995); Michael G. Brennan's 'Creating Female Authorship in the Early Seventeenth Century: Ben Jonson and Lady Mary Wroth', in *Women's Writing and the Circulation of Ideas: Manuscript Publication in England 1550–1800*, ed. George L. Justice and Nathan Tinker (Cambridge University Press, 2002), 73–93; Helen Ostovich's 'Hell for Lovers: Shades of Adultery in *The Devil is an Ass*', in *Refashioning Ben Jonson: Gender, Politics and the Jonsonian Canon*, ed. Julie Sanders, Kate Chedgzoy, and Susan Wiseman (Basingstoke: Macmillan, 1998), 155–82;

and Julie Sanders' *Ben Jonson's Theatrical Republics* (Basingstoke: Macmillan, 1998), 53–6. Sanders' chapter on 'The Alternative Commonwealth of Women' in that volume is also relevant here.

9. Christopher Gaggero, 'Civic Humanism and Gender Politics in Jonson's *Catiline*', *Studies in English Literature* 45.2 (2005): 401–24.

10. Maus' *Ben Jonson and the Roman Frame of Mind* provides a most thorough exploration of the topic. Other notable contributions to the discussion include William Blissett's 'Roman Ben Jonson', and Stella P. Revard's 'Classicism and Neo-Classicism in Jonson's *Epigrammes* and *The Forrest*', both in *1616 Folio*, ed. Brady and Herendeen, 90–110; 138–67; and John Mulryan's 'Jonson's Classicism', in *The Cambridge Companion to Ben Jonson*, ed. Richard Harp and Stanley Stewart (Cambridge University Press, 2000), 163–74.

11. Maus, *Roman Frame of Mind*, 20.

12. McCanles, *Jonsonian Discriminations*, 47.

13. His essay here builds on Dutton's distinguished body of commentary, see *Ben Jonson: To the First Folio* (Cambridge University Press, 1983); *Mastering the Revels: The Regulation and Censorship of Early Modern Drama* (University of Iowa Press, 1991); 'The Lone Wolf: Jonson's Epistle to *Volpone*', in *Refashioning Ben Jonson*, ed. Sanders, Chedgzoy, and Wiseman, 114–33; '*Volpone* and Beast Fable: Early Modern Analogic Reading', *Huntington Library Quarterly* 67 (2004): 347–70; 'Jonson, Shakespeare, and the Exorcists', *Shakespeare Survey* 58 (2005): 15–22; and 'Venice in London, London in Venice', in *Mighty Europe 1400–1700: Writing an Early Modern Continent*, ed. Andrew Hiscock (Oxford: Peter Lang, 2007), 133–52.

14. Miles, *Ben Jonson*, 171–5.

15. McCanles, *Jonsonian Discriminations*, 67.

16. See Evans, *Ben Jonson and the Poetics of Patronage*.

17. Leah S. Marcus' reading of Jonson as mirroring James both in personality and in 'style' is typical; she sees both men as self-divided proponents of classical restraint given to practices of excess: *The Politics of Mirth: Jonson, Herrick, Milton, Marvell and the Defense of Old Holiday Pastimes* (University of Chicago Press, 1986), 12.

18. Jonathan Goldberg, *James I and the Politics of Literature* (Baltimore: Johns Hopkins University Press, 1983). See particularly Orgel's *The Illusion of Power* (Berkeley: University of California Press, 1975) and also his *The Jonsonian Masque* (Cambridge, MA: Harvard University Press, 1967).

19. Butler has published widely on the subject but he takes up that specific argument in 'Courtly Negotiations', in *The Politics of the Stuart Court Masque*, ed. David Bevington and Peter Holbrook (Cambridge University Press, 1998), 20–40.

20. Butler, 'Courtly Negotiations', 26. In *Ben Jonson: Authority: Criticism* (1996) Richard Dutton also stressed such flexibility and ambiguity in the relationships between Jonson's texts and various forms of political authority; those negotiations, in his reading, reveal an author far less assured than

Richard S. Peterson's *Imitation and Praise in the Poems of Ben Jonson* suggested back in 1971.

21. Goldberg, *James I*, 65.

22. David Lindley notes that critics are increasingly engaging with the ways in which masques are 'problematically implicated in the shifting allegiances and political debates of the period' in his article 'Courtly Play: The Politics of Chapman's *The Memorable Masque*', in *The Stuart Courts*, ed. Eveline Cruickshanks (Stroud: Sutton Publishing, 2000), 43. See also Tom Bishop, 'The Gingerbread Host: Tradition and Novelty in the Jacobean Masque', in *The Politics of the Stuart Court Masque*, ed. Bevington and Holbrook, 88–120; Martin Butler 'Courtly Negotiations', and Stephen Orgel 'Marginal Jonson', in the same volume, 20–40, 144–75; Graham Parry, 'The Politics of the Jacobean Masque' in *Theatre and Government under the Early Stuarts*, ed. J. R. Mulryne and Margaret Shewring (Cambridge University Press, 1993), 87–117; and chapter three of Alison V. Scott's *Selfish Gifts: The Politics of Exchange and English Courtly Literature, 1580–1628* (Madison: Fairleigh Dickinson University Press, 2006), 125–58.

23. Katharine Eisaman Maus, for example, pertinently asks '[h]ow can the same person subscribe both to the view that seems to be Jonson's in the comedies and to the view that seems to be Jonson's in the masques and the poems of praise?' 'Facts of the Matter: Satiric and Ideal Economies in the Jonsonian Imagination', in *1616 Folio*, ed. Brady and Herendeen, 64–89, 73.

24. See Thomas Greene's oft-quoted essay on 'Ben Jonson and the Centred Self', *Studies in English Literature 1500–1900* 10 (1970): 325–48, in which he speaks of an implicit horror evident in Jonson's writing of 'a self too often shifted' (343). Also, Ian Donaldson's *Jonson's Magic Houses: Essays in Interpretation* (Oxford: Clarendon Press, 1997), 42.

25. Maus, 'Facts of the Matter', 73 and 74–5.

26. James Loxley, *The Complete Critical Guide to Ben Jonson* (London: Routledge, 2002), 160.

27. Maus, 'Facts of the Matter', 86.

28. Richard Burt, *Licensed by Authority: Ben Jonson and the Discourses of Censorship* (Ithaca, NY: Cornell University Press, 1993), 47. Both Maus and Burt pick up on points made by earlier commentaries that directly or indirectly examine Jonson's antitheatricality – most notably Jonas A. Barish's *The Anti-Theatrical Prejudice* (Berkeley: University of California Press, 1981) and Anne Barton's *Ben Jonson, Dramatist* (Cambridge University Press, 1984).

29. David Lindley, 'Embarrassing Ben: The Masques for Frances Howard', *English Literary Renaissance* 16 (1986): 343–59.

CHAPTER I

Feigning the commonwealth:
Jonson's Epigrams

A. D. Cousins

At the start of his *Epigrams* Jonson successively evokes three notions in which we know he had particular and recurrent interest.[1] Evoking and juxtaposing them, he offers at the start of his book a series of political representations that seem designed to govern the collection as a whole. They are of course not the only versions of the political generated in his book of epigrams. Nevertheless they are both those with which he chose to begin his work and arguably the most important insofar as, having been brought together in implicit affirmation of one another, they seem not so much to subordinate as to encompass the representations that follow. The notions are constancy, understanding, and kingship. Each is prominent in *Epigrams* and throughout Jonson's other writings – though necessarily with different degrees of emphasis, different frequency and inflection, depending on the demands of occasion and of genre. Each has therefore often received attention in commentary on the Jonson canon, although (as would be expected) that attention has been unequally given and at times has been indirect. Jonson emphasizes the notions but, just as they are not simple, neither does he simply evoke them; further, his juxtaposition of them is not least interesting because eutopian in the vision it unfolds.

The first of those notions, constancy, has usually been discussed (as far as the non-dramatic verse is concerned) in relation to Jonson's preoccupation with what he once called the 'gathered self'.[2] However, it has been considered ahistorically rather than otherwise. Acknowledging only sometimes, and sweepingly if at all, stoic or neostoic contexts of the notion, commentators have focused on its deployment by Jonson: on his iterative portrayals of the stable and integral self as an ideal mode of being.[3] Here, initially considering its evocation in the dedicatory address to the Earl of Pembroke that prefaces *Epigrams*, I want to contextualize the notion in terms of Jonson's making Pembroke a type of the stoic wise man and thence to locate it more specifically within the stoic and neostoic discourses circulating in early modern England. I want in particular to link it with Senecan and Lipsian formulations of what constancy is. Doing so clarifies the ensuing notion, understanding, which dominates *Epigram 1 To the Reader*. The formulations of constancy by Seneca and Lipsius stress elements and processes of cognition – right reason and judgment for example – that cannot be separated from what the opening epigram indicates true understanding and thus true reading involve. Moreover the subsequent epigram, which addresses Jonson's book itself, plays understanding against misunderstanding in such a way as to confirm those tacit connections between portrayal of Pembroke and identification of the preferred reader. Almost immediately however, following a careful gesture of indifference toward the marketplace, Jonson subsumes the notions of constancy and of understanding in the notion of kingship, which is not merely to say that his accounts of Pembroke and of the preferred reader are absorbed into his celebration of James I.[4] His portrayal of James as model king and poet, then as sacerdotal king, translates his evocations of constancy and of understanding into the domain of what might broadly be called the mythographic: into oblique association with the motif of opposites' reconciliation, with the motif of human life's having three aspects, and with commentary on Cicero's *Dream of Scipio*. As I have suggested above, in his sequentially evoking those notions Jonson offers a series of political representations that seem both eutopian and, in combination, greater than the sum of their parts.

   That having been proposed, I want now to examine how Jonson puts forward that series of representations and why his doing so can be called feigning the commonwealth. His emphasis on Pembroke's constancy in virtue (which is in effect to say, his imaging Pembroke as a type of the stoic wise man) indicates from the very start a version of the political recognizable at once in outline.[5] Its pointing towards that can be seen when Jonson writes: 'In thanks whereof [for "protection" by the earl, should it be needed] I return you the honour of leading forth so many good and great names as my verses mention on the better part' (lines 14–16). Jonson implies that his address to Pembroke – his image of Pembroke – introduces portrayal of a fellowship or community of English 'good and great names'. As Ian Donaldson describes the political representation being introduced there, citing the passage in *Discoveries* from which I take the title of my chapter:

Jonson creates in the *Epigrams* a kind of pantheon of national worthies, men and women whose virtues are deserving commemoration. The poet, wrote Jonson in *Discoveries* (1045–48), is one who 'can feign a commonwealth . . . can govern it with counsels, strengthen it with laws, correct it with judgments, inform it with religion and morals.' In the *Epigrams* Jonson 'feigns' a commonwealth of exemplary individuals in much this way – statesmen, scholars, soldiers, writers, artists – 'leading forth so many good and great names as my verses mention on the better part, to their remembrance with posterity'.   (*Epig.* Ded. 13–14)[6]

And – as Donaldson mentions also in a note to the sentence opening his remarks – Jonson had said to Drummond '[t]hat he had an intention to perfect an epic poem entitled *Herologia*, of the worthies of his country, roused by fame, and was to dedicate it to his country'.[7] One might add here not merely that Jonson's image of Pembroke, the first in his feigned 'commonwealth of exemplary individuals', is distinctly stoic but that the stoic colouring given the image is variously replicated in the portraits of some other 'worthies'. Jonson's attribution of stoic or neostoic values and tenets recurs throughout his imagining a community of national heroes.

   That process, as I have already foreshadowed and shall argue in detail below, tacitly links the nationalist political representation initiated via Jonson's image of Pembroke with his identification of his preferred reader. My argument can perhaps be more clearly made, for now, as follows. If in the Dedication Jonson launches the fiction of an heroic community existing within the larger community, in the first epigram (and again in the second) he identifies within the larger community a potential commonweal of true readers, of understanders, who by implication will therefore exist as well within the republic of letters – some may already, of course – to which he and William Camden and John Donne are for example intimated to belong. It is implicit that the stoic or neostoic ethics attributed across the community of worthies accord with the reading practices of those who, Jonson indicates, will form the community of true readers, whom he is rather summoning, shaping, than simply identifying. In any event, the two communities intersect, as ideal commonwealths within the commonwealth of Britain. Those versions of the political are then set *sub specie Jacobi*: they are set in perspective by the representations of James I as the ideal ruler, the model Christian prince. Jonson thus brings together a cumulatively eutopian and therefore cumulatively problematic sequence of political representations. I shall now consider the sequence itself.

PEMBROKE AND THE FEIGNED COMMONWEALTH OF WORTHIES

In his letter of dedication Jonson addresses his patron, William, Earl of Pembroke, as 'the great example of honour and virtue'. He then almost immediately continues by way of salutation: 'My Lord: While you cannot change your merit, I dare not change your title; it was that made it, and not I' (lines 1–2). Soon after comes this: 'I must expect at your Lordship's hand the protection of truth and liberty while you are constant to your own goodness' (lines 12–14).[8] The celebration of Pembroke stresses in each case that the earl, embodying 'merit' (namely, 'virtue') and 'goodness', does so with constancy – and thus refigures him as a latter-day stoic sage. Jonson's portrayal of the earl reflects what was a widespread contemporary interest in that ancient and heroic ideal of being, one personal yet also civil.[9]

It is an ideal that, given Jonson's initial and repeated emphasis on constancy, can be illuminated by reference to Seneca and to Lipsius. Writings by each were well known to him as they were to other early modern readers pursuing the *studia humanitatis*, and each wrote a work titled *De Constantia*.[10] Seneca argues in his essay on constancy:

But the wise man can lose nothing. He has everything invested in himself, he trusts nothing to fortune, his own goods are secure, since he is content with virtue, which needs no gift from chance, and which, therefore, can neither be increased nor diminished. For that which has come to the full has no room for further growth, and Fortune can snatch away only what she herself has given. But virtue she does not give; therefore, she cannot take it away. Virtue is free, inviolable, unmoved, unshaken, so steeled against the blows of chance that she cannot be bent, much less broken. (5.4–5)[11]

Self-sufficient in secure possession of that which does not change amidst the impermanence of things, the wise man himself becomes unchanging: not unadaptable but, rather, constant. To identify Pembroke with constancy and so – in the context of his supposedly flawless virtue – as a type of the stoic sage in accord with Seneca's idea of the wise man (for example), therefore functions in several ways. It of course flatters the earl by suggesting his moral self-sufficiency within his ultimate political dependence on the crown (I shall come back to that issue when I discuss Jonson's portrayals of James I). It is moreover a useful gambit for a poet-client who, claiming to attack vice from the moral high ground, seeks protection from whatever retaliation may ensue.[12] Finally, and as I have said above, it associates Pembroke with an heroic ideal of being that is at once personal and civil. Seneca remarks in *De Constantia* 8.2:

As he struggles and presses on towards those things that are lofty, well-ordered, undaunted, that flow on with even and harmonious current [*aequali et concordi cursu fluentia*], that are untroubled [*secura*], kindly, adapted to the public good [*bono publico nata*], beneficial both to himself and to others, the wise man will covet nothing low, will never repine.[13]

With regard to the civil aspect of that ideal as described in *De Constantia*, perhaps two things should be mentioned before I turn to consider Lipsius' thinking on constancy and how it – in combination with Seneca's – illuminates Jonson's evoking the notion.

A couple of Seneca's remarks on the social implications of the wise man's life might have been especially interesting to his Jacobean readers and not least to Jonson. Focused respectively on peace and on greed, those remarks could have been seen as having an immediate relevance severally to King James and to the economic changes occurring in his reign. The first remark concerns Stilbo, Seneca's main instance of the wise man. Of Stilbo he writes: 'Amid swords flashing on every side and the uproar of soldiers bent on pillage, amid flames and blood and the havoc of the smitten city [Megara, when captured by Demetrius], amid the crash of temples falling upon their gods, one man alone had peace' (6.2).[14] Later he asserts: 'Only the bad attempt to injure the good; the good are at peace with each other, the bad are no less harmful to the good than they are to each other' (7.2).[15] The wise man possesses inner peace and belongs to a community of the peaceful – a feature of the stoic sage that harmonizes with James I's insistent self-portrayal as a pacific man seeking to maintain a peaceful society. Jonson's image of his patron has, in other words, distant but important affinities with the king's imaging of himself. It also concurs with Jonson's self-presentation in *Epigrams*. I mean that in his collection Jonson at times directly or indirectly lays claim to or associates himself with some of the characteristics of the stoic wise man and, thence, a moral authority that he can share with Pembroke (at least to a degree), who has a political authority Jonson cannot share.[16] That brings me to the second of Seneca's remarks, which concerns enemies of the public good. Early in *De Constantia* Seneca condemns 'Publius Clodius on the one hand, Vatinius and all the greatest rascals on the other', for being 'carried away by blind cupidity' ('*caeca cupiditate*') and betraying the state.[17] Seneca's reference to '*caeca cupiditate*' recalls Cicero's '*caeca ac temeraria dominatrix animi cupiditas*', where *cupiditas* is identified more forcefully and more comprehensively as inimical to the common weal.[18] Seneca observes that the stoic wise man does not know cupidity for he has all he wants in having virtue ('he is content with virtue'). Jonson elaborately stresses, in the epigram to his bookseller, that he lacks the greed to become an active participant in the marketplace – that although he may be in the marketplace, he is nevertheless not of it. Gesturing towards dissociation from the economic forces and relations in which he knows his society and himself to be embedded, he distantly associates himself with that ideal mode of being with which he links Pembroke (as well as some friends, some further patrons). He indirectly lays claim to a moral authority that associates him with his feigned commonwealth of worthies.

Those remarks by Seneca having been considered, I want now to revisit Jonson's double staging of virtue, and of independence amidst dependence, in his letter of dedication. His doing so raises the question of what constancy is: it may well be the hallmark of the stoic sage, but what exactly is it? By way of answer one could begin with Seneca's words straight after those from *De Constantia* just now quoted at length: 'The man who, relying on reason, marches through mortal vicissitudes with the spirit of a god, has no vulnerable spot where he can receive an injury.'[19] He asserts concordantly in *De Vita Beata*: '[T]he right-thinking mind never alters.'[20] For Seneca, constancy – a fixed habit of virtue – is the consequence of right reason's governing the mind.[21] Then in seeking an answer one could usefully turn to Lipsius, Jonson's contemporary, since a related although less voluntaristic idea of constancy occurs in his *De Constantia*, a Christian rethinking of Seneca's essay when Lipsius' native Belgium was invaded by the Spanish. The continuity between Seneca's thought and that of Lipsius is clear. The latter writes: 'Constancy is a right and immovable strength of the mind, neither lifted up, nor pressed down with external or casual accidents.' Further: 'By strength, I understand a steadfastness not from opinion, but from judgment and sound reason.' No less evident however is the discontinuity, as soon starts to appear: '[T]he true mother of Constancy is Patience, and lowliness of mind, which is, a voluntary sufferance without grudging of all things whatsoever can happen to, or in a man. This being regulated by the rule of Right Reason, is the very root whereupon is settled the high and mighty body of that fair oak Constancy.' A little afterwards one reads – and there the contextualizing of Seneca is what matters:

Reason hath her offspring from heaven, yea from God: and *Seneca* gave it a singular commendation, saying, *That there was hidden in man part of the divine spirit*. This reason is an excellent power or faculty of understanding and judgment, which is the perfection of the soul, even as the soul is of man ... [Y]ou are deceived if you think all the soul to be *Right reason*, but that only which is uniform, simple, without mixture, separate from all filth or corruption: and in one word, as much as is pure & heavenly. For albeit the soul be infected and a little corrupted with the filth of the body and contagion of the senses: yet it retaineth some relics of his first offspring, and is not without certain clear sparks of that pure fiery nature from whence it proceeded . . . Those little coals do always shine and show forth themselves, lightening our darkness, purging our uncleanness, directing our doubtfulness, guiding us at the last to Constancy and virtue. As the Marigold and other flowers are by nature always inclined towards the sun; so hath Reason a respect unto God, and to the fountain from whence it sprang. It is resolute and immovable in a good purpose, not variable in judgment, ever shunning or seeking one and the self same thing.   (1.5)

Lipsius agrees with Seneca that constancy is the offspring of right reason and judgment – that it is generated by the quintessentially divine in humankind. His idea of what constitutes the divine within and beyond the human differs of course from Seneca's; likewise he differs from Seneca inasmuch as he closely joins right reason and judgment with patience and humility. Considered separately, but especially when considered together, the Lipsian and Senecan formulations of constancy illuminate Jonson's evoking that notion and thence his feigning both a commonwealth of worthies and a commonwealth of true readers (which is to say, of understanders). In particular they imply that what constitutes his community of national heroes as imaged throughout *Epigrams* needs to be looked at afresh: that his 'feigned commonwealth of exemplary individuals' cannot simply be called a 'community of the same'.[22]

   Seneca's and Lipsius' writings on constancy offered Jonson usefully broad, connected fields of reference when in his *Epigrams* he chose to ascribe constancy of virtue to a patron or friend (or maybe an addressee who was both). That is to say, if an alleged constancy of virtue metonymically identifies someone in *Epigrams* with the stoic sage, Jonson may variously associate the notion of constancy itself (via, for example, Seneca or Lipsius) with free will or grace, with Roman or Christian virtue, with *romanitas* or cosmopolitanism. On the other hand its relations with those things, which need not be viewed as mutually exclusive, may be left discreetly unclear, so that the person praised is seen to have a moral authority and dignity of an unspecified kind. The community of national heroes portrayed in his collection – even when viewed solely with reference to the attributed stoic or neostoic affiliations which initiate and recur throughout its portrayal – therefore inevitably, and interestingly, expresses difference as well as sameness. That accords with Jonson's portrayals of himself in relation to his addressees. As I have suggested above, in *Epigrams* Jonson tends to indicate the broad identity of himself with another on the basis of moral authority since, in most cases, authority of that kind can be his only basis for such a claim. Yet whatever the gestured sameness between him and the subject of his praise in any given poem, his indicating it co-exists with his suggesting – sometimes his insistence upon – distinctions between them.

To examine the community of worthies presented throughout *Epigrams* will illustrate what are in fact disparities of sameness and diversities of difference amongst those portrayed – and between them and Jonson.[23] Sameness is of course an epideictic given within the supposed community's members. All are imaged as in some form or another embodying moral excellence. That they do so unites them; yet how they do so distinguishes them. They have a diverse commonality and are individuated – as the hierarchic and competitive structure of Jonson's world either dictated or encouraged that they should be, depending on who was addressed, and since it allowed (or, he preferred) that only to a point might he *trope* identity with them. In those respects a revealing poem is the ninety-eighth epigram, *To Sir Thomas Roe*. It alludes to the notion of constancy evoked in the dedicatory epistle to Pembroke, thereby implicitly linking Roe with Pembroke in a commonality of virtue. At the same time, it links Jonson with Roe in ways that perhaps assert identity – yet potentially differentiate – between the poet and the recipient of his praise.

The poem starts, not by accident since it concerns a life praised for transcendence of the accidental and unexpected, with focus on how Roe has 'begun' the business of living:

> Thou hast begun well, Roe, which stand well to,
>   And I know nothing more thou hast to do.
> He that is round within himself, and straight,
>   Need seek no other strength, no other height;
>   Fortune upon him breaks herself, if ill,
>   And what would hurt his virtue makes it still.

(lines 1–6)

According to Jonson, Roe has 'begun' and continues in virtue; his life expresses right reason and judgment ('round within himself, and straight'). It is a life wanting nothing and therefore beyond both fear and desire (lines 4–6). The portrayal of Roe in such terms – all linked to the stoic notion of constancy – celebrates him as a type of the stoic sage and as one that seems more Senecan than Lipsian, for Roe has made himself what he is. Yet if he shares that ascribed role with Pembroke, who in the Dedication seems also to be a self-made man, the two are nevertheless unlike. So the final half of the poem indicates, at the same time as it ambiguously presents, Jonson's

relationship to Roe, which to a degree resembles Jonson's carefully nuanced
relationship with his patron:

> That thou at once, then, nobly mayst defend
> With thine own course the judgement of thy friend,
>   Be always to thy gathered self the same,
> And study conscience more than thou wouldst fame.
>   Though both be good, the latter yet is worst,
>   And ever is ill-got without the first.
>
> (lines 7–12)

In those lines Jonson warns Roe that his maintaining of constancy will be
challenged by the allure of 'fame'. (That is to say, Roe's consistency in virtue
will be challenged by what Seneca and Lipsius would have seen as a form of
opinio and hence not in fact a genuine good, whereas Jonson seems here to
class it a collateral good.)[24] Earlier, he had deferentially but of course
purposefully raised the topic of constancy in his address to Pembroke (at
the last, with an eye to his own possible need for protection). Neither in
the latter's case nor in Roe's, however, does Jonson overtly put forward
more than the mere appearance of admonition. What might be called
Jonson's decorously hesitant pointing towards counsel in the Dedication
diplomatically implies its own superfluousness. It has in fact been obliquely
deflected before being expressed, since Pembroke has been addressed at the
Dedication's outset as 'the great example of honour and virtue'. His having
been so emphasizes that, in Jonson's feigned community of worthies, all are
neither equal nor the same: even among the notional sages there is necessarily distinction. Pembroke is the exemplar of virtue; Roe possesses it but
is not its 'great example'. Pembroke is Jonson's patron and potential
protector – and an earl; Roe is titled but can be called 'friend' – 'friend'
being interestingly ambiguous. Stoic philosophy held that the wise alone
can truly be friends. Jonson's use of the word, when celebrating Roe as
stoic sage, may thus translate some of the moral authority attributed to
Roe back to Jonson himself (especially when 'friend' is read in conjunction
with 'judgement' and with what's said in reference to Roe at line 3). Yet it
may not: the celebration of Roe may be taken as intimating that, an admiring 'friend' in a less philosophically specific sense, Jonson acknowledges a
completeness which he himself cannot achieve.[25] In any event, since Roe
is allegedly a type of the sage, a man complete, he must already know
that 'fame' cannot be believed a genuine good and cannot be tempted by
it (cf. line 2). Jonson's counsel draws attention to what might tempt Roe
from constancy were Roe temptable – but because he isn't, Jonson's

counsel is rather praise. Although to readers other than Roe – and who are not among the wise or the unusually virtuous – the poem's concluding four verses may be counsel, to Roe they can merely be affirmation of what he knows, how he lives.[26] To put the Dedication next to the ninety-eighth epigram is arguably, then, to see this. The commonality indicated between Pembroke and Roe places them within the group that's first in Jonson's imagined community of national heroes. Their commonality is, however, the ground of their necessary individuation – from one another, from those who are also members of the feigned commonwealth of worthies but not of their group, and from Jonson.

   Pembroke and Roe appear to be further distinguished by the ninety-ninth epigram, in which Jonson casts his friend as a member both of the community of worthies and of what I have called the community of true readers (cf. lines 1–2). Uniting the good life and good letters, Roe seems to be attributed with a scope of life that Pembroke, for all his ascribed virtue, does not. However, in *Epigram 102 To William, Earl of Pembroke* one sees Jonson imaging his patron not merely as the exemplar of virtue but as the very incarnation of good letters. Therein Jonson actually distinguishes between his patron and his friend. *Epigram 102* starts with Jonson praising Pembroke at an epideictic level not so far short of that he assigns to King James – a level of praise he denies to Roe. In fact it starts with his troping Pembroke's name virtually as the epigram of epigrams:

> I do but name thee, Pembroke, and I find
>   It is an epigram on all Mankind,
>   Against the bad, but of and to the good;
> Both which are asked, to have thee understood.

(lines 1–4)

So Jonson's epigram is merely a gloss to the supreme epigram that is Pembroke's name – and which, following the logic of Jonson's hyperbole, effectively makes all others of its kind (including even those constituting *Epigrams*) all but unnecessary.[27] Moreover Pembroke's name and therefore he himself require to be truly read: by understanders. That's simultaneously made clear of Jonson's poem. The opening line alludes to discovery (via 'find'). Jonson indicates that his understanding of Pembroke's name is at once unique and spontaneous – natural discovery ('I do but name thee, Pembroke, and I find'). But his hyperbole itself inescapably and immediately implies that his 'find[ing]' is the opposite – rhetorical invention, the judged production of material and meaning. Jonson moderates the excess of his praise at the moment of articulating it. As elsewhere in his non-dramatic verse, distance from no less than commonality with a patron characterizes his role-play as client.[28]

What makes Pembroke's name the supreme epigram, according to Jonson, is the singularity of its owner's being at once senior man of state and stoic sage:

> But thou, whose noblesse keeps one stature still,
> And one true posture, though besieged with ill
> Of what ambition, faction, pride can raise,
> Whose life even they that envy it must praise,
> Thou art so reverenced, as thy coming in
> But in the view doth interrupt their sin:
> Thou must draw more; and they that hope to see
> The commonwealth still safe must study thee.
>
> (lines 13–20)

Pembroke is said in effect to be the 'hope' of '[t]he commonwealth' – *spes rei publicae*.[29] He is quite literally first in *Epigrams* among the *principes viri et feminae* of Jonson's feigned commonwealth of worthies; but not all those who follow him are also imaged as stoic sages. Roe is, so too Neville (in *Epigram 109*), for example. Others are portrayed with some stoic or more generally Roman colouring. Their portraits thus resemble the images of Pembroke, of Roe, and of Neville, being nonetheless not identical with them nor themselves the same. Jonson portrays still others, of course, with little or no Roman colouring. His attribution and praise of moral excellence are not bounded by Rome; neither, for that matter, is his concept of moral excellence uniform. With regard to that diversity, this could again be mentioned: when imaging himself, Jonson does not seek to efface his differences from his various addressees. Whether indicating commonality or emphasizing affinity, he always acknowledges difference.[30]

Examples of the diversity that I have been describing could well begin with Jonson's address to Sir Ralph Sheldon (*Epigram 119*). There Jonson's praise is eclectic. Opening with a list of follies great and small that Sheldon avoids, he then celebrates Sheldon's virtuous conduct by allusion sequentially to Seneca, Pliny, and Martial.[31] The scope of Sheldon's attributed virtue is unclear amidst the poem's variety of reference. However, it's clear that he has a virtuous habit of mind expressive of right reason. After the catalogue of follies avoided by some men for flawed reasons (lines 1–6), Jonson says:

> No, Sheldon, give me thee, canst want all these,
> But dost it out of judgement, not disease;

> Dar'st breathe in any air, and with safe skill,
> Till thou canst find the best, choose the least ill.

(lines 7–10)

Sheldon's consistency in virtue marks him as a type of the stoic wise man, yet precisely what type seems uncertain. Just before the lines quoted above, Jonson ends his catalogue of follies by ironically picturing 'that good man, / Whose dice not doing well, to a pulpit ran' (5–6) – thus at last, although briefly and indirectly, introducing Christian virtue into a poem that proceeds to laud its addressee's practice of moral choice. Immediately after the evocation of Sheldon's stoic constancy follows Jonson's allusion to Seneca. The praise accorded Sheldon's consistency in virtue seems, therefore, to imply his linking Christian with stoic virtue, just as the subsequent allusions to Pliny and Martial seem to help portray him as no less Roman in spirit than he is English by birth and environment. Jonson's eclectic portrayal of Sheldon indicates him to be a type of the stoic wise man baptized, a member of the commonweal of worthies who – in his neostoicism – is a Lipsian figure rather than one either Senecan or heterogeneously Roman. Yet the mingling of the Christian with the stoic, the English with the Roman, makes the image of Sheldon an elusive portrayal of virtue in action, perhaps because of Sheldon's recusancy or perhaps because Jonson wished to imply Sheldon's being a man of practical wisdom rather than primarily a devout man.[32] And Jonson expresses admiration for Sheldon, enthusiastic sympathy with his way of being in the world, but no sameness between them beyond likemindedness.

Carefully indistinct, if not elusive, is the epigram to Sir William Uvedale (*Epigram 125*):

> Uvedale, thou piece of the first times, a man
> Made for what nature could, or virtue can;
> Both whose dimensions, lost, the world might find
> Restored in thy body and thy mind!
> Who sees a soul in such a body set
> Might love the treasure for the cabinet.
> But I, no child, no fool, respect the kind,
> Which (would the world not miscall't flattery)
> The full, the flowing graces there enshrined;
> I could adore, almost to idolatry.

The hyperbolic rhetoric that allows Jonson at once to enthuse and to signal the performative distance of his writing celebrates a marvellous and reassuring reconciliation of opposites.³³ Uvedale, according to Jonson's mythic rendering of him, incarnates continuity between the flawed present and the golden past, harmonizes pleasure with virtue and thus matter with spirit, nature with grace. He is no stoic wise man but, rather, reassurance of perfection's not being lost to the world – and therefore the subject of wonder. One aspect of that is, of course, this: Uvedale's metonymic virtue expresses *omnia in parvo*, having a generous and fluid abundance that (by implication) makes classification superfluous. Jonson presents himself as the knowing admirer almost overcome with wonder at the *numen* of the man he praises, yet too knowing to be so. There are distances in the poem, not identity.³⁴

By way of final illustration I shall consider the seventy-sixth epigram, which is one of the poems focused on Lucy, Countess of Bedford.³⁵ Jonson's hyperbolic rhetoric of praise in that poem does not so much enthuse as play with the notion of enthusiasm – 'possession by a god' – itself:

> This morning, timely rapt with holy fire,
> I thought to form unto my zealous muse
> What kind of creature I could most desire
> To honour, serve and love, as poets use.
>
> (lines 1–4)

Jonson's layered irony can be seen in his amusedly anecdotal imaging of himself as divinely inspired – possessed by his muse – and in the graceful extravagance of his desire as it is articulated throughout most of what follows (lines 5–16). It can especially be seen in his alluding to Sidney's Astrophil. At the end of his poem he concludes his fantasy of the ideal and heroic woman with: 'Such when I meant to feign and wished to see, / My muse bade, *Bedford* write, and that was she' (lines 17–18). The initial sonnet of *Astrophil and Stella* finishes, as we know, with: 'Thus great with child to speake, and helplesse in my throwes, / Biting my trewand pen, beating my selfe for spite, / "Foole," said my Muse to me, "looke in thy heart and write"' (lines 12–14).³⁶ Upon looking into his heart Astrophil will find the likeness of Stella. His Muse's impatient command echoes a recurring trope from the *Rime*, in which Petrarch's speaker asserts that he is conscious of bearing within his heart the likeness of Laura.³⁷ Jonson does not presume to have his Muse tell him to look into his heart and find imaged there the object of his fantasy: he cannot identify himself as intimately with his patroness as the courtly Astrophil could with Stella. Instead, following a far less intimate – and peremptory – injunction, he inscribes the name of a woman whom he certainly may not claim to incorporate. His implicitly counter-Sidneyan conceit is that the truest poetry turns out, with reference to Bedford, not to be the most feigning.[38] Writing Bedford's name, Jonson suggests, is therefore not to 'form' his ideal but to acknowledge its pre-existing his attempt. Seeking to 'form' his ideal he has unwittingly gestured towards the *numen* of his patroness. One could elaborate usefully if briefly in this way. Out of Jonson's serio-ludic enthusiasm, his wryly recounted possession by his muse, comes the moment of (foreshadowed) recognition made climactic to the poem – recognition of his desire's perfection in Bedford. Like some being in a masque, she embodies an Idea: in this case his insufficient, indistinctly for-mulated idea that she has perfectly embodied before he could formulate it; an idea that he could begin to 'form', then express, only when possessed by his muse. In her androgynously heroic virtue Bedford may have qualities congruent with those of the stoic wise man but otherwise she is far removed from Pembroke, Roe, and Sheldon (less so from Uvedale, yet nevertheless she is at a great remove from him). And she is further from Jonson than Stella from Astrophil.

The seventy-sixth epigram attests, then, to the wide diversity – the required individuation – amidst commonality in Jonson's feigned common-weal of national heroes. The poem affirms that although his evoking the notion of constancy is foundational to the imagining of his fictive common-weal, constancy is not the only mark of Jonson's eutopian community of the various few. Jonson gives priority to that notion, yet much co-exists with it. One of those co-existent things is the notion of understanding. I shall now consider Jonson's evoking it and, hence, his feigning a second commonweal – the community of true readers.

FEIGNING THE COMMONWEALTH OF UNDERSTANDERS

After evoking the notion of constancy in his Dedication, Jonson proceeds in the first of his epigrams to evoke that of understanding. The initial poem addresses '*the Reader*' and warns: 'Pray thee take care, that tak'st my book in hand, / To read it well; that is, to understand.' The pointedness of the epigram lies in its rhyme's sharp emphasis on the disparity between physical and mental possession of Jonson's book. Less obtrusive is the emphasis on complementary (though not equal) authorities, attached to its sequencing of pronouns. The poem opens in admonition of the reader ('thee') to be careful, indicates Jonson's intellectual proprietorship of the book as transcending the reader's physical ownership or other possession

of it ('tak'st my book in hand'), and ends by implying that understanding
'it' – true reading of it – allows the reader to participate in something of
Jonson's authority over his work. To understand the book is of course to
possess it more than just physically. Yet the question remains as to what
Jonson's take on the notion of understanding may be – and the subsequent
epigram, *To My Book*, offers an answer, one which in effect reveals
Jonson beginning to feign, from the start of *Epigrams*, a commonwealth
of understanders.

It is clearly if tacitly suggested in the first epigram that understanding will
involve discrimination and that thereby the reader will implicitly become
linked with Jonson as *auctor*. The nature of discrimination, which is to
say, the natures of misunderstanding and of its opposite, is unfolded in
the subsequent poem:

> It will be looked for, book, when some but see
>   Thy title, *Epigrams*, and named of me,
> Thou shouldst be bold, licentious, full of gall,
> Wormwood and sulphur, sharp and toothed withal;
>   Become a petulant thing, hurl ink and wit
>   As madmen stones, not caring whom they hit.
>   Deceive their malice who could wish it so.
>   And by thy wiser temper let men know
>   Thou are not covetous of least self-fame
>   Made from the hazard of another's shame;
> Much less with lewd, profane and beastly phrase,
> To catch the world's loose laughter or vain gaze.
>   He that departs with his own honesty
>   For vulgar praise, doth it too dearly buy.

The place to begin is, for my purposes, with Jonson's conceit of the book as
a living thing. The question arises, a living thing of what kind? The answer
to that leads in turn to answering the previous question, namely, what
Jonson might take understanding itself to be.

Addressing the book as a creature of his begetting – one variant of a familiar early modern trope – Jonson starts by considering misunderstanders
and how their misjudgment will fantastically transform, will deform, his
book. '[S]ome' potential readers, he says, will pre-judge from the title of
his book and his authorship of it that *Epigrams* will 'be bold, licentious,
full of gall, / Wormwood and sulphur, sharp and toothed withal' (lines
3–4). Their misjudgment anticipates that his book will be a grotesque, monstrous in its extravagance, bitterness, and violence. In fact, they expect his
book to contain poems that will characterize it predominantly in terms

of confrontational subgenres of the epigram. They expect, then, epigrams containing foulness (*foetidas* – 'licentious' poems) and bitterness (poems 'full of gall' – *fel*). They expect, too, poems with a vicious sharpness (a hostile *argutezza* – or pointedness of wit).[39] Their malicious pre-judgment – their prejudice – transforms his work into a caricature generated by their misreading of title and author: by misunderstanding born of opinion (*opinio*). So in anticipation they indecorously associate it with violence, indecorum, and excess (those categories being suggested by the Latin origins of 'petulant').[40] All satire is hybrid, but the misreaders whom Jonson chooses himself to summon in anticipation will think – as he fables – that satire by him will be a crazy hybrid. They will think it to be creativity deformed by ungoverned emotions and tearing itself apart in unreasoned, unfocused anger ('hurl ink and wit' – its own substance – '[a]s madmen stones, not caring whom they hit'). Now of course there are extreme bitterness and corrosive anger in various poems of *Epigrams*; but here Jonson seeks, not surprisingly, to identify otherwise the qualities of his poems.

   Almost the first half of Jonson's poem emphasizes that misunderstanding expresses prejudice and false judgment – and thus opinion (as for example Lipsius describes it and as Jonson concordantly represents it elsewhere).[41] In their lack of discrimination, Jonson's imagined misunderstanders are ironically Pygmalion-like, choosing to (re)make *Epigrams* in the image of their own unattractive desires. The poem's beginning therefore implicitly and antithetically defines discrimination, which is at once to say, the notion of understanding: understanding expresses true judgment; true judgment expresses right reason. That indirect, conventional definition elucidates the trope used in the poem's second half to characterize Jonson's book as it allegedly is in truth, namely this: *Epigrams* embodies a 'wiser temper' (line 8). The transitional verse introducing that trope – the magisterially measured *adhortatio*, 'Deceive their malice who could wish it so' (line 7) – suggests the correction of misunderstanders against their wills. In conjunction with what immediately follows, the line suggests that Jonson's book, by its reasoned and prudent moderation, will make self-evident to misunderstanders what judgment, discrimination, understanding should have been and in fact are. Jonson asserts that his book repudiates *fel* and *foetidas* – and that it rejects 'depart[ure]' from 'honesty' (line 13). The book will confront potential readers who are misunderstanders with what could fairly be called the ethics of reading. However, for understanders it will offer confirmation of what they know and practise, not confrontation – stressing, as it does so, elements and processes of cognition inseparable from

those informing the Senecan and Lipsian formulations of constancy. Jonson
rewrites, in short, the start of Martial's *Epigrams*, where the Roman poet
wrote: 'I trust that I have followed in my little books such a mean (*tale
temperamentum*) that none who forms a right judgment of himself (*de se
bene senserit*) can complain of them.'[42]

   Since the ethics of reading indicated by *To My Book* clearly if obliquely
link those able to be understanders with those able to achieve constancy of
virtue, it is not unexpected that Jonson's feigned community of worthies
overlaps with the community of understanders which he begins to
summon into being through the interaction between his first and
second epigrams.[43] Though by no means all members of the former community are suggested to be members of the latter, several of Jonson's
addressees notably are. Roe is, for example; so too (by the logic of the
humanist topos foundational to *Epigram 102*) must be Pembroke. John
Donne is a member of the latter, Jonson implies, who belongs as well
to the former. Thus in the twenty-third epigram Donne is praised
at the outset for his virtuosity as a writer and last for the virtue of his
life. Jonson declares: '[E]very work of thy most early wit / Came forth
example, and remains so yet' (lines 3–4).[44] He subsequently brings
Donne's writing and life together when he refers to '[T]hy language,
letters, arts, best life, / Which might with half mankind maintain a
strife' (lines 7–8). He offers a comprehensive image of Donne's *virtu*;
in the ninety-sixth epigram, however, Jonson emphasizes Donne's
unique judgment, his unique creativity ('That so alone canst judge, so
alone dost make'). *Epigram 23* indirectly associates Donne with
Pembroke. *Epigram 96* directly associates Jonson with Donne, carefully
– not to say anxiously – dissociating Jonson from a merely popular
readership or audience. He carefully writes himself into his eutopian
community of understanders.

   By way of concluding at this point, I should like to focus briefly on
Epigram 14 To William Camden. There the elaborate humility of the
ninety-sixth epigram takes a different form, one appropriate to the celebration of a man who, Jonson suggests, is rather a culture-hero than a
distinguished man of letters. Like Pembroke, Camden needs to be rightly
understood. Jonson's poem begins:

> Camden, most reverend head, to whom I owe
>   All that I am in arts, all that I know,
> (How nothing's that?) to whom my country owes
>   The great renown and name wherewith she goes;

> Than thee the age sees not that thing more grave,
> More high, more holy, that she more would crave.
>
> (lines 1–6)

Naming Camden, Jonson identifies his own derivation. Moreover naming Camden he identifies the man from whom, he subsequently claims, Britain has itself come to derive identity: a man of unique *gravitas* and *pietas*. Jonson portrays Camden as a truly national hero, who belongs to the feigned commonwealth of worthies and likewise to that of understanders. He can return *ad fontes* (see line 8, below), fulfilling the humanist dream of tracing origins, and therefore he comprehensively understands the natures of texts and traditions. As Jonson writes, emphasizing Camden's credibility born of *auctoritas*:

> What name, what skill, what faith hast thou in things!
> What sight in searching the most antique springs!
> What weight, and what authority in thy speech!
> Man scarce can make that doubt, but thou canst teach.
>
> (lines 7–10)

Jonson concludes:

> Pardon free truth, and let thy modesty,
> Which conquers all, be once overcome by thee.
> Many of thine this better could than I:
> But for their powers accept my piety.
>
> (lines 11–14)

The poem ends – as at once praise of Camden and *gratiarium actio* – with an implicitly iterated honouring of Camden's *pietas* through which Jonson stages the imperfect repayment of his personal debt to Camden (lines 13–14). It is a gesture that emphasizes Jonson's association with a man he represents as the ideal humanist scholar – an understander and the educator of yet others.

To be part of the feigned common weal of understanders is, nevertheless, to inhabit a world where books are sold and bought, a world of commodities and marketplaces. Jonson's third epigram, *To My Bookseller*, acknowledges as much; on the other hand, the poem takes pains to indicate its author's unwillingness that *Epigrams* be valued and judged in terms of economic criteria. In fact it takes pains to suggest his indifference to the materiality of his book. Communication with understanders is, by implication, what really counts (lines 8–10). The poem begins with an allusion to *prudentia*, one that's simultaneously commonsensical and reductive:

> Thou that mak'st gain thy end, and wisely well
> Call'st a book good or bad, as it doth sell,
> Use mine so, too; I give thee leave.
>
> (lines 1–3)

Then comes the 'but':

> but crave
> For the luck's sake it thus much favour have:
> To lie upon thy stall till it be sought;
> Not offered, as it made suit to be bought.
>
> (lines 3–6)

There is a readership, Jonson announces, in which he has no interest:

> Nor have my title-leaf on posts or walls
> Or in cleft-sticks, advanced to make calls
> For termers or some clerk-like serving-man
> Who scarce can spell the hard names; whose knight less can.
>
> (lines 7–10)

Better his book should end as a simply material commodity, he says – sold to be wrapping paper (lines 11–12) – than it should begin as a commodity of merely another kind: a book seeking buyers, a readership, outside the understanders who may seek it. Jonson's fiction of transcending the marketplace, delivered with a carefully casual *hauteur*, itself of course requires one or more enabling fictions. In good part his feigning the eutopian commonwealths provides those. However, the subsequent epigrams focused on King James present, in effect, an overarching fiction. They fable exactly where the commonwealths of worthies and of understanders ultimately find their common apex; they crown, that is to say, Jonson's feigning a level of existence – an ideal political economy – beyond the economy of the marketplace.

FEIGNING THE KING

The epigram *To King James* celebrates, as do the masques, transcendence manifested through the reconciliation of opposites:

> How, best of kings, dost thou a scepter bear!
> How, best of poets, dost thou laurel wear!

But two things rare the fates had in their store,
And gave thee both, to show they could no more.
For such a poet, while thy days were green
Thou wert, as chief of them are said to have been.
And such a prince thou art, we daily see,
As chief of those still promise they will be.
Whom should my muse then fly to, but the best
Of kings for grace, of poets for my test?

Jonson's celebrating the king's possession of both 'scepter' and 'laurel' locates his image of James within the tradition that human life has three aspects: contemplation; action; pleasure. As we know, the first of those aspects has to do with philosophic thought not directed towards matters of state; the second is concerned with politics and the business of government; the third is focused on the senses and (or) sensuality.[45] Jonson asserts in addressing the king that James is the elect of 'the fates' and so has been pre-destined, one might almost say, to unite the life of political action with the life of the intellect. Plutarch had written:

And those who can unite political ability with philosophy I regard as perfect men, for I take them to attain two of the greatest blessings, serving the state in a public capacity, and living the calm and tranquil life of philosophy. For, as there are three kinds of life, the practical, the contemplative, and the life of enjoyment, and of these three the one devoted to enjoyment is a paltry and animal life, and the practical without philosophy an unlovely and harsh life, and the contemplative without the practical a useless life, so we must endeavor with all our power to combine public life with philosophy as far as circumstances will permit.

Thus, as Jonson has it, King James brings together what Macrobius calls – with reference to Cicero's *Dream of Scipio* – 'the rules of double perfection' ('*perfectionis geminae praecepta*').[46] Jonson's own words are again relevant here, some of those from *Discoveries* in which he associates poets with philosophy rather than with sensuous pleasure: 'We do not require in him [the poet] mere elocution; or an excellent faculty in verse; but the exact knowledge of all virtues, and their contraries.'[47] The fourth epigram's fiction of James as model king and poet therefore has several implications pertinent to Jonson's feigning of commonwealths.

First, Jonson's fiction of the king emphasizes that personal choice is not an issue as regards James' possession of sceptre and laurel (his reconciling political action with contemplation). A choice by the Fates has conferred

those upon him; in other words, no personal decision has made James
either or both king and poet. Moreover Jonson emphasizes that James
has been given rare capacities as well as rare gifts, rather than asserting
that he has exemplarily exercised agency in using the gifts bestowed on
him. James is not portrayed as if he had himself in some way re-enacted
the judgment of Paris or enacted Scipio's dream of judgment. The point
is, I think, that the king stands above such personal choices. He does
not have to do anything in order to become or to remain the best of
rulers and of poets. He was (pre)destined to be, and thus is, both.
Jonson's fiction distinctly implies as a consequence that James necessarily
forms the apex to the commonwealths of worthies and of understanders.
Submitting himself with graceful deference (since graceful deference, not
truth, is all) to the royal poet allows Jonson to affirm his participation
in what might be called a mythographic order of his own fashioning:
one feigned as beyond, though co-existent with, the economy of the
marketplace.[48]

Jonson's complementary assertion of that mythographic order can be
seen in his fifth epigram's representing James as sacerdotal king:

> When was there contract better driven by fate?
> Or celebrated with more truth of state?
> The world the temple was, the priest a king,
> The spoused pair two realms, the sea the ring.

At the personal level James unites sceptre with laurel; at the transnational,
he unites Scotland with England. Jonson fables a reconciliation of hitherto
opposed nations that centres upon the king but which has not ultimately
depended upon the king's personal decision any more than does James'
being model king and poet. Elected by the Fates, as Jonson emphasizes
once more (and in the poem's first line), James acts as the destined instrument of national unity. He performs a version of the sacred marriage in his
role as king-priest – itself an archetypal reconciliation. Jonson's participation in the mythographic fiction lies not solely in the fact of his fashioning it but, additionally, in his basing it on a trope used by James himself.
That is to say, Jonson amplifies the words of the 'best . . . of poets' and
now king-priest, fashioning himself as an instrument to the instrument of
the Fates.[49] He reworks those words into a masque-like poem where
James becomes the central figure in a cosmic pageant.[50] And James
stands, according to Jonson, in the midst of a vast circle within the circle

of the world: *nihil deest quod duceret orbem.* Thus Jonson could write, in *To the Ghost of Martial* (*Epigram 36*):

> Martial, thou gav'st far nobler epigrams
> To thy Domitian, than I can my James;
> But in my royal subject I pass thee:
> Thou flattered'st thine, mine cannot flattered be.

After that numinous image of James abruptly comes Jonson's contemptuous dismissal of alchemists ('If all you boast of your great art be true, / Sure, willing poverty lives most in you'). James, as portrayed in the fifth epigram, plays a role in the transformation of kingdoms; alchemists, as the next poem emphasizes, transform nothing although golden transformation is their claim. Jonson juxtaposes vision with lie. He suddenly sets the dystopian against the eutopian, the satiric against the epic.[51] And the contradictions of his Book express the heterogeneity of his Britain, which the understander will know how to read, the worthy how to inhabit. The understander will know, moreover, that although both Jonson and the alchemists are makers of fictions, those fictions differ markedly insofar as they are inventions (and inventions both linked to mythography). Jonson creates a fiction of national destiny, a political representation that crowns the feigning of commonwealths which informs his Book. That is to say, his setting Great Britain *sub specie Jacobi* is the apex to his re-imagining and rewriting of the nation – which offers a way to discern the eutopian or, at least, eutopian possibilities amidst the jumble of the actual. The alchemists' lie is only an idol of the theatre, for the marketplace.

Nevertheless, Jonson knows the precariousness of his eutopian fictions just as well as he knows the vulnerability of the fiction sold by alchemists. Perhaps the clearest example of that can be seen in *To My Muse* (*Epigram 65*). The poem has sometimes been thought a covert recantation of the praise expended on Cecil in the two epigrams immediately preceding it.[52] That may be so – the juxtaposition suggests subversion. But whether or not *To My Muse* is aimed at Cecil, its following straight on from the Cecil poems indicates Jonson's sensitivity to problems with his feigning of commonwealths in *Epigrams*. The first of the two grouped poems to Cecil (63) distinctly identifies him as a type of the stoic wise man. It is his 'virtue', Jonson writes, not his 'fortune' that has made Cecil a man of remarkable achievement; and he is a man of 'equal mind' (respectively, lines 2–4 and 8). Moreover he reflects or expresses '[t]he judgement of the king' (line 4). The second poem, also associating him with James, celebrates Cecil as the Treasurer who is in yet above the current 'age of [merely material] gold'

(line 4): as a man at once overseeing, but not subject to, the economy and fit
to receive such a gift as would have been 'treasure[d]' in the Golden Age
(lines 3–4). Then, in *To My Muse*, Jonson writes this:

> Away, and leave me, thou thing most abhorred,
> That hast betrayed me to a worthless lord,
> Made me commit most fierce idolatry
> To a great image through thy luxury.

(lines 1–4)

The poem may or may not be aimed at Cecil; it is certainly focused on
Jonson himself. In its opening lines he initiates an allegory through
which personal failure can be conceded and then, at the last, ironically
recuperated. Jonson creates a means through which he can negotiate a
specific failure by himself as understander, maker, feigner of commonwealths. In effect he berates himself for having wrongly included someone
in the list of 'good and great names' headed by Pembroke – for his having
included someone unworthy in his feigned commonwealth of worthies. He
suggests that his failure of understanding – his false making – have transformed him no less than they have the object of his praise. He has ceased
to be, with reference to that specific case, the revealer of a commonwealth
of national heroes, the maker who brings it into view and hence summons it
into being, and become the fashioner and passionate worshipper of a false
image. '[L]uxury' is a word particularly apt, of course, in the context of
Cecil's patronage, given his conspicuous *luxuria*. In any event, it is a
word Jonson uses to characterize his own excessive desire within a particular
client-relationship or act of clientage – his own self-betraying concupiscence.[53] Jonson was prepared to admit, his poem suggests via excoriation
of his muse, that the enemy to his eutopian versions of the political in
Epigrams could come from within himself quite as powerfully as it could
from others.

NOTES

1. I am using the term 'notion' as it is used in Ian Maclean's *The Renaissance
   Notion of Woman: A Study in the Fortunes of Scholasticism and Medical
   Science in European Intellectual Life* (1983; rpt Cambridge University Press,
   1992), at page 1. In what follows, and as I shall subsequently note where
   pertinent, my thinking about *Epigrams* has been guided partly by Erving
   Goffman's theorizing on role-play and on stigma. See, respectively: *The
   Presentation of Self in Everyday Life*, rev. edn (1959; rpt New York:
   Doubleday, n.d.); *Stigma: Notes on the Management of Spoiled Identity*

(1963: rpt Harmondsworth: Penguin, 1973). Thereafter those works are referred to severally as *The Presentation of Self* and as *Stigma*. As I shall likewise note where relevant, it has also in part been guided by Quentin Skinner's *Regarding Method* (Cambridge University Press, 2002).

2. Only once in his poems: see *Epigram 98 To Sir Thomas Roe*, line 9. Reference is to *Ben Jonson: Poems*, ed. Ian Donaldson (Oxford University Press, 1975). Now-contemporary commentary also refers to the 'gathered self' as the 'centred self'. See especially Thomas M. Greene, *The Light in Troy: Imitation and Discovery in Renaissance Poetry* (New Haven: Yale University Press, 1982), 275. In discussing that Jonsonian preoccupation Greene refers to a number of poems, including *Epigram 128 To Sir William Roe*.

3. For instance while examining Jonson's preoccupation, in his drama, with antitheses to the 'gathered self', Peter Hyland rather simply announces that the epigrams on Neville and Pembroke picture them as types of 'the classic Stoic hero'. See his *Disguise and Role-Playing in Ben Jonson's Drama* (Salzburg: Institute for English Speech and Drama, 1977), 19.

4. The epigram *To My Book* being followed by *To My Bookseller* and thereupon by the epigrams respectively *To King James* and *On the Union*. Later in this chapter I shall more closely discuss the sequencing of the poems.

5. On constancy – or consistency – in virtue as the hallmark of the stoic wise man, see for example Seneca, *Ep. 120*, 18–20 in *Ad Lucilium Epistulae Morales*, ed. and trans. R. M. Gummere, Loeb Classical Library, 3 vols. (1917–25; rpt Cambridge, MA: Harvard University Press, 1967–71), III. Cf. *ibid.*, III, 11–12 (1–4 are especially relevant to Jonson's Dedication). Further references to the letters are from that edition. See also: J. M. Rist, *Stoic Philosophy* (1969; rpt Cambridge University Press, 1977), 3–4; A. A. Long, *Hellenistic Philosophy: Stoics, Epicureans, Sceptics*, 2nd edn (1974; rpt Berkeley: University of California Press, 1986), 177, 202–4. On 177, Long writes: 'The Stoics distinguished good men from others by reference to the consistency of their *logos*.' He adds: 'Our moral progress is typified not by the extirpation of all emotion and desire, but by the occurrence of desires and feelings which are dispositions of a governing-principle increasingly consistent with right reason.' Cf. Malcolm Schofield, 'Stoic Ethics', in *The Cambridge Companion to the Stoics*, ed. Brad Inwood (Cambridge University Press, 2003), 242–4.

6. See Donaldson's 'Jonson's Poetry', in *The Cambridge Companion to Ben Jonson*, ed. Richard Harp and Stanley Stewart (Cambridge University Press, 2000), 125.

7. See *Conversations* 1.1–3, in *Ben Jonson: The Complete Poems*, ed. George Parfitt (New Haven: Yale University Press, 1975), 461.

8. Jonson's repetition of 'while' alludes to the possibility of change in Pembroke – and therefore to Jonson's vulnerability as his client – but the diplomatic intimation is of course that Pembroke *cannot* alter in his possession and practice of virtue, as the phrase 'great exemplar' suggests from the beginning (a point I shall return to later in this discussion).

9. See: Gerhard Oestreich, *Neostoicism and the Early Modern State*, ed. Brigitta Oestreich and H. G. Koenigsberger, trans. David McLintock (Cambridge University Press, 1982), 28–75; Giles D. Monsarrat, *Light from the Porch: Stoicism and English Renaissance Literature* (Paris: Didier-Erudition, 1984), 21–80; Achsah Guibbory, *The Map of Time: Seventeenth-Century English Literature and Ideas of Pattern in History* (Urbana: University of Illinois Press, 1986), 105–35; Mark Morford, *Stoics and Neostoics: Rubens and the Circle of Lipsius* (Princeton University Press, 1991), 14–138; Robert C. Evans, *Jonson, Lipsius and The Politics of Renaissance Stoicism* (Durango: Longwood, 1992), 1–27 and 111–30; Richard Tuck, *Philosophy and Government 1572–1651* (Cambridge University Press, 1993), 31–119; Adriana McCrea, *Constant Minds: Political Virtue and the Lipsian Paradigm in England, 1584–1650* (University of Toronto Press, 1997), 3–39 and 138–70. That it is an *heroic* ideal can be clearly seen when, in *De Constantia* for instance, Seneca cites Ulysses and Hercules as exemplars of the stoic wise man (which he does in 2.1). See Seneca, *De Constantia*, in *Moral Essays*, ed. and trans. John W. Basore, Loeb Classical Library, 3 vols. (1928–35; rpt Cambridge, MA: Harvard University Press, 1963–70). Further references to *De Constantia* and to others of the *Moral Essays* will be from that edition. On Jonson's use in general of Roman authors, see: Katharine Eisaman Maus, *Ben Jonson and the Roman Frame of Mind* (Princeton University Press, 1984); Julie Sanders, *Ben Jonson's Theatrical Republics* (Basingstoke: Macmillan, 1998), 11–33. On Jonson's use of Roman authors in *Epigrams*, see Stella P. Revard, 'Classicism and Neo-Classicism in Jonson's *Epigrammes* and *The Forrest*', in *Ben Jonson's 1616 Folio*, ed. Jennifer Brady and W. H. Herendeen (Newark: University of Delaware Press, 1991), 138–67.
10. Justus Lipsius, *Two Bookes of Constancie*, trans. Sir John Stradling, ed. Rudolf Kirk, annot. Clayton Morris Hall (New Brunswick: Rutgers University Press, 1939). All reference – in modernized spelling – will be to that edition and given in the body of the chapter.
11. '*Sapiens autem . . . vinci possit.*'
12. Cf. Quentin Skinner, 'Motives, Intentions and Interpretation', in his *Regarding Method*, 90–102, at page 98. In the same volume, see his 'Interpretation and the Understanding of Speech Acts', 103–27, 104–7. See also J. G. A. Pocock, 'Texts as Events: Reflections on the History of Political Thought', in *Politics of Discourse: The Literature and History of Seventeenth-Century England*, ed. Kevin Sharpe and Steven Zwicker (Berkeley: University of California Press, 1987), 21–34.
13. '*Ad illa nitens . . . nihil flebit.*'
14. '*Inter micantis ubique . . . uni homini pax fuit.*' Cf. 5.6–6.1.
15. '*Iniuria in bonos . . . quam inter se.*'
16. A tactic Jonson uses in *To Penshurst*, as I have noted in my article with R. J. Webb, 'Appropriating and Attributing the Supernatural in the Early Modern Country House Poem', *Early Modern Literary Studies* 11 (2005): 1–26, at 4. Cf. Seneca's *Ep.* 31.11 and his *Ep.* 44.1–5. In *Epigrams*, of

course, Jonson doesn't lay claim only to characteristics of the stoic sage. Moreover, what might be called his process of moral association is carefully nuanced – as I discuss below.

17. The passage runs, in full: 'And then I made answer that on behalf of the state you [Serenus] had good reason to be stirred – the state which Publius Clodius on the one hand, Vatinius and all the greatest rascals on the other, were putting up for sale, and, carried away by blind cupidity, did not realize that, while they were selling, they too were being sold' (2.1 – '*Tum ego respondi . . . vendunt et venire*').

18. In his fable of the first orator as humankind's prime culture hero. See Cicero, *De Inventione* 2.2, in *De Inventione, De Optimo Genere Oratorum, Topica*, ed. and trans. H. M. Hubbell, Loeb Classical Library (1949; rpt Cambridge, MA: Harvard University Press, 1968). Cf. *De Tranquillitate Animi* 2.7.

19. '*Qui rationi innixus . . . ubi accipiat iniuriam*' (8.3).

20. Also: '[T]he life that is happy has been founded on correct and trustworthy judgement, and is unalterable' ('*Beata ergo vita . . . stabilita et immutabilis*' – 5.3). And: 'The happy man, therefore, is one who has right judgement; . . . the happy man is he who allows reason to fix the value of every condition of existence' ('*Beatus ergo est . . . ratio commendat*' – 6.2).

21. Again, cf. Rist, *Stoic Philosophy*, 3–4.

22. See Stanley Fish, 'Authors-Readers: Jonson's Community of the Same', *Representations* 7 (1984): 26–58. Fish demonstrates that sameness is at times articulated in Jonson's non-dramatic verse by way of a distinctive epistemology. As he puts it, when discussing a poem addressed by Jonson to Nicholas Breton: 'In this felicitous epistemology, perception is not mediated or "asquint" because it is *self*-perception; there is no obstruction between the eye and its object because there is literally nothing (no thing) between them. The dilemma of representation – its inability to be transparent, to refrain from clothing or covering – is no longer felt because representation is bypassed in favour of the instantaneous recognition, in another and in the work of another, of what one already is' (31).

23. Stanley Fish writes in his 'Authors-Readers' that, '[I]n short, Jonson establishes [in the poems *de facto* revealing a "community of the same"] an *alternate* world of patronage and declares it (by an act of poetic fiat) more real than the world in which he is apparently embedded. He invokes the distinctions that structure (or at least appear to structure) his material existence – distinctions of place, birth, wealth, power – but then he effaces them by drawing everyone he names into a community of virtue in which everyone is, by definition, the same as everyone else. He calls his heroes and heroines by their proper titles – Lady, Sir, Lord, Knight – but then he enrols them in his list under the title they all indifferently share' (38). My argument now being unfolded concurs at some points with and at others diverges from that of Fish's essay.

24. For Seneca, see *De Vita Beata* 12.1–2; for Lipsius, *De Constantia* 1.4–6.

25. Given Jonson's *impresa* of broken compass and incomplete circle. Goffman's categories of 'the own and the wise' illuminate Jonson's ambiguous

self-presentation in this poem (via his *impresa*), just as they more obviously illuminate his writing about those, such as 'Playwright' (in *Epigram 100*), whom he castigates. See *Stigma*, 31–45. Also helpful here, as in relation to the poems on Cecil and James I, is Goffman's discussion of 'Discrepant Roles' in his *The Presentation of Self*, 141–166.

26. Cf. Skinner's 'Interpretation and the Understanding of Speech Acts', in his *Regarding Method*, 108.

27. On this poem see also: Richard S. Peterson, *Imitation and Praise in the Poems of Ben Jonson* (New Haven: Yale University Press, 1981), 56; Richard Dutton, *Ben Jonson: To the First Folio* (Cambridge University Press, 1983), 79–81; Robert C. Evans, *Ben Jonson and the Poetics of Patronage* (Lewisburg: Bucknell University Press, 1989), 108–18.

28. Again, see my and R. J. Webb's 'Appropriating and Attributing the Supernatural', 2 and 6.

29. '*Spes*' often occurs in close conjunction with '*res publica*' in Roman texts. See Cicero's *Ad Familiares* 2.9.2 for instance; and there's a use of the phrase by Cicero's brother in *Commentariolum Petitionis* 13. I owe the second reference to Dr Alison Scott.

30. A case in point: even though, in *Epigram 109 To Sir Henry Neville*, he implies his morally authoritative indifference to distinctions of class – a point made explicit in *Epigram 9*, though 'strict' (line 2) is ambiguous – Jonson nevertheless duly acknowledges Neville's 'pedigree' as no negligible thing (line 4).

31. See Ian Donaldson's notes to the poem, on page 69 of his edition (*Ben Jonson: Poems*).

32. On Sheldon's recusancy see Donaldson, *ibid*. As regards Sheldon and wisdom, Herford and Simpson note a view quite contrary to Jonson's: 'Chamberlain told Carleton that "Sir Rofe Shelton" was a buffoon'. See C. H. Herford and Percy and Evelyn Simpson, eds., *Ben Jonson*, 11 vols. (1952; rpt Oxford: Clarendon Press, 1970), XI, 26.

33. On this poem see also Peterson, *Imitation*, 87–9.

34. As regards distance of another kind, see *Epigram 105 To Mary, Lady Wroth*. There Jonson again uses a *renovatio* topos – but of course uses it differently: Wroth figures as the embodiment of *numen* who would, were it necessary, enable renewal of classical representations of the feminine divine.

35. On this poem see also Sara J. Van den Berg, *The Action of Ben Jonson's Poetry* (Newark: University of Delaware Press, 1987), 94–5.

36. Reference is to *The Poems of Sir Philip Sidney*, ed. William A. Ringler, Jr (Oxford: Clarendon Press, 1962).

37. See my *Shakespeare's Sonnets and Narrative Poems* (Harlow: Longman, 2000), at page 116, and also Ringler's note to line 14 of Sonnet 1, on page 459 of his edition of Sidney.

38. Although self-evidently it also is.

39. On the subgenres of the early modern epigram, see Rosalie L. Colie, *The Resources of Kind: Genre-Theory in the Renaissance* (Berkeley: University of

California Press, 1973), 68–9; Alastair Fowler, *Kinds of Literature: An Introduction to the Theory of Genres and Modes* (1982; rpt Oxford: Clarendon Press, 1985), 183–4, 229. Behind their accounts lies chiefly Julius Caesar Scaliger's *Poetices Libri Septem* (Lyon, 1561), 3.126.

40. According to Lewis and Short, *Petulans* suggests, in addition to petulance as such, impudence; wantonness. *Petulantia* (which of course has similar or identical associations) suggests, of things: exuberance; luxuriousness.

41. In his *Two Bookes* Lipsius writes: 'Therefore we define right reason to be, *A true sense and judgment of things human and divine.* (So far as the same appertains to us.) But opinion (being the contrary to it) is defined to be, *A false and frivolous conjecture of those things*' (1.4). For Jonsonian representation of opinion, see *Hymenaei*, in *Selected Masques*, ed. Stephen Orgel (1970; rpt New Haven: Yale University Press, 1975), 70–5, especially at lines 650, 835–9.

42. Martial, *Epigrams*, ed. and trans. Walter C. A. Ker, Loeb Classical Library, 2 vols. (1919; rpt Cambridge, MA: Harvard University Press, 1990), '*Spero me secutum . . . se bene senserit.*' It's observed by Van den Berg that Jonson's first four epigrams parallel those opening Martial's Book One (see *Action*, 89–90).

43. That is to say, which he begins to summon in opposition to an anticipated gathering of misunderstanders.

44. In lines 1–2, Jonson says: 'Donne, the delight of Phoebus and each muse, / Who, to thy one, all other brains refuse'. In his edition Ian Donaldson glosses the compressed second line as 'who, in favour of your brain, refuse to inspire all other brains'. Perhaps it additionally means (or means instead?): 'who rely on your brain rather than on the inspiration or authority of all other brains'. Jonson stresses the singularity of Donne, as line 3 also indicates.

45. See: Plutarch, *The Training of Children*, trans. R. C. Trench, in *The Essays and Miscellanies*, 3 vols. (New York: Crowell, 1909), II, 11 – to be quoted below; Fabii Planciadis Fulgentii, *Opera*, ed. Rudolfus Helm (Lipsiae: Teubneri, 1898), *Mitologiarum Libri Tres*, 2.1. 65–7; Marsilio Ficino, *The 'Philebus' Commentary*, ed. and trans. Michael J. B. Allen (Berkeley: University of California Press, 1975), 480 and 482.

46. See Macrobius, *Commentarii in Somnium Scipionis*, ed. Jacobus Willis (Leipzig: Teubner Verlagsgesellschaft, 1970), 2.17.9. Edgar Wind quotes Macrobius' phrase in connection with Plutarch and Fulgentius when discussing 'Virtue Reconciled with Pleasure' in his *Pagan Mysteries in the Renaissance*, rev. edn (Harmondsworth: Penguin, 1967), 81–96, 81–2. On page 82 he writes: 'In the *Dream of Scipio* by Macrobius, which ends with a discourse on *tripartita philosophia*, the hero is warned against the voluptuous life and urged to pursue the active and contemplative virtues – *perfectionis geminae praecepta.*'

47. Parfitt, *The Complete Poems*, 405, at lines 1280–3.

48. For another reading of the poem's conclusion see Michael McCanles, *Jonsonian Discriminations: The Humanist Poet and the Praise of True Nobility* (University of Toronto Press, 1992), 165.

49. In his note on the poem, on page 9 of his edition, Ian Donaldson remarks: 'James himself had compared the Union of England and Scotland to a marriage.' In Herford and Simpson, *Ben Jonson* (XI, 3) James is quoted: 'What God hath conioyned then, let no man separate. I am the Husband, and all the whole Isle is my lawfull Wife.'

50. As Donaldson points out, in the note mentioned above, 'Jonson echoes the analogy [to a marriage] again in *Hym*[*enaei*].'

51. Robert Wiltenburg also reads the fifth epigram with reference to the epic and the cosmic. See his *Ben Jonson and Self-Love: The Subtlest Maze of All* (Columbia: University of Missouri Press, 1990), 67–8. He writes of *Epigrams* in terms of 'a renewed "city", a society of the virtuous' (72). His view of Jonson's Book overlaps with mine at some points.

52. See, for instance, Donaldson's note to the poem (at page 35 of his edition). The forty-third epigram is the first of Jonson's poems to Cecil.

53. On the epigrams to Cecil, see Evans, *Patronage*, 95–107. See also Dutton, *To the First Folio*, 144–55.

CHAPTER 2

The Jonsonian masque and the politics of decorum

Alison V. Scott

Since Stephen Orgel's groundbreaking publication *The Illusion of Power*, the politics of Jonson's masques have largely been treated in terms of New Historicism, with criticism often focusing on 'tracing how the binary structure of the masque – its division between dominant masque and subordinated antimasque – parallels the polarised conceptual, discursive and political oppositions along these two axes'.[1] Despite the obvious advantages of the historicist approach, it has in practice led to masques being reinserted 'back into a scenario of power and its inescapable confluences that . . . increasingly looks formulaic and transhistorical', as Martin Butler has observed; and the most recent commentaries have thus sought new ways of thinking about the genre.[2] David Lindley made an early attempt in that vein to avoid over-simplifying the paradoxical impulses of the masque, noting that 'the struggle within the poet's work to sustain the transmutation of the circumstances of the Jacobean court and its politics into self-sufficient myth' is the 'true fascination of the genre'.[3] Similarly, Butler's later readings of individual masques interrogate the poet's struggle with or 'negotiation' of the transformation of contingent, courtly realities into constant, transcendental myth. I want to extend those discussions here by considering a further dimension of the poet's political struggle, namely the way in which Jonson draws attention in his masques to the paradoxical nature of the genre's political work (truthfully reflecting and truthfully praising James and his court), and then deliberately evokes classical ideas of *kairos* (timeliness) and decorum (seemliness) in order to forge a feasible reconciliation of those contraries – in effect, to keep multiple truths in play at once.

As James Loxley suggests, the politics of Jonson's masques revolve around the attempt to reconcile the 'contingent circumstances' of a given masque with the 'unchanging truths' every masque is obliged to affirm.[4] The Ciceronian and Stoic notion of *kairos* – denoting creativity in responding to a given situation – thus proved a particularly useful principle for Jonson to invoke. Part of the broader concept of decorum, denoting a process of accommodation in relation to a given circumstance, *kairos* enabled a defence of the masque against accusations of base flattery and superfluity; and that allowed Jonson to claim a moral seriousness for the genre (or at least for his own contributions to and innovations within it).[5] Decorum, a 'doctrine of truth to type' that Herford and Simpson understood Jonson to hold 'as the essence of his art', thus provides a means for Jonson to reconcile the political and ethical tasks of the poetry of the masque rhetorically, so that the panegyric speaks true in a most powerful if not absolute way.[6] More specifically, as a form of political weaving that 'can achieve a combination of opposites which does not eliminate conflict but rather uses it to the city's advantage', *kairos* allows Jonson to keep the satire of the antimasque in play at the same time as he crafts an affirmation of majesty within the decorous masque proper.[7] Furthermore, in positioning his audience in opposition to the vices and incongruities of the anti-masque figures, he manufactures a collective agreement on the truth of the masque's praise, but does so within a framework that is neither singular nor absolutist.

In the important essay that I have already mentioned, Butler summarizes the positions of Stephen Orgel and Jonathan Goldberg in relation to the political work of courtly masques.[8] In Orgel's case, Butler challenges the assumption that the masque circulates within given power structures, affirming 'more or less the same thing' on every occasion – the authority and majesty of the king.[9] In Goldberg's case, Butler is concerned that the 'stunning analysis of the masques as at one and the same time outrageously subversive and outrageously self-abasing' – an argument that asserts that masques perform subversion in order to enable a display of containment – has similar totalizing effects to that of Orgel's reading, it performs 'more or less the same ideological manoeuvres'.[10] While not disputing that masques were unusually 'embedded in the collective practices of their society', Butler challenges the notion that 'masques always performed the same political work', arguing that to assume that they did so is to overstate 'the generic unity of the masques' and to underestimate 'the hybrid character of Jacobean absolutism'.[11]

Masques do not always perform the same political work and to assume that they did is indeed to simplify the genre and its intersections with power at court. On the other hand, it is very difficult to dispute Orgel's observation that Jonson's masques generically affirm 'more or less the same thing'.[12] That programme of affirmation thus needs to be understood as one aspect of the broader and otherwise shifting political work of the masque. Moreover, such political work is carried out within, or else demands a generic framework that – as Goldberg elucidates – simultaneously subverts and gratuitously affirms the values and order of the court. As such, it threatens criticism of and lavishes praise upon the king at the same time, being shaped by and shaping the idealized image of majesty. Loxley sees those oppositions within the politics of the masque as being mirrored in the binary structure of masque and antimasque; and suggestive therefore of the subversion/containment debate that, as Butler contends 'has followed New Historicism' everywhere.[13] As formulaic as the transformation of antimasque into masque (the unmasking as such) can appear, however, it fluctuates and evolves markedly over time; and while the Jonsonian masque does generally affirm 'more or less the same thing' then, it does so within a framework of decorum that prescribes the interpretation/understanding/consumption of the masque in the context of a specific political moment and/or a distinct social occasion.[14] Jonson rhetorically positions his audience/reader as Apollonian (in line with the ideals of the masque proper) rather than as Dionysian (in terms of the disproportions and distortions of the antimasque), at the same time as he entertains them with Dionysian revels. As *The Vision of Delight* suggests then, the 'shows' are 'new ... strange ... and sweetly vary', but as the audience 'expect the pleasing'st sight', the 'vision of delight' is necessarily engendered. To borrow Nietzsche's terms, the 'separate art worlds of dreams and intoxication' must be delineated; that may give the impression that the Apollonian dream has eclipsed the Dionysian intoxication, but in fact the 'Apollonian consciousness ... like a veil' hides the 'Dionysian world from ... vision' in order that the vision can be one of 'delight'.[15]

As Butler demonstrates, the masque has to be understood as a vehicle through which power is not merely affirmed but rather 'negotiated'.[16] Working with Leinwand's revision of Greenblatt's notion of *negotiation*, in which Leinwand aims in part to 'attribute change to something other than subversion' in order to avoid a totalized reading of Renaissance drama, Butler argues that masques were sites for many social transactions. Negotiations, as Greenblatt's *Shakespearean Negotiations* demonstrates, are understood to be rhetorical acts that 'give and take between differently empowered participants in the political process'; the 'courtly negotiations' of the masque rely on a form of reciprocity and they enact dialectic.[17] In that sense, the 'oscillation of symbolic transactions' mirrors the dialectic enacted within the masque via the juxtaposition of antimasque and masque proper, an opposition which itself invokes a whole series of related binaries (misrule and rule, chaos and harmony, satire and panegyric) that are highlighted, but not necessarily fully understood in the subversion/ containment historicist readings of Jonson's masques. Recognizing that, Lesley Mickel attempts to move beyond the boundaries of the subversion/ containment debate in her study of Jonson's antimasque.[18] Her conclusion – that the masque at once subverts and then contains that subversion – however, demonstrates the difficulty of trying to approach the masques from a fresh perspective. Nevertheless, Mickel advances a useful reading of the relationship between masque and antimasque as dialectic, 'that is, in essence, a process of negotiation . . . [that] seeks neither to undermine the state nor to laud it without qualification, but to produce a conditional endorsement of the monarchy'.[19] Her Foucauldian reading suggests how we might resist the notion that the antimasque effects subversion only to be brought into inevitable containment by the masque proper, while also recognizing that the process of negotiation is not free enough to resist endorsement (a form of containment) outright.[20] Yet, the obvious and important question arising from that is, upon what condition the endorsement of monarchy relies, or what principle is invoked in order to retain a play of opposites while still performing the necessary endorsement and celebration of patron/s and sovereign?

I should like to suggest that the condition upon which the masque's affirmation hinges relates to the decorum of the occasion. More specifically, that Jonson utilizes the notion of reciprocity in negotiation to transfer some of the responsibility for creating and sustaining that decorum onto the audience of the masque – endorsing the masque's panegyric essentially becomes a sign of the understanding and good judgment that Jonson's poetry repeatedly inscribes as a moral virtue.[21] The condition upon which the endorsement that Mickel speaks of – and which relates to the poet's struggle as perceived by Lindley, and to Butler's concept of 'courtly negotiations' – becomes a matter of perception/interpretation and also one of discrimination in consumption. In that way, Jonson enables satire and panegyric, subversive and assenting readings of the court to co-exist, so that the masque always appears to affirm essentially the same thing, and yet also performs distinct political work on particular occasions and for particular patrons/addressees.

'Who hath not heard, who hath not seen, / Who hath not sung his name?' ring the rhetorical questions in a song from Oberon, and the response is of course only the 'soul that hath not, hath not been' (lines 227–9). The audience is automatically complicit in the masque's praise, and the question of whom they sing is of course loaded. But the point is that the masque sings simultaneously of James and Henry and as each spectator mentally debates or answers the question of the direction of the praise, the meaning of the masque is shaped and its political work multiplies.[22] Ostensibly, of course, Jonson praises Prince Henry – Oberon. Yet, at the same time, the praise belongs to James, and it is James' wisdom that is ultimately affirmed (lines 227–8). Importantly, each song/way of perceiving the masque's praise has its own separate but related moment: praise for Oberon and his song belong to the 'hum'rous moon' which 'will not stay' (line 13) and, in fact, appears responsible for putting much of fairyland to sleep:

> Look! does not his palace show
> Like another sky of lights?
> Yonder with him live the knights
> Once the nobles of the earth,
> Quickened by a second birth,
> Who for prowess and for truth
> There are crowned with lasting youth,
> And do hold, by Fate's command,
> Seats of bliss in fairyland.
> But their guards, methinks, do sleep!
> Let us wake 'em. Sirs, you keep
> Proper watch, that thus do lie
> Drowned in sloth!
>
> (lines 101–13)

In their intoxicated slumber, the elves argue that the sylvans risk being 'stol'n' from themselves (line 158), but the sylvans insist there is no need for them to be guarding until the break of day – the elves' 'expectance is too soon' (line 172). When the first crow of the cock sounds, it marks Oberon's time – the intoxication of the antimasque evaporates and Oberon appears in his chariot. Powerful and glorious as he is, however, Oberon is a creature of the moon and must give way to 'the herald of the day' (line 348), which is obviously James' space and both represents and enacts Apollonian perspective. The 'high-graced Oberon' is necessarily reminded that 'it is time' (lines 342–3) that the 'brightness of this night' were gone (line 367) – '[g]entle knights, / Know [. . . the] measure of . . . nights' (lines 340–1). At once, Jonson asserts that he knows the measure of his praise, and challenges his audience to exercise similar prudence in their interpretation of the masque's vision; the masque's decorum is thus successfully negotiated with specific regard to timeliness or *kairos*.

In his analysis of *The Vision of Delight and Pleasure Reconciled to Virtue*, Goldberg suggests that arriving at the proper measure of the masque is akin to perceiving; and in perceiving, the spectator affirms 'a view of a view' because the transformation of the masque 'literalizes and embodies the mysteries that lie in the king's eyes, the mysteries that can be read from his view'.[23] The decorous vision of delight, which is, in effect, the mysterious vision of the masque proper that can only be truly seen (and then understood) from the correct position, is a vision that requires distance to be established between spectator and spectacle. The audience must step back far enough to see themselves – not in the antimasque figures of otherness and states of intoxication – but in the masque's figures of harmony and state of dream or mystery. The masque is thus always a negotiation between what Camille Paglia has termed the 'objectification' of Apollo and the 'identification' of Dionysius: it must manifest the order, gravity, and distance of Apollo, and yet, the revel itself and the act of revelling remain Dionysian.[24] The transformation of the masque thus signals the point at which revelling/participation/identification must cease, and seeing from a distance, admiring the 'Apollonian "One" ... as work of art' must take place.[25]

In that sense, the transformation of the masque and the transformation of the audience's vision are mirrored; they must both take place in order that the 'real' vision of delight becomes visible. Moreover, that 'real' vision stands in direct contrast to the Dionysian antimasque where 'space is collapsed ... [and the] eye cannot maintain point of view'.[26] Daedalus' first song in *Pleasure Reconciled to Virtue* illuminates the interdependence of that crucial objectivity and the idea of measure, which in this case is imagined explicitly in terms of precision and clarity of movement, facilitating the correct reading of the scene:

> Then, as all actions of mankind
>   Are but a labyrinth or maze,
> So let your dances be entwined,
>   Yet not perplex men unto gaze;
> But measured, and so numerous too,
>   As men may read each act you do,
> And when they see the graces meet,
>   Admire the wisdom of your feet.
> For dancing is an exercise
>   Not only shows the mover's wit,
> But maketh the beholder wise,
>   As he hath power to rise to it.

(lines 232–43)

The dance of the masque proper stands in direct opposition to the anti-masque's 'perplexed dance of straying and deformed pilgrims taking several paths' (*Masque of Augurs*, lines 248–50); it stands as a symbol of understanding and clarity, where the confusion of the antimasque dance is clearly connected with distorted perception and articulation – 'de more absurd it be and vrom de purpose, it be ever all de better' insists Vangoose in his pointedly broken English (*Masque of Augurs*, lines 243–4). Daedalus' dance will enact decorum, which explicitly involves moderation, for 'by far the most significant concept [in terms of the decorum of dance] was that of measure or misura'.[27] Evoking John Davies' description of dance as 'moving all in measure' where 'Time the measure of all moving is' and Time and measure are the twin offspring of 'Reason' (gotten together, but with Time being 'first borne'), Jonson obviously connects the notion of physical measure with eloquence, understanding, and truth, effectively transfiguring the art of dance into the art of rhetoric.[28] The masque's key persona – Hercules – as Wayne Rebhorn notes in a discussion of Hercules Gallicus in Alciati's Emblemata – was often used by writers and artists to evoke the force of eloquence and to foreground rhetoric's key virtue of prudence.[29] Alciati's emblem 'Duodecim certamina Herculis', in fact, 'allegorizes his first two labors specifically in ways that link him to rhetoric: it declares that the first one represents the triumph of eloquence . . . over unconquered strength (the Nemean lion) and the second, the defeat of sophistry (the Hydra)'.[30] Elucidating contemporary commentary on Alciati's 1591 edition, Rebhorn notes that the emblem 'conflates Hercules' twelve labors with Hercules Gallicus, stressing the superiority of words to swords . . . This Hercules . . . possessed both prudence and eloquence'.[31] Those dual virtues shape Jonson's Hercules – the 'active friend of Virtue' (line 146), connecting with the dance's twin virtues of time and measure to collectively oppose the indecorum of the bouncing belly:

> Bottles? mere vessels? half a tun of paunch?
> How? And the other half thrust forth in haunch?
> Whose feast? the belly's? Comus'? and my cup
> Brought in to fill the drunken orgies up?
> And here abused? that was the crowned reward
> Of thirsty heroes after labor hard?
> Burdens and shames of nature, perish, die;
> For yet you never lived, but in the sty
> Of vice have wallowed, and in that swine's strife
> Been buried under the offense of life.
>
> (*Pleasure Reconciled to Virtue*, lines 86–95)

The monstrous antimasque of bottles and tuns is cast in the vein of the infamous Gryllus who, of course, prefers to remain a swine under Circe's spell, rather than be restored to his natural and rational state.[32] The 'offense of life' is thus manifest in excess and a beastly lack of reason; it is opposed by Hercules' heroism in the service of virtue, which takes the dual form of prudence and eloquence – the kind of 'self-control' that Cicero identifies as giving 'as it were a sort of polish to life', a polish which he then names as 'decorum'.[33] Hercules' rhetorical questions about the pleasures of the antimasquers thus resonate as a challenge for the audience – who will indulge in the very excessive and distorting pleasures they are being warned against after the performance – to '[have] power to rise' to the decorum of the occasional and shun the Dionysian pleasures that threaten to 'extinguish man ... Or so quite change him in his figure' (lines 98–9).[34] But the threat to reason and prudence is not only figured in the transformation of men into monsters, but also in the transformation or distortion of perception. The ambiguous Bowl-Bearer thus gestures that the antimasque's song of the belly-god 'is well, and . . . is not well' (line 41) and he asks pardon for his 'two senses' (his eyes) which cause him to 'see double'; he then moves directly to question what the audience of the masque 'see':

Ha! You look as if you would make a problem of this. Do you see? Do you see? a problem: why bottles? and why a tun? and why a tun? and why bottles to dance? I say that men drink hard and serve the belly in any place of quality ... are living measures of drink, and can transform themselves, and do every day, to bottles or tuns when they please.   (lines 63–70)

The Bowl-Bearer engages of course with Augustinian ideas of concupiscence, with which the audience would have been entirely familiar: drunkenness was understood to be a beastly vice because it 'subverteth' the understanding and causes man to lose the 'knowledge and governance of himself'.[35] The antimasque literalizes that loss of self in the presentation of the men transformed to measures of drink, but as part of its revelry it also explains that transformation to the audience in terms of the Bowl-Bearer's subverted perspective on the scene (he has apparently drunk like a frog that day). As the audience naturally sees what the drunken Bowl-Bearer perceives, they are drawn into a dangerous position of (false) Dionysian identification with the excessive pleasures that, in his wisdom, Hercules has already resisted. At the same time, the Bowl-Bearer challenges the audience to question what they see, seemingly answering a charge of an aesthetic indecorum or incongruence – 'why bottles? and why a tun?' He does so by asserting that men transform themselves (and therefore bring bottles and tuns to life) by drinking without measure, by keeping time by 'the truest clock i' the world' – the belly (line 75). The Bowl-Bearer then attempts to annul a potential objection to the device of the anti-masque by appealing to a form of false measure, that is the clock of the belly who 'break'st all thy girdles' in sensuous overindulgence (line 33). However, his antimasque of 'living measures of drink' (line 68) not only inverts the ideal of measure as moderation, it effects a distortion of perception that causes a form of double vision – an inversion of the 'view in a view' that Goldberg associates with the affirming and Apollonian vision of the masque proper.[36]

Once the Bowl-Bearer has posed his problems of measure, Hercules appears on stage to denounce the antimasquers as unnatural 'monsters' and indecorous 'contraries'; his resistance to the excesses of the belly and to the double vision of the Bowl-Bearer effects the masque's transformation, so that when he instructs the scene of vice to vanish, it does.[37] He is rewarded with rest only to be threatened with death by a second antimasque of pygmies. As Goldberg observes, '[h]is seductive sleep almost does him in; the pygmies surround him and are about to brain him', he must wake up and return to the active thoughts that drive the false rites and the monsters away.[38] What is significant here is that Hercules' heroism revolves around acts of perception – he recognizes 'vicious hospitality' from true, he responds to the chorus' request that he awaken and 'look', and he manifests virtue where Virtue is described as 'looking on' (lines 83, 141, and 192). The audience is invited to adopt this active virtue of perception as model behaviour, that is, as the means with which to reconcile virtue with pleasure and thus to comprehend and reflect the decorum of the masque:[39]

> An eye of looking back were well,
> Or any murmur that would tell
> Your thoughts, how you were sent
> And went,
> To walk with Pleasure not to dwell.

(lines 291–6)

> She [virtue], she it is, in darkness shines.
> 'Tis she that still herself refines,
> By her own light, to every eye
> More seen, more known when Vice stands by.

(lines 308–11)

The Platonic ideals of the masque and the virtues of the king and court are thus highlighted against the backdrop of 'darkness' that is the antimasque.

Virtue makes itself visible then, but it is visible only because the 'eye of looking back' correlates with Hercules' prudence, effectively moderating pleasure. In remembering the darkness of the antimasque, then, it is implied that the audience will be more likely to choose Hercules' path of virtue and consequently arrive at Virtue's seat (line 314). If the affirming message of Jonson's masque is conditional, as Mickel argues, it thus hinges on a decorum of perception or seeing that is strongly connected with ideas of prudence and self-control: as Cicero insists, decorum 'embraces . . . temperance . . . [and] moderation in all things'.[40] It is politically prudent for masque writer and spectator to perceive things in a particular way, as befitting the occasion. Prudence and measure are also located within the masque as virtues, and as all virtues emanate from the king, a self-reflexive cycle of affirmation is established which can only be disturbed by an act of indecorum that would render its perpetrator a cultural outsider and a non-understander. As Goodfellow observes in *Love Restored*, there is only one way to view a masque and that is to declare 'confidently . . . [that you are] part o' the device' (line 129).

If masques are 'courtly negotiations' as Butler argues – and if they therefore pivot on acts of decorous perception – they are also, as Francis Bacon points out, mere trifles and 'toys'.[41] That reputation for superfluity clearly contradicts the idea that they are grounded on prudence and measure, and the masque's association with triviality and transience colours its negotiating, impacting on the trifles of the masque in various ways. Though Patricia Fumerton has argued that 'the "trifling" arts of the cook, architect, and ultimately poet combined in the masque to stage a profoundly "trivial" or insubstantial Jacobean self', Jonson's rhetoric of decorum contradicts that notion by lending gravity to the contested triviality of the masques.[42] The so-called trifles of the masque are in fact as vital to the decorum of the masquing occasion and, ultimately, to the idealized image of the king and court as the ornamental details of Vitruvian architecture were vital to proprietary or 'that perfection of style which comes when a work is authoritatively constructed on approved principles'.[43] Even Bacon's essay 'Of Masques and Triumphs' admires the masque's 'alterations of scenes', as 'things of great beauty and pleasure; for they feed and relieve the eye, before it be full of the same object'. The masque does not stage a trivial self then, but rather stages the redemption from triviality through measure which, while primarily aesthetic, clearly evokes the moral categories of temperance and prudence in line with Cicero's definition of decorum.[44] In that way it avoids glutting the eye with 'petty wonderments', it is 'graced with elegancy' as opposed to being 'daubed by cost', and it effects variety without descending into vulgarity.[45]

Within the world of the masque and within the broader world of the
court, we can see that the related concepts of moderation and self-control,
seemliness and timeliness remain pivotal. The masque's internal negotiation
of opposites and its scripting of a properly measured audience response to or
vision of the masque are, in part, rhetorical manoeuvres designed to coun-
teract the genre's associations with triviality. Gentle knights are such in
Oberon because they understand the measure or boundaries of the orgies
of the night. Those knights thus practise decorum and they are Jonson's
means of reflecting the ideal decorum of the court, which is subsequently
affirmed when the audience demonstrates its understanding of the
masque, and its own understanding of the measures of the night. The
gentle knights, the prudent audience, the overseeing Apollo, and the discriminating poet are thus aligned in terms of a decorum, which, according to
Cicero, is enacted in a prudent response 'to the particular and contingent in
human affairs'.[46] That emphasis on the measure of the masque and the
prudence of the poet/audience in its creation and consumption directly
opposes the widespread assumptions that masques were superfluous and
wasteful – emblems, as it were, of *vanitas*.[47] In fact, the extravagance of
the occasion, of the audience's consumption, of James' spending, and
even of the poet's praise is justified in terms of decorum. Excess is
redescribed as concentrated but restrained delight appropriate to majesty
and royal magnificence, '[f]or what is noble should be sweet, / But not dis-
solved in wantonness' (*Pleasure Reconciled to Virtue*, lines 282–3).[48] James
maintains supremacy in that equation because it is his particular perspective
that determines the boundaries of the decorous, but the presentation of the
masque as part of a collective decorum obviously allows Jonson to vary the
specific political work of each masque within that broader framework of
constant affirmation.

In Oberon, as we have seen, Jonson wants to praise Henry and to win his
support without appearing to topple James from his correct position as
principal object of the masque's panegyric. He uses the idea of measure in
the specific form of *kairos*, then, because it enables the construction of a
particular time and space in which praise for the prince is fitting, while
still allowing the assertion that such a space must ultimately give way to
James' overarching power. In *Pleasure Reconciled to Virtue*, the idea of
measure is invoked with specific, moral reference to the importance of temperance – it is acceptable to 'walk with Pleasure, [but] not to dwell' (line
296). Then, in *Neptune's Triumph*, measure is noticeable for its absence as
Jonson interrogates the excesses of his own invention – the antimasque –
but does so in order to advance indirect criticism of foreign or excessive

taste for novelty. He distinguishes the Jonsonian masque and its audience from those tastes, implicitly implying their contrasting understanding of what is fitting, at the same time as he illuminates the threat that 'indiscrimination' poses for the court's and the masque's decorum.

The Poet in *Neptune's Triumph* perceives antimasques as 'at best outlandish nothings' and refuses to craft one because it would be 'heterogene to all device' or, in other words, it would be superfluous and unseemly (lines 159–60).[49] The Poet's assertion of decorum, however, is paradoxically spoken from the indecorous space of the antimasque, while his resistance to the world of the antimasque actually enables the production of the Cook's olla podrida or 'metaphorical dish' (lines 173 and 169). That metaphorical antimasque is a hotchpotch of 'rotten' ingredients (persons); the Cook thus recalls Athenaeus' 'modern cooks' who are criticized in *The Deipnosophists* for their incongruous combinations of ingredients, 'for what possible good can come when one individual quality is mixed with another and twisted together in a hostile grip?' (3.102).[50] Like the Bowl-Bearer of *Pleasure Reconciled to Virtue*, the Cook claims to practise a form of *kairos* in the sense that his dish is designed to suit prevailing tastes and meet the expectations of the occasion; however, it is clearly a sham *kairos* because it conversely effects a breach of decorum.[51] Evoking the Platonic association of poetry and cookery, the Cook thus asserts that 'a good poet differs nothing at all from a master-cook' (lines 24–5), but in stressing the incongruous nature of the Cook's product, Jonson implicitly challenges the notion that Cook and Poet are equally subject to the 'tyrannous mistress' of expectation. While the Cook is clearly excessive and produces only what is designed to 'please the palates of the guests', the Poet is more measured in his approach, concerned not merely with expectation but with the 'understanding' that genuine *kairos* requires (line 39).[52] That concern separates him from the associations with sophism that the reader is obviously meant to recognize in the figure of the Cook. Quite unlike the Cook, the Poet is not primarily concerned with satisfying the 'palate of the times' (line 29) – that is with Plato's 'gratification' of the senses (462d) – rather, he carefully considers the integrity or the soul of his art, answering the Cook's question as to why the masque had been delayed (which was a real political question of concern to his would-be audience) in terms of decorum: 'It was not time / To mix this music with the vulgar's chime' (lines 115–16).

While never denying the power of expectation and the need to satisfy the tastes of the consumer, Jonson insists that the Poet advances a higher truth that is not subject to the judgment of the body, but rather to 'pure affections', at the safe return of Albion to 'Neptune's Triumph'. The Poet duly considers 'how temperance may be bred' in the audience/reader 'and how virtue as a whole may be produced and vice expelled'; the licence of the Cook is thus potentially corrected by the Poet.[53] However, the Cook and his indecorum are still invading the stage only twenty-five lines before the masque concludes, his antimasque of sailors occurring only fifteen lines before the end of the triumph. Decorum is never quite established, and this masque more than any other thus suggests – both in its structure and in its content – the ambiguous appeal of the antimasque and its vices within contemporary society. At the same time, however, the masque challenges the audience to prefer the 'serious' piece rather than the 'rotten' piece of the entertainment, and challenges them thus to paradoxically affirm their own construction as a virtuous élite requiring no 'correction'.[54] The masque performs at once the same and different political work to that of Oberon with its loaded rhetorical question '[w]ho hath not sung his name?' (line 228) because it constructs a similar decorous group of understanders who comprehend and celebrate the values of the masque proper (and therefore the majesty of James), but it does so specifically to evade the political difficulties that the occasion of *Neptune's Triumph* brought to bear.[55]

In the personae of Cook and Poet, Jonson is able to express and play with contraries. Orgel has argued that those contraries can be more or less simplified into an opposition between the Poet's truth and the Cook's falsehood in creating a 'metaphorical dish' from which dancers emerge to appeal 'not to "a palate of the Understanding" but to the sensual appetite'.[56] Those dancers represent people who gossip about rather than seek to comprehend state business and therefore '[k]now all the things the wrong way'; they recall Plato's warning that if the body rather than the soul were to become judge, 'everything would be jumbled together, without distinction'.[57] Certainly Orgel is right to argue that Jonson is satirizing a particular form of courtier from which the audience is implicitly meant to be able to distinguish themselves, but I do not read the relationship between Poet/Cook and between masque/antimasque as being either as simple as truth/falsehood, or necessarily as 'genial' as Orgel claims.[58] To my mind, the potential criticism of the excesses of courtly taste is not 'assimilated' within the larger world of the Poet's masque, rather it represents the indecorum that the court – with its own love of novelty and variety – and the masque, which as Jonson explains derives a principal part of its life from 'variety' (*Masque of Queens*, lines 9–10), might potentially fall into. It is that indecorum, and not the Cook per se, that represents distorted knowledge or the wrong reading of the masque. The threat to truth is not thus absolute or fixed, but is rather posed by the spectators' tastes and judgment. In short, if the audience of the masque desires 'things the wrong way' and prefers the rotten olla podrida of the Cook to the mysteries of the Poet, then their improper consumption of the masque will prove deforming, and its truth will be rendered false.[59] The antimasque is not necessarily assimilated in the way Orgel suggests; in fact, if it had been performed, it would have functioned as a rhetorical means by which to persuade the audience to 'read, reflected in his son's [Charles'] return' 'the pomp of Neptune's triumph' and 'the glories of his great designs' (lines 253–5), and to refrain from turning the joyful event into 'enquiry after news' (line 186) as the people of 'present palates' might be expected to do (line 168).

The antimasque is then provocatively presented as 'heterogene' to the decorum of the masque, while at the same time providing the means by which the decorum of the masque and of the court it praises can be delineated. In that sense, Jonson plays with the idea that decorum is both interior and exterior to the text – constructed as it were by the reader's per-ception. In that way, he is able to shift some of the responsibility for the masque's 'commend[ing of] their kind' to the audience. Richard A. Lanham's notion that decorum is 'a stylistic criterion [that] finally locates itself entirely in the beholder and not the speech or text' is useful here. Lanham asserts that '[n]o textual pattern per se is decorous or not. The final criterion for excess, indecorum, is the stylistic self-consciousness induced by the text or social situation'.[60] The idea that it is the beholder who ultimately bestows decorum enables politic flexibility: the masque's affirmation of majesty can be understood as true praise as distinct from flat-tery (because the audience effectively agrees that it is so), at the same time as the antimasque's representations can be recognized as criticism of the real court, and then effectively ignored. As Lanham explains:

[D]ecorum is a *creative* as well as a *pious* concept . . . it creates the social reality which it reflects. Decorum, not to put too fine an edge on it, amounts to a pious fraud, the 'social trick' par excellence. We create, with maximum self-consciousness and according to precise rules, an intricate structure of stylistic forces balanced carefully as to perceiver and perceived, and then agree to forget that we have created it and to pretend that it is nature itself we are engaging with.[61]

Jonson is not adapting his masques to a 'preexistent social reality' but is, to borrow Lanham's description, 'reflecting on how that reality has been con-stituted by the idea of decorum'.[62] His decorum is twofold: on the one hand he claims to seek and uphold the truth Ciceronean-style,[63] and at the same time he claims to respond to contingent truths by adapting his praise to circumstance and judging, as Quintilian puts it, 'how much the ears of . . . [his] audience will tolerate'.[64] That allows him to reflect a singular affirming image of majesty as truth, while at the same time implying the conditions upon which that truth hinges. The audience/reader of the Jonsonian masque thus experiences the mystical truth of majesty, at the same time as he/she is rhetorically persuaded to accept that 'truth', at the same time as he/she is asked to practise a form of discrimination in order to deduce or construct the decorum or 'truth' of the masque for themselves.[65]

As Ciceronean decorum effectively unites *honestas* and *utilitas* and by implication allows the notions of absolute and contingent truth to co-exist, it is a particularly useful approach for Jonson as masque writer – it enables a defence against accusations of flattery and superfluity. Jonson remains, nevertheless, acutely aware of the Platonic perception of the conflict between moral goodness and political utility. In *Gorgias*, as I have already mentioned in relation to my discussion of *Neptune's Triumph*, Plato's Socrates asserts that rhetoric, like cookery, is 'but a habitude or knack', opposed to dialectic and equating to flattery (463b); many of Jonson's masques engage with Plato's idea that rhetoric 'is a producer of persuasion for belief, not for instruction in the matter of right and wrong' (455a). Most obviously, Jonson's claim that masques 'ought always to carry a mixture of profit with them no less than delight' (*Love's Triumph*, lines 6–7) effectively refutes *The Republic*'s denial that poetry can instruct to virtue, and challenges the interdependent construction of a binary opposition between knowledge and persuasion that we see in *Gorgias*.[66]

Evoking Plato's denigration of sophism and poetry's association with that 'irrational' habitude, Jonson necessarily engages with the sophism that Plato seeks to dismantle, and therefore with the Gorgianic views of *kairos* that characterize the sophistic conception of truth. One critic at least has described Gorgianic *kairos* as 'a process of continual interpretation' that construes truth as 'immanent not anterior to the situation'; and that obviously connects with Lanham's idea that decorum 'creates the social reality which it reflects'.[67] Of course, as certain 'rules' of masque-making precede the occasion then some part of the masque's truth has to be anterior, but Jonson certainly plays with the notion that the *kairos* of the occasion licenses another truth, which is constructed by the interplay between the masque and the court it reflects on a given occasion, and is constructed as part of the decorum of that occasion.[68] On the one hand, then, Jonson presents himself in the vein of the *Phaedrus*' wise man who is capable of discerning the immutable truth that is arrived at through dialectic; yet, on the other, he utilizes the opposing sophistic argument that meaning or truth is relative to the context (time, place, audience) in which it is uttered.[69] 'Poetry . . . is not borne w'h euery man; Nor euery day', Jonson reminds us, and in the masque no less than in the epigram, poetry is a humanist tool used 'To Make the Spectators Understanders' (*Love's Triumph*, 1), which, nevertheless, relies in part upon the spectator's inherent and agreed capacity to judge correctly the truth of what they see.[70]

In his epigram *To My Muse* Jonson regrets his praise of a 'worthless lord' since that lord's behaviour has made his praise indistinguishable from flattery. Here, truth adapts as it were to circumstances and transforms into a more appropriate 'tax', but that adaptation is essentially spontaneous and therefore distinct from political *utilitas*. Though, in the first instance, it appears that the poet has failed to judge correctly what is appropriate, the epigram is in fact designed to reveal that his sense of decorum is intact. It achieves that end by appealing both to the sophistic idea of changing truth and to the Platonic idea of immutable truth: the epigram pivots on a moment in which an enduring truth (the poet's praise was never flattery) is paradoxically revealed via a form of dialectic (it is tax rather than praise). Most important, the rhetoric of the epigram denies a fissure between propriety and praise and attempts thus to preserve the poet's ethical discrimination. On one level, it is preserved and the poet is absolved of the misdemeanour of praising an unworthy lord (acquitted of flattery), but on another level the transformation of praise into tax is transparently self-interested – the rhetorical rewriting of the poet's lapse into indecorum appears overly convenient and thus itself potentially indecorous. As Robert Evans notes, the poem thus asserts the poet's power, at the same time as it insinuates his 'vulnerability . . . [and] implicitly confessing his need to defend himself'.[71]

To My Muse highlights how the meaning of praise can be renegotiated according to circumstance or, more specifically, in relation to the subject's behaviour and/or the readers' understanding. The epigram thus evokes Ciceronean decorum to excuse the poet's *utilitas* as a response to his subject's indecorum, designed to preserve rather than undermine *honestas*; the lord is consequently demoted in a hierarchy based on seemliness and congruity. As Bacon distinguishes classes of masques – those that aspire to 'elegancy' and those that are merely 'daubed with cost' – so Jonson implies that there are different classes of subjects and a hierarchy of consumers of his work. The masques are no exception. In the preface to *Hymenaei*, for instance, proper (learned and decorous) consumption is distinguished from improper (frivolous) consumption, and a hierarchy is created consisting of those who exercise good taste and comprehend the masque's removed mysteries, and those of more airy tastes who are merely absorbed in its outward shows, and for whom Jonson cannot be held responsible:

> And howsoever some may squeamishly cry out that all endeavor of learning and sharpness in these transitory devices, especially where it steps beyond their little or . . . no brain at all, is superfluous, I am contented these fastidious stomachs should leave my full tables and enjoy at home their clean empty trenchers, fittest for such airy tastes, where perhaps a few Italian herbs picked up and made into a salad may find sweeter acceptance than all the most nourishing and sound meats of the world.

> For these men's palates let me not answer, O muses. It is not my fault if I fill them out nectar and they run to metheglin. (*Hymenaei*, lines 17–27)

The rhetorical manoeuvre mirrors that of 'To My Muse', but here there is no doubt at all that the poet has acted decorously, and the responsibility for the transformation of his praise into tax as such is placed firmly with those of inappropriate and 'airy tastes' who transmute 'nectar' into a base consumable inappropriate for the lofty occasion – 'metheglin'. Critics of the masque are thus excluded from its mysteries on the basis that they lack the discrimination to understand the demands of the occasion – in short, to practise decorum. By contrast, Jonson recognizes that such consumers are unseemly in the context of the masque and, as he suggests in *Hymenaei*, he is happy for them to go home (lines 21–2).

Threatening spectators with dismissal from the decorum of the masque is obviously a rhetorical strategy that aims at standardizing audience response to the masque in order to enable the masque's affirming function. At the same time, however, it stresses that spectators have to exercise their own judgment to respond appropriately and to 'understand'. Such discrimination and sound judgment manifested itself in serious consideration of the masque as humanist poetry.[72] In the preface to *Hymenaei* then, Jonson highlights the importance of studying the masque's 'inward parts' in addition to enjoying the 'outward show'. Of course, the reader of the preface demonstrates that *studiositas* in the very act of reading, and proves him/herself therefore part of the understanding élite of 'royal princes and greatest persons' that Jonson praises (lines 9–10). That is one of several related ways in which he prescribes *studiositas* rather than *curiositas* as the proper state for consuming his masques; and, significantly, the curious find themselves reflected, not in the mysteries and decorum of the masque as its understanders are, but rather in the burlesque and indecorum of the antimasque.[73]

That is most obviously and, indeed, literally the case in *Time Vindicated to Himself and to His Honors*, which begins with an antimasque of 'Fame' and 'the Curious' – the latter containing 'the Eyed, the Eared and the Nosed' – who 'come to spy. And hearken. And smell out' (line 6). The concern that they will inquire into '[m]ore than . . . [they] understand' (line 7) mirrors the Poet's question in *Neptune's Triumph* – '[w]hat if they expect more than they understand?' (line 39); and understanding is connected throughout to the idea of *kairos*. Fame remarks early in the piece, 'Time' has sent him 'to summon / All sorts of persons worthy to the view / Of some great spectacle he means tonight / T' exhibit, and with all solemnity' (lines 24–7), but the Curious spurn such solemnity and desire the liberty to 'do what . . . [they] list' regardless of the demands of the occasion (line 61). Moreover, they demand novelty from the time, reminding Fame that she 'promised . . . [them they] should have anything. / That Time would give . . . [them all they] could imagine' (lines 170–2). Fame denies she promised them any such thing and they fall to arguing about what they want from her until she insists that they agree among themselves and, when they do, she will grant them what they want (lines 197–8). That coherence is of course impossible, for the Curious are uncivil and riotous, they cannot understand and do not desire what is suitable for the occasion and, therefore, they cannot arrive at consensus. In that sense they 'abuse the Time' as Fame observes (line 209), and Fame is forced to fit out their fancies with a second antimasque of tumblers and jugglers which 'Time faintly permit[s]'. That antimasque, satisfying curiosity and consequently driving them away, enables harmony and coherence – the aesthetic and ethical decorum of the occasion. While 'the curious are ill-natured, and, like flies, / Seek Time's corrupted parts to blow upon' like 'spectators who know not what they would have', the 'sound ones' that represent Jonson's 'understanders' rather 'live with fame and honor' and witness thus the transformation of the masque (lines 218–24).

Like the newsmongers of *News from the New World*, and the gossips of *Neptune's Triumph* that '[k]now all the things the wrong way', 'the Curious' 'only hunt for novelty, not truth' (line 214). The preface to *Hymenaei* connects undiscerning spectators with such irreverence for the truth, and in the preface to *The Haddington Masque* critics of the masque are actually slighted for their affront to the truth, as manifest in their incorrect interpretation of and response to Jonson's work, which is viewed as symptomatic of a 'tyrannous ignorance' (lines 11–14). As Cicero reminds us, decorum demands that we 'discern the truth and . . . uphold it' in all things and so, while Jonson intended his masque to 'honorably fit' the occasion, his critics – like 'the Curious' antimasquers of *Time Vindicated*, and like the newsmongers of *News from the New World* – exhibit a recognizable shortcoming.[74] As the critics or misunderstanders of the masque are considered to have 'airy tastes', hankering after foreign and insubstantial things, so the 'Eyes', 'Ears', and 'Nose' of *Time Vindicated* desire novelty. 'What gambols? What devices? What new sports?' demands 'Eyes' in eager anticipation of an outlandish spectacle. When Fame eventually drives the Curious away, he compares them directly with unappreciative spectators such as those Jonson refuses to cater for in the preface to *Hymenaei*: 'Why, now they are kindly used, like such spectators / That know not what they have' (lines 218–19). Antimasquers and critics of the masque are thus both depicted in terms of *curiositas*: they pursue 'pleasures arising from the knowledge acquired through all the senses'.[75]

Jonson's description of the Curious blowing upon Time's corrupted parts evokes, of course, not only Augustine's notion that the Curious seek knowledge in the wrong places, but also Cicero's earlier depiction of those that 'miss the truth . . . fall into error [. . . and are] led astray' which is as 'improper as to be deranged' (1.94). The image of the Curious laying eggs in the corrupt parts of the body of Time emphasizes how rotten their particular creativity is. In direct contrast to those spectators who live free from the 'molestation' of curiosity, the Curious parasitically seek out opportunities to misuse and deface Time and to waylay Fame. Curiosity's abuse of Time in *Time Vindicated* thus manifests monstrosity and incivility, and that abuse resonates as a breach of decorum and, more specifically, of *kairos*: the Curious desire to see/ hear/smell 'fit freedoms / For lawless prentices on a Shrove Tuesday, / When they compel the Time to serve their riot / For drunken wakes and strutting bear baitings, / That savour only of their own abuses' (lines 208–12). In short, they want to witness what is unseemly in the context of masque where Time must agree with Love (line 261). Once curiosity is dispelled, however, Time is vindicated and Time and Love are able to conspire to 'breed delight, and a desire / Of being delighted, in the nobler sort' (lines 282–6). Jonson thus affirms the virtues of his audience by juxtaposing their responses to sensual delights with those of the Curious antimasquers and, by implication, with those like detractors he criticizes in *Hymenaei* who are possessed of 'fastidious stomachs' and yet 'know not what they have'.

The Curious desire insubstantial things, they have as it were 'airy tastes'; antimasque characters are thus repeatedly associated not only with sensual pleasures but also with insubstantial knowledge – trivia or miscellanea. They typically seek gossip, news, novelty, indulgence, and change, while the audience is constantly reminded that they must resist such subversion and be 'somewhat better discoverers' than the stock antimasque figures (*Love Restored*, line 160):

> [A] writer should always trust somewhat to the capacity of the spectator, especially at these spectacles, where men, beside inquiring eyes, are understood to bring quick ears, and not those sluggish ones of porters and mechanics that must be bored through at every act with narrations.   (*Masque of Queens*, lines 95–8)

The transition from antimasque to masque is thus often marked by a form of apology for the potentially indecorous triviality and/or unseemliness of the preceding show. Jenkin performs this role in *For the Honor of Wales*, apologizing for the 'absurdities' he indicates will now cease (lines 334–6); the Gentleman in *The Irish Masque* functions likewise, dismissing 'coarser manners' from the stage (line 135). Meanwhile, the transformation of the masque in *The Fortunate Isles* is marked by Johphiel's apology for the antics of Merefool and his indulgence in the antimasque of knaves and ruffians. When Merefool exclaims with regret, 'What, are they vanished! . . . I do like their show' (lines 281–2), Johphiel admonishes him, 'Go, you are / And will be still yourself, a Merefool' (lines 286–7), before turning to address the 'Great King' and beg James' 'pardon, if the desire to please have trespassed' (lines 289–90).

The rhetorical strategy of Johphiel's apology is complicated. It operates in part as *ante occupatio*, anticipating possible objections that a noble audience might have to the foolery that has preceded the masque proper, and apologizing for any trespass to decorum in order to refute that any real trespass has in fact been made. However, the apology also works in further and even contrary ways to *ante occupatio* because it excuses the antimasque's indecorum (and Johphiel/Jonson's involvement in it) on the basis that it was designed to please, a move which doesn't so much anticipate and refute criticism, but rather highlights the audience's complicity in any breach of decorum that might have occurred. The implication is that if members of the audience have indiscriminately delighted in the antimasque, they must now remember themselves and return to perceiving things in a particular and decorous way. In combining those strategies, Jonson demonstrates the importance of audience response to his assessment of the *kairic* moment, emphasizing how the decorum of the occasion is effectively negotiated between spectacle and spectator, and positioning his masque as a mediator between the two.[76] Johphiel's apparent attack on the antimasque is actually then defensive of Jonson's position as a writer working within a complex framework of demands and expectations, trying to create and accommodate the decorum of the occasion. As in the epigram *To My Muse*, in the preface to *Hymenaei*, and in the exchange between Poet and Cook in *Neptune's Triumph*, Jonson suggests that his invention is constrained by the desires of his audience and by the decorum of the occasion, but then claims credit for expertly satisfying one without compromising the other. In *Love Restored*, he goes one step further by having Plutus – an imposter to the masque – criticize masquing in terms of a sham *kairos* invoked as a means of licensing indecorum:

Thou and thy like think yourselves authorized in this place to all license of surquidry. But you shall find custom hath not so grafted you here but you may be rent up and thrown out as unprofitable evils. I tell thee, I will have no more masquing; I will not buy a false and fleeting delight so dear. The merry madness of one hour shall not cost me the repentance of an age.   (lines 27–33)

The criticism that Plutus levels at the 'fleeting delights' of the masque are commonplace criticisms against which Jonson was used to defending himself and his masque writing, but they are also criticisms of the court that he articulated himself. In his *Discoveries*, for example, he remembers with apparent disgust, and in language that echoes Plutus' criticism, the spectacle and 'pomp of a whole kingdom' that accompanied a foreign king visiting England. He specifically remarks on the foolishness of pursuing pleasure through such temporal displays: 'shall that which could not fill the expectation of a few hours, entertain and take up our whole lives, when even it appeared as superfluous to the possessors, as to me that was a spectator?' (lines 1415–25). Though Plutus' criticisms of courtly excess are upheld in other contexts by Jonson, the point here is that they are inappropriately expressed in the social context of the masque, which should not depend on 'so earthly an idol' as money. At the same time, of course, Jonson uses the character of Plutus to suggest the potential of the masque to manifest excess, imbalance, and indecorum. The 'merry madness of one hour' that Plutus speaks of manifests a similar misuse of time and measure as Jonson perceives in the visit of the foreign king, and a comparable distortion to proper time and judicious restraint to the Belly-God's sensuous clock in *Pleasure Reconciled to Virtue*. Yet, Plutus is no friend of virtue like Hercules, but rather a divisive god of money who threatens to implode the very mysteries that the masque generically reflects and affirms. He specifically accuses the masquers and audience of considering themselves 'authorized in this place to all license of surquidry', that is to say, of arrogantly excusing their

indulgences and excesses by claiming them appropriate to the occasion –
essentially by licensing their pleasures on the basis of decorum.[77] In that
way, the masque stages the unmasking of the masque as licentious, before
unmasking its critic as the god of money who is idolized only by the
unwise and the disingenuous. As with the other masques I have discussed
here, Jonson's poetic licence clearly relies on the 'social trick' of decorum
that is created and sustained by both 'perceiver and perceived'.[78] Adopting
that line, he enables the antimasque to be read at once as an entertainment
designed to indulge an audience desiring novelty, and as an instructive satire
of the 'vanities in . . . high places' and the 'light follies' that might potentially
cause unworthy spectators to intemperately 'fall and feed' on the revels
(*Love Restored*, lines 136–7).

   The ten ornaments of courtly virtue in *Love Restored* 'keep their measures
true, / And make still their proportions new, / Till all become one harmony'
(*Love Restored*, lines 246–8), and that movement epitomizes the Jonsonian
masque as a whole. As the preface to *The Masque of Queens* outlines, the
antimasque is Jonson's means of counterbalancing the masque in order to
shape and maintain the form and the decorum of the whole, and in
order to keep multiple truths in play at once. The Jonsonian masque is
thus 'one and entire' in that its 'parts grow or are wrought together' in
just proportion to illuminate the whole (*Discoveries*, lines 2773–6). It is,
then, constant and evolving, fixed and flexible in its meanings at the
same time; able therefore to appear to affirm basically the same thing on
each masquing occasion as Orgel contends, at the same time as attending
to political work specific to each individual context as Lindley and Butler
have argued. The politics of the Jonsonian masque are thus always at
once engaged with Platonism and Sophism, the affirmation of immutable
truth and the adaptation to contingent truth; and they invoke and construct a Ciceronian decorum that unites political utility with ethical discrimination and honesty. Jonson, in fact, says as much himself when he
illuminates the difficulties of producing an appropriate royal entertainment
in his preface to *The Haddington Masque*. It falls to 'us that are trusted with
a part . . . in these celebrations', he claims, 'to do nothing in them beneath
the dignity of either'. With that in mind, he prints the masque which in his
'first conception' he 'intended honorably fit', nevertheless asserting that he
knows 'truth to be always of one stature' in defence against those 'who have
never touched so much as to the bark or utter shell of any knowledge', but
who will grant themselves regardless 'peremptory license to judge' the truth
and the decorum of his work. As in *To My Muse*, Jonson appears on one
level supremely confident of his ability to assert the correct reading of his

text via the rhetoric of decorum, while on another he acknowledges the vulnerability of his text to transformation by ignorant and indecorous readers who 'know not what they have'.

NOTES

1. James Loxley, *The Complete Critical Guide to Ben Jonson* (London: Routledge, 2002), 203. Loxley notes that Martin Butler's work has complicated the '"absolutist" models of Orgel and Goldberg' (202) in one way, while explorations of 'the way in which masques participate in writing or rewriting the broader political discourses of race and gender' (203) – including the work of Barbara Lewalski, Suzanne Gossett, Marion Wynne-Davies, Clare McManus, Yumna Siddiqi, Kim Hall, and James M. Smith – have sought to complicate those models in a different way. In his introduction to the criticism of the masque, he concludes that 'for . . . recent critics, the masques still speak eloquently of royal power . . . [but] they do so in such a way as to reveal the workings and limits of a politics of identity, a politics that develops along the interlocking axes of gender, race and nation' (Loxley, *Complete Critical Guide*, 204).

2. Martin Butler, 'Courtly Negotiations', in *The Politics of the Stuart Court Masque*, ed. David Bevington and Peter Holbrook (Cambridge University Press, 1998), 20–40, 22. Heather Dubrow remarks on a similar problem in relation to the Stuart Epithalamium: 'if neglecting tensions in the genre . . . is dangerous, studying them involves its own perils', see *A Happier Eden: The Politics of Marriage in the Stuart Epithalamium* (Ithaca, NY: Cornell University Press, 1990), 3–4.

3. See David Lindley, 'Embarrassing Ben: The Masques for Frances Howard', *English Literary Renaissance* 16 (1986): 343–59, 358–9.

4. Loxley, *Complete Critical Guide*, 197.

5. See Phillip Sipiora and James S. Baumlin, eds., *Rhetoric and Kairos: Essays in History, Theory, and Praxis* (Albany: State University of New York Press, 2002), xii–xiii. As James L. Kinneavy suggests, in his essay 'Kairos in Classical and Modern Rhetorical Theory', included in the same volume, *kairos* eventually merges with the idea of decorum to become 'a major issue in much of classical rhetoric in antiquity, particularly with the Pythagoreans, the Sophists, Plato, and Cicero' (59).

6. *Ben Jonson*, ed. C. H. Herford and Percy and Evelyn Simpson, 11 vols. (1925–52; rpt Oxford: Clarendon Press, 1965–70), X, 116 – the note refers to Face's use of the term 'decorum' in the final lines of *The Alchemist*. Michael McCanles observes that 'the true poet is defined for both Horace and Jonson as one whose capacity for true ethical discrimination . . . is registered in artistic decorum: knowing what is decorous', *Jonsonian Discriminations: The Humanist Poet and the Praise of True Nobility* (University of Toronto Press, 1992), 90.

7. See M. S. Lane, *Method and Politics in Plato's Statesman* (Cambridge University Press, 1998), 173. Orgel notes of course in his introduction to *The Complete Masques* (New Haven: Yale University Press, 1969) that the genre had a dual commitment 'to satiric comedy on the one hand and the poetry of praise on the other' (3). All references to the masques are taken from Orgel's edition unless otherwise stated.

8. See, in particular, Stephen Orgel, *The Illusion of Power* (Berkeley: University of California Press, 1975), and Jonathan Goldberg, *James I and the Politics of Literature* (Baltimore: Johns Hopkins University Press, 1983); also Orgel's *The Jonsonian Masque* (Cambridge, MA: Harvard University Press, 1967).

9. Butler, 'Courtly Negotiations', *ibid.*, 23.

10. *Ibid.*, 25, 24.

11. *Ibid.*, 26.

12. Even recent readings of masque contexts accept that 'Jonson never lost sight of the central function of the masque as ritual', James M. Smith, 'Effaced History: Facing the Colonial Contexts of Ben Jonson's *Irish Masque at Court*', *English Literary History* 65.2 (1998): 297–321, 307.

13. Butler, 'Courtly Negotiations', 25.

14. Hugh Craig notes that later antimasques 'show a marked increase in riot and exuberant subversion' and that 'antimasque figures in . . . later entertainments, though monstrous and deformed, usually prove to be civilized and sometimes noble creatures under a spell', 'Jonson, the Antimasque and the "Rules of Flattery"', in *The Politics of the Stuart Court Masque*, ed. David Bevington and Peter Holbrook (Cambridge University Press, 1998), 176–96, 183. It is also the case that Jonson increased the number of antimasques over time – multiple antimasques, which challenged in part the simple binary of masque/antimasque, featured strongly after 1616 and the performance of *Mercury Vindicated*.

15. Nietzsche, 'The Birth of Tragedy', in *The Birth of Tragedy and The Case of Wagner*, trans. Walter Kaufmann (New York: Vintage, 1967), 33 and 41. As Goldberg notes, the masque is about how the spectacle should be seen, about the perspective of the king that the masque presents (*James I*, 61).

16. Butler's essay thus contributes to arguments surrounding the masque's intersection with courtly factions and appeals to other members of the royal family. Leeds Barroll, for example, has argued that Queen Anne used the masque to present herself as powerful in her own right, see 'The Court of the First Stuart Queen', in *The Mental World of the Jacobean Court*, ed. Linda Levy Peck (Cambridge University Press, 1991), 191–208; Tom Bishop has considered the masque in the multivariate court in his essay 'The Gingerbread Host: Tradition and Novelty in the Jacobean Masque', in *The Politics of the Stuart Court Masque*, ed. Bevington and Holbrook, 88–120. While that important volume of essays is 'interested most of all in the ways in which masques negotiated among a range of commitments' (Introduction, 9), I examined Jonson's marketing of his masques as gifts for multiple recipients in *Selfish Gifts: The Politics of Exchange and English Courtly*

Literature, 1580–1628 (Madison: Fairleigh Dickinson University Press, 2006), 147–58. The 'faultlines' he speaks of recall the slippages Jonathan Dollimore speaks of in his introduction to *Political Shakespeare: New Essays in Cultural Materialism*, ed. Jonathan Dollimore and Alan Sinfield (Ithaca, NY: Cornell University Press, 1985), 12. See also Theodore B. Leinwand's discussion of 'Negotiation and New Historicism' (which Butler uses), *PMLA* 105.3 (1990): 477–90. Leinwand discusses the New Historicist/cultural materialist binary of subversion/containment in relation to Foucault's positing of a more fluid structure of cultural power relations in which containment and subversion exist in a constant state of negotiation highlighting 'microencounters [or] sites at which power is not so much possessed as exercised' (478).

17. Butler, 'Courtly Negotiations', 26.
18. Legley Mickel, *Ben Jonson's Antimasques: A History of Growth and Decline* (Aldershot, UK: Ashgate, 1999).
19. *Ibid.*, 17.
20. See Leinwand, 'Negotiation and New Historicism', 478.
21. Readers thus interpret the masque and its praise correctly when they read within the decorum of the occasion which dictates that majesty must be affirmed; in this sense Jonson inscribes a community of 'true readers' that correlates with what Cousins terms 'the commonwealth of understanders' in his chapter in this volume.
22. On the masque as Henry's and James' see Robin Headlam Wells' article '"Manhood and Chevalrie": *Corialanus*, Prince Henry, and the Chivalric Revival', *Review of English Studies* n.s. 51 (2000): 395–422; and my *Selfish Gifts*, 149–51.
23. Goldberg, *James I*, 62.
24. Camille Paglia, *Sexual Personae: Art and Decadence from Nefertiti to Emily Dickinson* (London: Penguin, 1991), 96–7.
25. *Ibid.*, 97.
26. *Ibid.*, 98.
27. Sharon Fermor, 'Decorum in Figural Movement: The Dance as Measure and Metaphor', in *Decorum in Renaissance Narrative Art: Papers delivered at the Annual Conference of the Association of Art Historians, London, April 1991*, ed. Francis Ames-Lewis and Anka Bednarek (London: Birkbeck College, 1992), 78–88, 80; Sir John Davies, 'Orchestra' stanza 23, in *The Poems of Sir John Davies*, ed. Robert Krueger (Oxford: Clarendon Press, 1975), 96. Jonson uses similar metaphors to speak of 'style' and the importance of avoiding perplexity and confusion in *Discoveries*; he recommends that we 'should speak what we can the nearest way, so as we keep our gait, not leap' (2009–11), see also 2011–20. All references to *Discoveries* are taken from *Ben Jonson*, ed. Ian Donaldson, The Oxford Authors (Oxford University Press, 1985).
28. Fermor, 'Decorum in Figural Movement', 80.

29. Wayne Rebhorn, *The Emperor of Men's Minds: Literature and the Renaissance Discourse of Rhetoric* (Ithaca, NY: Cornell University Press, 1985), 51, 67, see also 68–71, especially fig. 3 which depicts 'HIC HERCULES EST GALLICUS' from Achille Bocchi's *Symbolicarum Quaestionum . . . Libri quinque* (Bologna, 1574), book 2, symbol 43.

30. *Ibid.*, 67.

31. *Ibid.*

32. See Plutarch's *Moralia*, trans. Harold Cherniss and William C. Helmbold, Loeb Classical Library, 15 vols. (1957; rpt London: Heinemann; Cambridge, MA: Harvard University Press, 1968), XII, 986b–c.

33. *De Officiis* 1.93. References are to the translation by Walter Miller, Loeb Classical Library (1913; rpt London: Heinemann; Cambridge, MA: Harvard University Press, 1968).

34. As Dudley Carleton remembers, *The Masque of Blackness* was 'concluded with a Banquet in the great Chamber, which was so furiously assaulted, that down went Table and Tresses before one bit was touched' (Herford and Simpson, *Ben Jonson*, X, 448); moreover, the confusion of the post-masque festivities provided a haven for pickpockets and other undesirables, Carleton recounting the 'infinit . . . losses . . . of chaynes, Jewels, purces, and such like loose ware' and the loss of one woman's 'honesty' (*ibid.*, 449). Carleton describes the indecorums of the masque that Jonson will obviously omit, and he indicates as much to his correspondent (Chamberlain) by conceding that the 'maske at night requires much labor to be well described' and so, as there was 'a pamphlet in press' which would 'saue [. . . him those] paynes', he would speak of the occasion in general terms, which effectively amount to gossip (*ibid.*, 449).

35. Montaigne, 'Of Drunkennesse', in *The Essayes of Montaigne*, trans. John Florio (1603; rpt New York: Random House, n.d.), 299.

36. Paglia, in reference to Plutarch's calling Apollo 'the One', distinguishes between the singular Apollonian vision and the multiple Dionysian vision which denotes 'mob-rule and the slurry of uncountable objects rumbling through nature' (*Sexual Personae*, 97).

37. I am influenced here by Goldberg's assertion that the antimasque is 'a vision of vice' from Hercules' perspective (*James I*, 63).

38. Goldberg, *James I*, 63.

39. See *ibid.*, 63–4; also Leah S. Marcus, *The Politics of Mirth: Jonson, Herrick, Milton, Marvell, and the Defense of Old Holiday Pastimes* (University of Chicago Press, 1986) – Marcus notes of *Pleasure Reconciled*, that '[t]he world of the masque and the world of the court' merge, so that the courtiers 'symbolically enact their choice of the hard path of Virtue, a choice which their subsequent behavior at court will presumably make manifest' (124).

40. *De Officiis*, 1.93. The principle of decorum was associated with the golden mean from Aristotle onwards. Cicero thus states that 'the very essence of propriety is found in the division of virtue . . . [called] temperance', *De Officiis*, 1.100; and Quintilian asserts that 'all extravagance of any kind is

indecorous', *Institutio Oratoria*, trans. H. E. Butler, Loeb Classical Library, 4 vols. (London: Heinemann; Cambridge, MA: Harvard University Press, 1961), 11.1.91. On the association between decorum and the related virtue prudence, see the second chapter of Victoria Kahn's *Rhetoric, Prudence, and Skepticism in the Renaissance* (Ithaca, NY: Cornell University Press, 1985).

41. 'Of Masques and Triumphs', in *Francis Bacon: The Major Works*, ed. Brian Vickers (Oxford University Press, 2002), 416. Tom Bishop rightly notes that, though Bacon 'condescends to the masque as trivial and superfluous, [he] concedes that its proper function is to offer a regime of pleasure for the eye of the court', 'The Gingerbread Host', 100.

42. Patricia Fumerton, *Cultural Aesthetics: Renaissance Literature and the Practice of Social Ornament* (Chicago University Press, 1991), 112.

43. See Vitruvius, *The Ten Books of Architecture*, trans. Morris Hicky Morgan (New York: Dover Publications, 1960), book 1.5, at pages 14–15.

44. Obviously, the relationship between Vitruvius' *decor* and the rhetor's *decorum* is uncertain, but I tend to agree with Alina Payne's observation that it was 'not a concern for Renaissance readers; when they read Vitruvius they read him along with Cicero, Horace, and Quintilian, using one Roman text to explicate another in the accepted fashion of humanist exegesis. And in such a context, *decor* inevitably recalled *decorum*.' *The Architectural Treatise in the Italian Renaissance: Architectural Invention, Ornament, and Literary Culture* (Cambridge University Press, 1999), 53–4.

45. The politics of the paradoxical critique/defence are illuminated by the fact that Bacon himself sponsored masques and so wished, as Jonson did, to delineate the kind of masque in which he had an interest as more appropriate to majesty than mere generic 'toys'. Bacon apparently spent some £2,000 on *The Masque of Flowers*, which marked the occasion of the Earl of Somerset's wedding. See also Elizabeth McClure Thomson, ed., *The Chamberlain Letters* (New York: G. P. Putnam's Sons, 1965), 75.

46. See Kahn, *Rhetoric, Prudence, and Skepticism*, 35; and Cicero, *Orator*, 71, trans. H. M. Hubbell, at volume 5 of *Cicero*, Loeb Classical Library, 28 vols. (London: Heinemann; Cambridge, MA: Harvard University Press, 1939).

47. Orgel, *Illusion of Power*, 59.

48. Jonson's politics of genre were thus inherently focused on the conflicting agenda of reflecting the ideology of restraint manifest in James' own writings and speeches – which of course aimed to reform the 'continental excesses' of the court (Marcus, *Politics of Mirth*, 122) – at the same time as entertaining James with the visions of delight he demanded, and that themselves manifested the very excesses James outwardly counselled against.

49. As Richard Helgerson notes, like the epigram, the masque suffered from its relation to systems of patronage, 'the very relation that made them so useful to Jonson as signs of his social elevation . . . rendered their author liable to the familiar charge of flattery', *Self-Crowned Laureates: Spenser, Jonson, Milton and the Literary System* (Berkeley: University of California Press, 1983), 176.

50. Athenaeus, *The Deipnosophists*, trans. Charles Burton Gulick, Loeb Classical Library (London: Heinemann; Cambridge, MA: Harvard University Press, 1961), 3.102–3.

51. Quintilian reminds that 'statements which are in sufficient harmony with the facts will none the less lose all their grace unless they are modified by a certain restraint' (*Institutio Oratoria*, 9.1.91) and Horace's *De Arte Poetica* begins with a discussion of the poet's licence and the need, within that licence, for restraint in composition so that 'wild, and tame' are not brought to 'cleave / Together' (Herford and Simpson, *Ben Jonson*, VIII, 305).

52. The distinction is an important one as Jonson makes clear in *Discoveries*, lines 823–31.

53. Plato, *Gorgias*, 504d. References are to W. R. M. Lamb's translation, *Plato: Lysis, Symposium, Gorgias*, Loeb Classical Library (1925; rpt London: Heinemann; Cambridge, MA: Harvard University Press, 1967).

54. Plato, *Gorgias*, 507d.

55. The masque was intended to be performed some three months after Charles' and Buckingham's return from Spain and the masque has to account for this delay. In the end, of course, the masque was cancelled outright, Chamberlain explaining that 'the cause is thought to be the competition of the French and Spanish ambassadors, wch could not be accomodated in presence, and whetersoeuer of them were absent yt wold sound to his disgrace, and so much the Spanish ambassadors did intimate upon notice that the French was first inuited, and forbare not to say (that among many other) they should take this for the most notorious affront' (Herford and Simpson, *Ben Jonson*, X, 659).

56. Orgel, *Jonsonian Masque*, 96.

57. Plato, *Gorgias*, 465d.

58. Orgel, *Jonsonian Masque*, 97. Bruce McComiskey has argued that Socrates' denigration of Gorgias in Plato's *Gorgias* is not that simple either because Socrates assumes that Gorgias defines truth in terms of Platonic epistemology, when in fact, Gorgias deals with truth in relativist terms, *'Gorgias' and the New Sophistic Rhetoric* (Carbondale: Southern Illinois University Press, 2002), 24–5.

59. Cousins discusses how Jonson's epigram 'To my Book' anticipates how misunderstanding might 'deform' his book in his chapter in this volume.

60. Richard A. Lanham, *A Handlist of Rhetorical Terms* (Berkeley: University of California Press, 1991), 45.

61. *Ibid.*, 46.

62. *Ibid.*

63. Cicero, *De Officiis*, 1.27.

64. Quintilian, *Institutio Oratoria*, 11.1.91.

65. Jonas A. Barish provides an early reading of a similar sort of two-way effect of the wonder of the masque when he argues that the '"magnificence" of the event combines with the climactic recognition of the king's visible presence to infuse a sense of "wonder", into participants and spectators; the "wonder", in turn,

creates a frame of mind uniquely favorable to the absorption of all the virtues appropriate to them as loyal subjects', *Ben Jonson and the Language of Prose Comedy* (Cambridge, MA: Harvard University Press, 1960), 244. Obviously, I read the participants and spectators as, in part, performing a more active role than Barish's use of the term 'absorption' implies, but I remain indebted to the reading.

66. See *Republic*, trans. Robin Waterfield (Oxford University Press, 1998), 606e–607a; *Gorgias* 459a–d; also McComiskey, *'Gorgias' and the New Sophistic Rhetoric*, 25–6. As McComiskey argues, Socrates is able to discredit sophism in *Gorgias* only by assuming that Gorgias accepts that binary opposition, which his works clearly demonstrate he did not; through that opposition, however, Socrates is able to argue that Gorgianic rhetoric cannot effect instruction and functions therefore merely in terms of gratification.

67. Eric Charles White, *Kaironomia: On the Will to Invent* (Ithaca, NY: Cornell University Press, 1987), 14–15.

68. The 'rules' of masque writing are, of course, mocked in the opening scene of Beaumont and Fletcher's *The Maid's Tragedy*.

69. White, *Kaironomia*, 14–15.

70. Jonson's statement about the poet's giftedness comes in a letter to Anne, appended to a presentation copy of *The Masque of Queens*. That letter is reprinted in Herford and Simpson, *Ben Jonson*, VII, 280–1. McComiskey argues that, contrary to Plato's presentation of Gorgias, 'Gorgianic rhetoric *is* concerned with the greatest good . . . the good of the community' (*'Gorgias' and the New Sophistic Rhetoric*, 27–8); I am obviously indebted to that argument in my reading of Jonson's own treatment of the subject and to his observation that while Plato's word for knowledge – episteme – 'implies an understanding that exists prior to any given situation in which it might be applied . . . Gorgias' term *eidô* . . . implies an understanding that is derived empirically from a situation, and its etymology is related to sight' (25). James S. Baumlin notes that the rhetoric of decorum assumes that 'truth itself changes according to the circumstances in which one finds oneself', 'Ciceronian Decorum and the Temporalities of Renaissance Rhetoric', in *Rhetoric and Kairos*, ed. Sipiora and Baumlin, 158; see also Kahn, *Rhetoric, Prudence, and Skepticism*, 35.

71. Robert Evans, *Ben Jonson and the Poetics of Patronage* (Lewisburg: Bucknell University Press, 1989), 66.

72. McCanles, *Jonsonian Discriminations*, 90–1. Richard Dutton discusses the preface to *Hymenaei* in relation to Jonson's desire to assert the seriousness of his art, demonstrating that the masque was designed to put the audience into a state of '"wonder", in which (the hope was) they might "profit" from the "remov'd mysteries" which bear so crucially on everyday human conduct', *Ben Jonson: To the First Folio* (Cambridge University Press, 1983), 95. Dutton remarks wryly that it is 'open to doubt whether the average Jacobean courtier would respond with such proper humility to these flattering spectacles' (96).

73. See Thomas Aquinas, *Summa Theologica*, trans. Fathers of the English Dominican Province (New York: Benziger Bros, 1947–8), 2.2.167.

74. Cicero, *De Officiis*, 94.

75. Aquinas, *Summa Theologica*, 2.2.167.

76. Amélie Frost Benedikt observes that Gorgias' explanation of *kairos* stresses that 'one cannot evaluate the kairic fit of an action to a particular moment without considering the response of others', 'On Doing the Right Thing at the Right Time: Toward an Ethics of *Kairos*', in *Rhetoric and Kairos*, ed. Sipora and Baumlin, 231.

77. In *The Architectural Treatise*, Alina Payne notes that *decor* and *decorum* both 'prescribed the limits of authorial freedom (or licence) and privileged convention (*consuetudo*) in gauging appropriateness relative to an audience' (58).

78. Lanham, *Handlist of Rhetorical Terms*, 46.

CHAPTER 3

The politics (and pairing) of Jonson's country house poems

Robert C. Evans

The politics of Ben Jonson's two country house poems – 'To Penshurst' and 'To Sir Robert Wroth' – are an important but complicated topic. The first difficulty, of course, is how the term 'politics' shall be defined. Will it be used to refer to whatever political views Jonson himself may have intended to express in these poems? Or will the term refer to the various possible political responses the poems could provoke among Jonson's contemporaries? Or, alternatively, will the term primarily suggest much-later and more-recent reactions to the poems by representatives of political approaches – such as Marxism, new historicism, cultural materialism, etc. – unknown (or at least unnamed) in Jonson's day? Or, finally, will the term refer primarily to 'macropolitics' (i.e., to issues of ideology, formal governance, or power relations among large social groups) or to 'micropolitics' (i.e., to power relations among individuals)? Any of these aspects of the topic would be worth exploring, and many have indeed been the subjects or motives of previous analysis. Politics of some sort are almost impossible to ignore in discussions of these poems; the works invite (almost demand) political responses. Reactions to the poems, however, will depend (and have depended) very much on the contexts readers bring to them.

A brief glance at the history of criticism of these poems will suggest the variety of responses their 'politics' have provoked. Thus G. R. Hibbard, writing in 1956 in the seminal article on the country house genre, finds in such poetry evidence of 'strong ethical thought' that 'voices and defines the values of a society conscious of its own achievement of a civilized way of living, and conscious also of the forces that threatened to undermine and overthrow that achievement. The function of the poet in this society' (Hibbard continues) 'was to make it aware of itself; and because the poet had a function the relation between poet and patron in these poems is sound and wholesome'.[1] Hibbard considers Jonson's celebration of Penshurst 'the fullest statement we have of that traditional piety which is

73

the basis of his satire';[2] the poem reveals 'the function of the house in the community as the centre of a complex web of relationships which makes up the fabric of civilized living'.[3] According to Hibbard (paraphrasing Jonson's poem), the 'tenants of the Sidneys are not exploited; the relationship is a reciprocal one of duties and responsibilities on both sides, freely and gladly entered into. The tenants come [to the estate] because they want to, not because they must . . . The bonds between tenant and lord are an extension, as it were, of the bonds between child and parent'.[4] Hibbard nowhere questions or disputes the idyllic picture just described; he makes it clear that Jonson admires life at Penshurst, and it seems equally clear that Hibbard himself admires the life Jonson depicts. Hibbard thus speaks eloquently for one very strong faction of analysts of these poems – a faction that takes the poems at face value, and a faction that seems untroubled by the politics the poems imply. For Hibbard and many other critics, the poems are chiefly concerned with ethics rather than with 'politics' in the stricter senses of that term.

Writing in 1963, Paul Cubeta is mainly concerned with discussing parallels and distinctions between Jonson's works and their classical antecedents; according to Cubeta, Jonson in his country house poems 'defines an area of experience where ideal human activity can still thrive even though urban society has become morally corrupt'.[5] In statements such as this, as well as in the title of his essay ('A Jonsonian Ideal: "To Penshurst"'), Cubeta, like Hibbard, seems untroubled by the politics (macro- or micro-) implied by the poems, and the same seems true of Gayle Edward Wilson in a 1968 article on 'Jonson's Use of the Bible and the Great Chain of Being in "To Penshurst"'.[6] Whereas Cubeta had related Jonson's poems to classical sources, Wilson emphasizes the Christian dimensions of 'To Penshurst'. The effect of both articles is to distance the poems from any specifically contemporary political issues of Jonson's day (or any later era). Hibbard reads the poems as ethical statements; Cubeta connects them to their classical forebears; Wilson connects them to sacred religious texts. These approaches are continued, and greatly extended and enriched, in Alastair Fowler's important article of 1973, which argues that the patronage relations that lie at the heart of the poem on Penshurst 'brought out the best in Jonson'.[7] Fowler discusses the organization of 'To Penshurst' from multiple and richly reinforcing points of view, making his essay one of the best ever written on the poem, but the sentence from his piece that is most relevant to our present purposes is the one in which, like Hibbard, he argues that the work 'reflects unusual awareness of the civilized forms achieved by society at its best, and the threat presented to them by excessive display'.[8] For all the analysts cited so far, Penshurst represents not only a 'Jonsonian ideal' but also a more general ideal – and, in particular, a general political ideal – that almost anyone might admire and embrace.

The tone of analysis begins to alter, however, in the important work of Raymond Williams. In his seminal 1973 study *The Country and the City*, for instance, Williams calls Penshurst and other idyllic places like it 'lucky exceptions' to the generally darker side of power relations (and especially the relations between classes) during the English Renaissance, and he continues: 'There were, we need not doubt, such houses and such men [i.e., such owners of estates], but they were at best the gentle exercise of a power that was elsewhere, on their [i.e., the poems'] own evidence, mean and brutal.'[9] Indeed, Williams finds evidence, in 'To Penshurst', of an 'easy, insatiable exploitation of the land and its creatures – a prolonged delight in an organized and corporative production and consumption – which is the basis of many early phases of intensive agriculture: the land is rich, and will be made to provide'.[10] Williams concedes that the poem does endorse a kind of charity, particularly toward the poor, but he finds it 'a charity of consumption only'.[11] In other words, the poor are invited to share (occasionally) in products (owned by the rich) that come from land, which is also owned by the rich but worked by the poor. According to Williams, in the culture Jonson inherited, a more healthy 'charity of production – of loving relations between men actually working and producing what is ultimately, in whatever proportions, to be shared – was neglected, not seen, and at times suppressed, by this habitual reference to a charity of consumption, an eating and drinking communion, which when applied to ordinary working societies was inevitably a mystification. All uncharity at work, it was assumed, could be redeemed by the charity of the consequent feast.'[12] In the poem 'To Penshurst', Jonson, as an author who is also a guest of the Sidneys, finds himself in the awkward position of simply 'consuming what other men had produced'.[13] His poem, like others in the genre, effects a 'magical extraction of the curse of labour' by

a simple extraction of the existence of labourers. The actual men and women who rear the animals and drive them to the house and kill them and prepare them for meat; who trap the pheasants and partridges and catch the fish; who plant and manure and prune and harvest the fruit trees: these are not present; their work is all done for them by a natural order ... and what we are shown is the charity and lack of condescension with which they are given what, now and somehow, not they but the natural order has given for food into the lord's hands. It is this condition, this set of relationships, that is finally ratified by the consumption of the feast ... Jonson looks out over the fields of Penshurst and sees, not work, but a land yielding of itself.[14]

Jonson, in other words, helps perpetuate and glorify (according to Williams) a kind of cheat or fraud; he does not present a real picture of country life but rather offers 'social compliment; the familiar hyperboles of the aristocracy and its attendants'.[15] Less than twenty years had elapsed between the publication of Hibbard's article and the publication of Williams' book, but the distance (and difference) in tone, assumptions, and conclusions of their analyses could hardly be greater. Williams, in a few pages, had laid down a critical and political challenge that could not be ignored – a challenge to which nearly all later critics would feel some need to respond.

The response begins already in a footnote in the 1973 article by Fowler, who argues that labourers such as waiters and cheesemakers are not, in fact, extracted from the poem but are clearly present in its lines. Fowler also contends that Williams inappropriately mixes genres, since 'To Penshurst' is not meant to be read as a 'work-song'.[16] In place of Williams' vision of 'the familiar hyperboles of the aristocracy and its attendants',[17] Fowler argues that Jonson, 'far from having a servile relation to his patron, . . . takes for granted an easy friendship and even an advisory responsibility. Through recommendatory panegyric he guides the aspirations of the ruling class.'[18] Fowler's rejoinders to Williams continue in his important 1986 article 'Country House Poems: The Politics of a Genre', where he notes that

after many readings of Jonson's two poems, I continue to find labour represented in them – considering the genre, conspicuously so. In 'To Penshurst', Jonson does not extract the 'fisher' (l. 38), 'the farmer and the clown [countryman]' (line 48), 'some' (perhaps tenant farmers or clowns) with gifts of capon, cake, nuts, apples from their own land, and 'some that think they make / The better cheeses' (lines 52–3). And in 'To Sir Robert Wroth' . . . there is a whole seasonal round of occupations and labours.[19]

Later, in the same article, Fowler suggests that Williams' interpretations may be rooted in anachronistic ideas or in a misreading of specific generic motifs, and he also argues that in any case poets such as Jonson in poems such as 'To Penshurst' 'never pretend to give a naturalistic account of demesne farming. Most write emblematically, developing symbols of the role of husbandry and frugality in repair of the fall.'[20] Fowler strongly stresses this religious interpretation, arguing that 'Williams' talk of idealization in terms of an ethereal Golden Age or curseless Eden is unthinkable in Jonson's Christian and georgic traditions . . . Far from extracting labour, [Jonson] (and after him other estate poets) brought it into question in the first place. By writing about houses as estates, and in the georgic mode, they encouraged thinking about them in relation to husbandry and improvement.'²¹ Perhaps most intriguingly, Fowler disputes Don Wayne's 1984 view of the 'gifts' presented in 'To Penshurst' as examples of '*rent in kind*'; instead, Fowler argues that 'by 1612 rents in south-east England were completely monetarized, and would not have been presented as gifts'.²²

This is a crucial assertion, for if the 'gifts' presented to the Sidneys at Penshurst really *are* freely given and voluntary presents from the local peasantry, then the attractive picture Jonson presents of the estate is greatly strengthened. If, however, the 'gifts' are merely enforced, obligatory examples of 'rent in kind', then Williams' view of the poem gains significant support. Unfortunately, Fowler does not cite any source for his 1986 claim that rents in 1612 were paid in Kent as money rather than as goods, nor does he cite any source when he repeats the claim (twice) in his superb 1994 anthology *The Country House Poem*, where he once again disputes not only Don Wayne but also Michael Schoenfeldt on this particular point.²³ In her 2002 study *Maps and Memory in Early Modern England*, Rhonda Lemke Sanford does cite a 1578 source describing the practice of paying 'rents in kind' in England, but she, in turn, does not refute Fowler's specific claim that such practices had ceased in Kent in 1612 and are thus irrelevant to discussion of 'To Penshurst'. She simply assumes that 'the appearance of unmotivated gift-giving and goodwill belies the fact that this is most likely Rent Day and each subdivision of the land that was named earlier must be accounted for through payment of rent by its tenant'.²⁴ There are, however, various reasons for doubting this view, aside from the undocumented arguments Fowler offers.

In the first place, Jonson explicitly mentions that the products the peasants offer are given to 'salute' the lord and lady of Penshurst (line 49) and (even more tellingly) that they are meant to express 'loue' (line 57).²⁵ If the products were simply 'rents', it is hard to imagine why Jonson would stress their status as emblems of respect and even genuine affection, unless he were being extraordinarily cynical or ironic. In the second place, when describing the products, he offers a list that concludes with these words: 'some that think they make / The better cheeses, bring 'hem' (lines 52–3). These lines seem to imply that the peasants have some free discretion in choosing the kinds of products they will present to the Sidneys – phrasing that seems at odds with the kinds of stipulated contractual arrangement one associates with 'rents'. If one were merely paying an obligatory rent, why go to the trouble of going out of one's way to make 'better cheeses' when any ordinary cheese (or something else) would do?

The reference to the 'better cheeses' has always struck me as a wonderfully humorous example of what Milton would call 'modest pride' – that is, precisely the sort of attractive pride a person might exhibit after carefully preparing a favourite recipe for someone the preparer respected. It is hard to see why peasants would take any great pride in preparing an obligatory payment of rent. Thirdly, would peasants be likely to entrust to 'their ripe daughters' (line 54) such an important task as the payment of their rents? And, finally, if the visiting peasants are merely rent-payers, why does Jonson go out of his way to stress that none of them wishes ill to the walls of the estate (line 47)? Why emphasize that 'all come in' (line 48; if they were merely paying rent, of course they would all come in)? Why stress the 'hospitalitie' of the Sidneys (line 60), and why implicitly include the peasants among the 'guest[s]' (line 61) who are welcomed at the estate? If Jonson were thinking of the occasion he describes as an occasion of rent-paying, his references to hospitality and guests would seem inappropriate, and his comment that the Sidneys were 'farre aboue / The neede of such' rents would then be a very thinly veiled criticism of their inherent rapaciousness and would conflict with the whole tone of the rest of the poem. It is possible, of course, that Jonson knows he is referring to rent-paying but that he cynically puts the best face on this fact. He then would indeed be guilty, in this respect as in others, of the kind of 'absurdity' and 'poetic mendacity' Sanford alleges against him in the ways he presents matters of labour, ownership, wealth, and even gender relations.[26] In these words and assumptions of Sanford, we have come a long way from the sunny views of G. R. Hibbard, and even a long way from the fairly charitable tone of Raymond Williams.[27]

Even this brief overview of the history of critical commentary on Jonson's country house poems will suggest how strongly reactions to the 'politics' of these works depend on the contexts in which critics choose to interpret them. As Andrew McRae notes, 'Country house poems have variously been read as reactionary pastoral [by Williams], progressive georgic [by Fowler], and a subtle espousal of values "indicative of the rise of capitalism" [by Wayne]'.[28] Critics who stress the religious aspects of the poems (such as Wilson, Fowler, and Harp) tend to be untroubled by the politics the poems imply, since such critics tend to see the poems as ultimately concerned with larger, more 'transcendent' or more 'spiritual' issues and as using a religious perspective to celebrate and promote ideal social relations rooted in Christian love. Likewise, critics who stress the ethical aspects of the poems (such as Hibbard) also tend to find the politics of the poems untroubling, agreeing with William McClung that 'the historical changes in

English country-house life throughout the seventeenth century have been less influential upon "country-house poetry" than the moral tradition, in Latin and in English verse, that insistently opposes moderation and charity to ostentation and pride'.[29] Critics such as Williams and Sanford, however, are impatient with approaches that stress religion, ethics, or literary-generic conventions; they insist on reading the poems in light of the actual social conditions (especially class relations) of Jonson's day, and, judging the poems by ideal egalitarian standards, inevitably these critics find the works politically unappealing.[30]

In the pages that follow, I wish to suggest that one fruitful way to approach the politics of Jonson's two country house poems is to read the poems in tandem – as a deliberate pairing. Reading 'To Penshurst' in light of 'To Sir Robert Wroth' (and vice versa) may help shed new light on the political dimensions of each work, and doing so may also help resolve some difficulties that arise when attention is focused too exclusively on 'To Penshurst' in isolation. Reading the poems as a linked pair may also help promote a fuller appreciation of the poem to Wroth, which is usually overshadowed by (and largely ignored because of) its better-known neighbour.[31] Jonson seems almost to invite us to read the poems together: they are, after all, of roughly equal length; they share obvious thematic concerns; they were both addressed to members of the same extended family; and they were first printed side by side in the 1616 first Folio. Their phrasing is so similar at times that we cannot read one poem without immediately thinking of the other. Thus the references in 'Wroth' to 'proud porches' and 'guilded roofes' (line 15) instantly remind us of the references in 'Penshurst' to 'polished pillars, or a roofe of gold' (line 3). Likewise, when Jonson uses such words as 'exercise' (line 30) or 'thy friends' (line 25) in 'Wroth', we can't help but be reminded of his use of the very same words in 'Penshurst' (line 21). The 'cop'ces' in 'Wroth' (line 38) remind us of the 'copp's' (lines 19, 26) in 'Penshurst'; the references to 'PAN' and 'SYLVANE' in 'Wroth' (line 47) cannot help but recall the use of the same words in 'Penshurst' (lines 11, 16); meanwhile, the allusion to 'COMVS' in 'Wroth' (line 48) inevitably resembles the allusion to 'BACCHVS' in 'Penshurst' (line 11). Even the concluding advice, in 'Wroth', that the lord of the manor should learn to 'dwell' at his estate recalls the famous final words of 'Penshurst': 'thy lord dwells' (line 102). It would be possible to list many other specific or general resemblances between the two poems, but by now the main point is clear: these works are so similar that Jonson had to have had one in mind while writing the other, and they are also so similar that we, as readers, cannot help but think of one when we read its partner. This would be true even if the poems were not so obviously and deliberately paired (as they clearly were) in the printing of the first folio.

Of course, one way to interpret the many specific and general similarities between the two poems is to assume that in one poem Jonson had merely run out of steam and was simply copying himself. Perhaps (this argument might go) he wrote 'Penshurst' first and then merely churned out 'Wroth' as an uninspired imitation.[32] I find this possible argument unpersuasive for several reasons. First, 'Wroth' is a vigorous poem in its own right; indeed, its tone is (if anything) even more impassioned than that of 'Penshurst'. Jonson's emotions seem to have been fully engaged when he composed the work; he does not seem simply to have been repeating stale procedures. Second, 'Wroth', despite its many undeniable similarities to 'Penshurst', is also a significantly different work, as I hope to show. Neither poem is a copy of its neighbour. Therefore, rather than viewing one poem as a hackneyed knock-off of the other, I wish to argue instead that Jonson knew exactly what he was doing when he composed two works that were so obviously similar, and in particular that he knew precisely what he was doing when he placed them right next to each other in the first folio. Their side-by-side placement practically forces us to read them together, as commentaries on each other. Indeed, as long ago as 1973, Anthony Mortimer considered it 'important to read these poems as complementary and to see how far comparison reveals the genuine significance of both', and later in the same article he argued that the poems 'illuminate each other as essential, complementary approaches to the same poetic vision'.[33] Rarely, however, have the poems been discussed at length as a pair, and even more rarely has the poem on Wroth been given much sustained attention. By focusing particularly on that poem, however, we may arrive at a more complex understanding of the political dimensions of both works. And, by examining two of the earliest and most influential of all country house poems together, as a pair, we may come to a fuller grasp of some of the political dimensions and implications of the country house genre as a whole.[34]

In discussing the poems, I shall focus mainly on 'Wroth', not only because it tends to be relatively neglected, but also because I am more interested in the light (especially the political light) it can shed on 'Penshurst' than vice versa. The broad similarities (but also contrasts) between the two works are evident immediately. Both works open, for instance, with direct address: in 'Penshurst' Jonson speaks to the estate itself; in 'Wroth' the first line mentions Sir Robert explicitly; his estate itself does not really begin to come into focus for another twelve lines or so. Satire is strongly emphasized at the start of both poems: in 'Penshurst' other country homes are satirized, but in 'Wroth' the range of satire is much broader, with attacks on both 'the citie, and the court' (line 3) and on both the 'Sheriffes dinner' and the 'Maiors feast' (line 6). The court in particular comes in for heavy attack in the opening lines of 'Wroth' as Jonson mocks the general obsession with 'the better cloth of state; / The richer hangings, or crowne-plate' and as he particularly satirizes the superficialities of courtly masquing, especially the way people throng 'to have a sight / Of the short brauerie of the night; / To view the iewells, stuffes, the paines, the wit / There wasted, some not paid for yet!' (lines 9–12). These lines themselves exhibit a kind of wit for which 'Wroth' is too infrequently praised: one notes, for instance, the wonderfully ironic juxtaposition of 'short' and 'brauerie', the superb way in which a mere two words ('There wasted') unexpectedly undercut the long catalogue that precedes them, and also the double meaning implied by the words 'some not paid for yet'. This phrase can suggest, on the one hand, that the finery worn by participants at masques is often bought on credit by pretenders who want to display a kind of wealth they don't truly possess; or it can suggest that the court itself buys on credit and makes no speedy effort to settle its debts; and it can even suggest that Jonson himself (the person chiefly responsible for the 'wit' of the masques and for many of the intellectual 'paines' they involved) was routinely late in receiving payment.

However one chooses to interpret such phrasing, the main difference between the opening of 'Wroth' and the opening of 'Penshurst' is clear: 'Wroth' is a much more insistently and broadly satiric poem. It begins with a wholesale indictment not just of a few country houses but of a whole corrupt society. It attacks not just the ostentatious architecture of some immodest buildings but the real 'vice' and trivial 'sport' of some of the most powerful people in Jonson's society – the sort of people likely to attend sheriffs' dinners, mayors' feasts, and royal masques. 'Wroth' even implicitly mocks the particular people responsible for paying for the masques, and more generally it mocks the sort of people who value the court mainly as a place of wealth, display, and personal ambition rather than as a centre of disinterested service to the nation. Certainly 'Wroth' does not offer (at least in its opening lines!) what Raymond Williams dismisses as 'the familiar hyperboles of the aristocracy and its attendants'.[35] Instead, quite the opposite is true: Jonson indicts irresponsible aristocrats and courtiers with a kind of boldness, ferocity, and sarcasm that still has the power to shock. He can hardly be accused here of any sort of 'poetic mendacity',[36] and indeed it seems significant that the poem to Wroth is never discussed in Sanford's book, from which that phrase is taken. The poem *is* mentioned several times in passing by Williams, and the opening lines are even quoted, but even Williams does not discuss the poem at length, and even he chooses to emphasize what he calls its later 'lattice of compliment'.[37] This emphasis seems unfair, for much of the poem (as we shall see) is anything but complimentary.[38]

'Wroth' is a more insistently and obviously political poem than 'Penshurst', and perhaps it is (ironically) for that reason less politically effective. 'Penshurst' (for the most part) attractively celebrates an ideal; 'Wroth' (for the most part) brashly excoriates corruption. 'Penshurst' can seem almost magical in extolling rural harmony, and certainly it is full of an appealing good humour that is too often overlooked (or under-emphasized) in discussions of its politics.[39] 'Wroth', by contrast, is a more serious, more edgy, and even a more bitter poem. 'Penshurst' is a more appealing work to read and is one of the most often anthologized and analysed of all Jonson's writings; 'Wroth' (as all the evidence shows) is a much harder sell; even Jonsonians tend to neglect it.[40] 'Penshurst' makes its political points mainly through indirection and implication, and even when it spells them out it does so mostly in positive terms. 'Wroth', by contrast, hammers home its political points – and thus it runs the risk, occasionally, of seeming ill-humoured, unsubtle, and therefore both rhetorically and politically overbearing. Take, for instance, the reference in 'Wroth' to the 'paines' and 'wit' of masquing that are 'not paid for yet!' (lines 11–12). It seems hard to read these lines and not imagine, in part, a personal complaint by Jonson himself, whose payments as chief masque-writer were sometimes in arrears. Jonson thus seems to be using 'Wroth', if only momentarily, to express a merely personal gripe. The passage in 'Penshurst' that is comparably personal is much more appealing, and much more extensive (lines 61–75). It presents Jonson humorously as a bibulous glutton, and even the lines that may contain a sharper personal edge require knowledge of biographical facts not widely available to Jonson's first readers (at least not to readers of the printed version).[41] Jonson's personal complaints are thus more subtle in 'Penshurst' than in 'Wroth', and perhaps for that reason they are more rhetorically appealing and politically effective. Anyone reading 'Wroth', however, would be hard put to accuse Jonson of lacking political courage. 'Wroth' thus casts an intriguing light on the charges of political sycophancy sometimes levelled against 'Penshurst'. By placing the two poems side by side, and thus by practically inviting us to read them together, Jonson implicitly anticipates and answers such charges before they can even be levelled. (In postmodern lingo, he is 'always already' aware of the potential allegations against him.) 'Wroth' is the poem in which he clearly spells out political values and attitudes that are mostly implied in its companion, 'Penshurst'.

Only beginning in line 13 (and only then for a while) does 'Wroth' come to resemble 'Penshurst' in obvious ways. In that line Jonson momentarily turns away from urban corruption and begins to focus on Wroth's rural 'home'.[42] As in 'Penshurst', he describes the livestock of the estate (line 16), its woods and meadows (line 17), its flowing river (line 18), its appealing climate (line 19), and the peace and rest all these promote (lines 13, 20). Even more extensively than in 'Penshurst', he mentions the hunting that is a prime rural pastime (lines 23–36), and he also alludes (as in the companion piece) to visits by that chief enthusiast of the hunt, King James himself (line 23). In writing 'Wroth' as when describing Penshurst, Jonson also stresses the agriculture of the estate (lines 37–46), and, if anything, in 'Wroth' he goes out of his way to mention the labour – and labourers – involved in such production: meadows are 'mowed', sheep are 'fleeced' (line 39), trees are 'cut out in log' (line 45), and 'boughes [are] made / A fire now' (lines 45–6). Admittedly he refers to Wroth's 'vn-bought provision' (line 14), and it isn't hard to imagine how easily such a phrase could be 'de-mystified' and how even the references to labour and labourers could be seen as implying exploitation. But at least labour is openly acknowledged here; there is no 'magical extraction of the curse of labour' nor any 'simple extraction of the existence of labourers', as Williams alleged (not entirely convincingly) was true of 'Penshurst'.[43] In 'Wroth' the 'shearers' of both the meadows and the sheep participate in 'feasts' (line 40), and later the mixing of classes is even more explicitly celebrated:

> The rout of rurall folke come thronging in,
> (Their rudeness then is thought no sinne)
> Thy noblest spouse affords them welcome grace;
> And the great Heroes, of her race,
> Sit mixt with losse of state, or reuerence.
> Freedome doth with degree dispense.
> The iolly wassall walkes the often round,
> And in their cups, their cares are drown'd.

(lines 53–60)

The joyful 'thronging' described here differs considerably from the competitive 'throng[ing]' mentioned earlier, when Jonson was satirizing the superficialities of courtly masquing (line 9). It's entirely possible, of course, that these 'rurall folke' are compelled to come to Wroth's estate to pay their rents in kind, although no such payment is even hinted at, nor are any gifts of the

sort described in 'Penshurst' (lines 48–60) even alluded to.[44] It's also possible that the 'welcome grace' offered by Lady Wroth is merely a pretence or
supercilious ruse she adopted whenever she was occasionally forced to interact with sinfully rude peasants. It seems more likely, however, that Jonson
here (as in 'Penshurst') really does admire the kind of 'Freedome' that
'doth with degree dispense', and that we are meant to admire it, too. It is
possible, of course, to read both this poem and 'Penshurst' in light of
later egalitarian ideals and find them wanting, but then it is always easy
to judge any earlier work by the standards of a later day and convict it of
mendacity for failing to live up to an ideal the writer never even imagined.
The point worth emphasizing here, however, is that 'Wroth' provides a
useful antidote to the political criticism levelled against 'Penshurst'. In
'Wroth', labour – and labourers – *are* emphasized; in 'Wroth', no gifts
are mentioned that might be construed as 'rents'; and in 'Wroth' Jonson
even acknowledges that labourers may have 'cares' that need to be
'drown'd' in drink (line 60). If 'Penshurst' seems charmingly magical,
'Wroth' seems bluntly realistic, and by pairing the poems Jonson helps
remind us that his own political vision is not escapist, naive, or sycophantic,
let alone mendacious (a point that is also obvious from reading the body of
his works as a whole).

Indeed, no sooner does Jonson present this rural ideal of 'iolly' (if tem-
porary) freedom from rigid class distinctions than he immediately plunges
us back into an exceptionally grim and realistic account of widespread
social corruption – corruption that helped give value and meaning to
such relatively ideal and idyllic places as Penshurst and Wroth's estate. It
is easy, perhaps, to criticize 'Penshurst' for mystifying and underplaying
the less attractive aspects of life in Jacobean England, but no such charge
can plausibly be levelled at 'Wroth', and when the two poems are read
side by side, any allegations that Jonson was engaged in mere 'social compliment' seem distorted and unfair.[45] I have already cited the line in 'Wroth'
that refers to the ways people's 'cares are drown'd' in drink, but what makes
the line particularly interesting is its ambiguity. Jonson doesn't make precisely clear *whose* cares he means. At first it appears that he must be referring
to the 'rout of rurall folke' (line 53), but as he describes the specific 'cares' he
has in mind, it seems plausible that he is referring also to their social
'betters', perhaps even to members of the Wroth and Sidney families themselves. It is possible, perhaps, that peasants or small farmers would sometimes need to worry about 'which side the cause shall leese [i.e., lose]' or
'how to get the lawyer fees' (lines 61–2), but it seems perhaps even more
likely that these would be the kinds of 'cares' that would afflict members

of the middle or upper classes. Jonson's ambiguity seems deliberate: he seems to imply that both the 'folke' and their social superiors had reason to fear the kind of competitive, predatory economic and social conflict implied by the reference to lawyers. Jonson's political vision, not only in this poem but in 'Penshurst' and elsewhere, is one that disdains mere monetary motives and calculating legalistic ambition, and if in 'Penshurst' such disdain is mostly implied, 'Wroth' spells it out quite plainly.

For the next twenty or so lines of the poem, in fact, Jonson ceases to pay much attention to Wroth's estate itself, focusing instead on the varied kinds of social corruption that gave estates like Wroth's, and Penshurst, both their real and their symbolic value. The catalogue of vice he here unleashes is astonishing even by his own fierce satiric standards, for he runs the risk of offending almost every segment of society. Anyone who reads 'Penshurst' and imagines Jonson a toady has merely to turn the page and read these lines from 'Wroth' to be disabused of that notion. In these lines Jonson, normally a great admirer of martial valour, nonetheless attacks badly motivated soldiers who fight for all the wrong reasons – soldiers who 'watch in guiltie arms, and stand / The furie of a rash command' (lines 67–8). Such soldiers, presumably, engage in combat not on behalf of any higher values but for reasons of personal pride, profit, or ambition; far from fighting for causes sanctioned by reason, they are motivated by rashness, 'furie', and an egotistic desire to 'brag' (line 72). Having potentially annoyed many soldiers and former soldiers among his readers, Jonson next opens an even lengthier frontal assault on perverse and mercenary lawyers (lines 73–80). Indeed, these corrupt lawyers seem far more repulsive than the earlier braggart soldiers because Jonson so vividly and insistently reminds us of their actual victims, who include disinherited children and defenceless 'orphanes' and 'widdowes' (lines 77, 79). Then, having savaged corrupt lawyers, Jonson next attacks others whose only goal in life is to 'heape a masse of wretched wealth, / Purchas'd by rapine, worse than stealth' (lines 81–2). Perhaps this group also includes lawyers, but such satire additionally seems directed at perverse members of the mercantile class, such as monopolists, unscrupulous businessmen, or perhaps even those involved in piracy or colonial enterprises. Finally, Jonson also goes after flatterers and time-servers, presumably associated with the court, whom he calls 'organes to great sinne' and whom he condemns (in a splendidly ironic echo of line 21) for being 'glad to keepe / The secrets, that shall breake their sleepe' (lines 87–8). Whereas 'Penshurst', at around the same point in that poem, celebrates the arrival at the estate of the king and the crown prince, 'Wroth' at a comparable point indicts courtly corruption. Is Jonson thus being a flatterer in

'Penshurst' and a satirist in 'Wroth'? I think not. Instead I would argue that in one poem he chooses to teach mainly by praising virtue and that in the other poem he instead chooses to instruct mainly by condemning vice. 'Wroth' and 'Penshurst', in other words, are the concrete embodiments of the two conventional halves of epideictic rhetoric: they promote the same ethical (and political) values, but they do so in distinct but complementary ways. In attempting to come to grips with the politics of Jonson's country house poems, we need to read (and be aware of) *both* of his major contributions to the genre.

'Wroth' ends, appropriately enough, by focusing on Sir Robert himself. The closing passage credits Wroth with having the good sense (and good morals) to appreciate his fortunate condition, but it also offers counsel and instruction, especially in the final eight lines (lines 99–106). Here, as in the final lines of 'Penshurst', Jonson emphasizes faith in God as the ultimate source and guarantee of the positive values for which the estate is celebrated, but once again his approaches in the two poems are distinct. In 'Penshurst' Jonson merely mentions in general terms that the Sidneys, their children, and the household staff pray together thrice each day, but in 'Wroth' Jonson specifically instructs Sir Robert not only what to pray for but even how to pray. Perhaps Jonson had less personal confidence in Wroth than in the Sidneys; perhaps not.[46] In any case, the difference in tone and manner is appropriate to the more general differences between the two works. 'Penshurst' is a more assured poem in every sense of that word; 'Wroth' is less secure in all ways.[47] 'Penshurst' appeals to our sense of optimism and love of humour, to our longing for – and enjoyment of – peace and happiness. 'Wroth' is the more brutally realistic and even cynical work. In 'Penshurst' Jonson lets us think, for a moment, that we may briefly have escaped to a kind of Eden; in 'Wroth' he never for a second lets us forget our fallen world, and our fallen condition. 'Wroth', in a sense, is the work many critics of 'Penshurst' seem to wish Jonson had written when he composed his poem to the Sidneys. Perhaps that is one reason (though hardly the only reason) that 'Wroth' is so often ignored by analysts: in 'Wroth', unlike in 'Penshurst', there is very little to deconstruct or demystify; Jonson has already done much of that work for us. In 'Penshurst' Jonson imagines what a harmoniously ordered (if, of course, still imperfect and non-utopian) society might be like; in 'Wroth' he makes it clear that he knows how far reality remains from such an ideal. What both poems finally make clear is that for Jonson, politics could not be divorced from ethics, or ultimately from religion. It does not seem either accidental or surprising that at the conclusions of both works, Jonson stresses the need for virtue in individual persons, or that he stresses that the roots of such virtue lie in faith in God. For all his awareness of broader social corruption, Jonson seems to have had little confidence that sweeping social changes or whole-sale political revolution could ever fundamentally improve the human con-dition, let alone human nature. His was a fundamentally conservative political vision – a vision that is finally sceptical of utopian dreams and schemes because it is sceptical about the perfectibility of human beings.[48] 'Penshurst' gives us a glimpse of a society operating with about as much charity and goodwill as Jonson could hope to imagine in his day; 'Wroth' reminds us that such charity and goodwill were precious and rare and could never be taken for granted. In neither work does Jonson issue or suggest any grand prescriptions for social reform; he merely implies, as he implies throughout his writings, that a good society is impossible unless individual persons try to hold themselves to transcendent moral, and even spiritual, standards. To many, especially today, this vision may seem naive, retrograde, and perhaps even reactionary. Certainly it is not utopian, but in the past two centuries we have, perhaps, too often had reason to regret the appalling results of attractive utopian visions.

NOTES

1. G. R. Hibbard, 'The Country House Poem of the Seventeenth Century', *Journal of the Warburg and Courtauld Institutes* 19.1–2 (1956): 159–74, 159.
2. *Ibid.*, 163.
3. *Ibid.*, 164.
4. *Ibid.*
5. Paul Cubeta, 'A Jonsonian Ideal: "To Penshurst"', *Philological Quarterly* 42.1 (1963): 14–24, 15.
6. Gayle Edward Wilson, 'Jonson's Use of the Bible and the Great Chain of Being in "To Penshurst"', *Studies in English Literature* 8.1 (1968): 77–89.
7. Alastair Fowler, 'The "Better Marks" of Jonson's *To Penshurst*', *Review of English Studies* n.s. 24 (1973): 266–82, 266.
8. *Ibid.*, 279.
9. Raymond Williams, *The Country and the City* (New York: Oxford University Press), 29.
10. *Ibid.*, 30. For a similar point, see Kari Boyd McBride, *Country House Discourse in Early Modern England: A Cultural Study of Landscape and Legitimacy* (Aldershot: Ashgate, 2001), 114–15.
11. Williams, *The Country and the City*, 30.
12. *Ibid.*, 31.
13. *Ibid.*
14. *Ibid.*, 32.
15. *Ibid.*, 33.

16. Fowler, 'The "Better Marks"', 275n.1.
17. Williams, *The Country and the City*, 33.
18. Fowler, 'The "Better Marks"', 279–80.
19. Alastair Fowler, 'Country House Poems: The Politics of a Genre', *The Seventeenth Century* 1 (1986): 1–14, 7.
20. *Ibid.*, 8.
21. *Ibid.*, 9. One of the most interesting and detailed of all religious approaches to 'To Penshurst' is provided by Richard Harp in 'Jonson's "To Penshurst": The Country House as Church', *John Donne Journal* 7.1 (1985): 73–89.
22. Fowler, 'Country House Poems', 10.
23. Alastair Fowler, *The Country House Poem: A Cabinet of Seventeenth-Century Estate Poems and Related Items* (Edinburgh University Press, 1994), 11 and 58.
24. Rhonda Lemke Sanford, *Maps and Memory in Early Modern England: A Sense of Place* (New York: Palgrave, 2002), 85.
25. References to Jonson's poetry are to the texts in volume VIII of *Ben Jonson*, ed. C. H. Herford and Percy and Evelyn Simpson, 11 vols. (Oxford: Clarendon Press, 1925–52). For ease of reference I will sometimes abbreviate 'To Penshurst' as 'Penshurst' and 'To Sir Robert Wroth' as 'Wroth'.
26. Sanford, *Maps and Memory*, 85.
27. At one point, for example, Sanford comments on the famous lines from 'Penshurst' concerning the construction of walls at the estate: 'And though thy walls be of the country stone, / They'are reared with no mans ruine, no mans grone, / There's none, that dwell about them, wish them downe' (lines 45–7). Sanford contends that this passage 'underscores the absurdity' of any 'assumption of effortless abundance. These walls, we are led to believe, were "rear'd with no mans ruine, no mans grone"; but the very idea that walls made of "country stone" could possibly be built so effortlessly flies in the face of logic and should therefore make us question the purportedly effortless abundance that has preceded the introduction of this detail into the poem' (*Maps and Memory*, 84). Jonson, however, never claims or implies that the building of the walls was 'effortless'; indeed, as a former bricklayer himself, he would have known quite well how much effort was involved. He merely suggests that the building of the walls was not exploitative or ruinous (physically or financially) to the workers involved or to the neighbours of the estate. Presumably he means to imply that the labourers were fairly compensated for their efforts (by the standards of the day), that no property or materials belonging to neighbours were seized, and that although hard work was surely involved, no one suffered anything more than hard work in the building of the walls. To read the passage as Sanford reads it is to make Jonson guilty, I fear, not only of 'absurdity' but of an uncharacteristic naiveté.

    Alastair Fowler (in 'The Beginnings of English Georgic', in *Renaissance Genres: Essays on Theory, History, and Interpretation*, ed. Barbara Kiefer Lewalski (Cambridge, MA: Harvard University Press, 1986): 105–25) asserts that 'The view that landowners imagined their laborers merely as property hardly does justice to the good relations that sometimes obtained between ranks (as they still were – not classes)' (121–2). Elsewhere ('Country House Poems') Fowler makes the interesting suggestion that 'labour may not be prominent in estate poems because it was not prominent always in estates. (Landowners did not generally farm their estates for profit, and sometimes did not farm them at all.)' (7). For a different response to the challenges raised by Williams (a response that emphasizes the 'labour' of women, especially pregnant women), see Hugh Jenkins, *Feigned Commonwealths: The Country-House Poem and the Fashioning of the Ideal Community* (Pittsburgh, PA: Duquesne University Press, 1998), 54–62.

28. Andrew McRae, *God Speed the Plough: The Representation of Agrarian England, 1500–1660* (Cambridge University Press, 1996), 286.

29. William A. McClung, *The Country House in English Renaissance Poetry* (Berkeley: University of California Press, 1977), 180.

30. As Alistair Duckworth notes, 'Often, it seems, Williams expects from his authors a degree of radical consciousness unlikely even in nineteenth-century writers'; see 'Raymond Williams and Literary History', *Papers on Language and Literature* 11 (1975): 420–41; for the quoted passage, see 424. Duckworth's overview of Williams' work seems fair and balanced; it is hardly the kind of 'demolition of Williams' literary criticism' that William A. McClung calls it in his chapter on 'The Country-House Arcadia', in *The Fashioning and Functioning of the British Country House*, ed. Gervase Jackson-Stops, Gordon J. Schochet, Lena Cowen Orlin, and Elisabeth Blair MacDougall (Washington, DC: National Gallery of Art, 1989), 277–87, 277.

31. Fowler (in 'The Silva Tradition in Jonson's *The Forrest*', in *Poetic Traditions of the English Renaissance*, ed. Maynard Mack and George deForest Lord (New Haven: Yale University Press, 1982): 163–80) calls the poem to Wroth 'not so powerful as "To Penshurst" but underrated nevertheless' (167) – an assessment with which I agree.

32. Heather Dubrow does in fact 'hypothesize that "To Penshurst" preceded "To Sir Robert Wroth" and influenced it', although her valuable article – one of the best on the country house genre – in no way implies that 'Wroth' is merely a pale imitation of 'Penshurst'. See her essay 'The Country-House Poem: A Study in Generic Development', *Genre* 12 (1979): 153–79; for the quoted passage, see 164.

33. Anthony Mortimer, 'The Feigned Commonwealth in the Poetry of Ben Jonson', *Studies in English Literature* 13.1 (1973): 69–79; for the quoted passages, see 73–4 and 79.

34. Fowler (in 'The Silva Tradition') touches briefly on the idea of 'Penshurst' and 'Wroth' as 'companion poem[s]' (171), but he is more concerned in that article with the structure of *The Forest* as a whole.

35. Williams, *The Country and the City*, 33.

36. Sanford, *Maps and Memory*, 85.

37. Williams, *The Country and the City*, 27–8, 31, 48, 72.

38. For an argument that even 'Penshurst' is more implicitly critical (and less complimentary) than it seems, see Martin Elsky, 'The Mixed Genre of

Jonson's "To Penshurst" and the Perilous Springs of Netherlandish Landscape',
Ben Jonson Journal 9 (2002): 1–35, esp. 22–6.

39. On this point, see Judith Dundas, 'A Pattern of the Mind: The Country House
Poem Revisited', *Connotations* 8.1 (1998–9): 22–47, esp. 22 and 30.

40. Evidence of the relative neglect of 'Wroth' abounds and is reflected, for
instance, in two recent comprehensive books on the country house genre.
Thus McBride's study (*Country House Discourse*) mentions or discusses
'Penshurst' on forty-three pages but mentions or discusses 'Wroth' on four.
Likewise, Jenkins' book (*Feigned Commonwealths*) mentions or discusses
'Penshurst' on fifty-seven pages but mentions or discusses 'Wroth' on twelve.
To note these facts is not to disparage either book, since the disparities they
reflect are typical. For further evidence of the relative neglect of Wroth, see
John Burdett and Jonathan Wright, 'Ben Jonson in Recent General
Scholarship, 1972–1996', *Ben Jonson Journal* 4 (1997): 151–79, esp. 176. An
exception is the very valuable article by Martin Elsky ('Microhistory and
Cultural Geography: Ben Jonson's "To Sir Robert Wroth" and the
Absorption of Local Community in the Commonwealth', *Renaissance
Quarterly* 53.2 (2000): 500–28), although my approach here differs from his.

41. For these facts and their sources, see the note on lines 61–6 of 'Penshurst'
provided in Fowler's collection *The Country House Poem* (61).

42. Fowler (in 'The Silva Tradition') calls the ensuing lines 'one of the warmest
portrayals of rural life in our literature' (167).

43. Indeed, surviving manuscripts of 'Wroth' refer even more insistently to labour
than does the text printed in the first folio; the manuscripts mention 'eares [of
corn] cut downe in their most height' and 'ploued land up cast'. See *Ben Jonson*,
ed. C. H. Herford and Percy and Evelyn Simpson, 11 vols. (Oxford: Clarendon
Press, 1925–52), VIII, 98, notes to lines 41 and 43.

44. On this point, see also Mortimer, 'The Feigned Commonwealth', 77.

45. Williams, *The Country and the City*, 33.

46. On this matter, see the note on Wroth in Fowler's collection *The Country
House Poem* (66). See also McClung, *The Country House*, 138.

47. See also Mortimer, 'The Feigned Commonwealth', 77.

48. On this point, see the discussion of Jonson in Isabel Rivers, *The Poetry of
Conservatism, 1600–1745: A Study of Poets and Public Affairs from Jonson to
Pope* (Cambridge: Rivers Press, 1973).

CHAPTER 4

Style, versatility, and the politics of the epistles

John Roe

It has become usual to see Ben Jonson as a poet caught in a contradiction. On the one hand he is eager to pursue his own ideals and create a world of classical serenity beyond the grubby and corrupting reach of contemporary forces; on the other hand, he appears to be a shrewd exploiter of patronage, a market man who knows how to pander to the whims and prejudices of those in a position to help him materially. A modified version of the latter perspective insists that Jonson operated in a world of treachery and jeopardy, and that as a man of letters necessarily subjugated to the authority of others, he needed to watch his step. If he seems at points sycophantic, then he can hardly be blamed for practising manoeuvres designed to ensure his safety. In this chapter on the epistolary verses I shall pursue some of these alternative views of Jonson and try to decide whether or how they may be reconciled.

In his epistle to a fellow author, the jurist John Selden, Jonson makes a virtue of apology:

> I have too oft preferred
> Men past their terms, and praised some names too much;
> But 'twas with purpose to have made them such.[1]

No reader would deny the plausibility of this appeal. There is a moral art to flattery, and that is to procure a general social benefit by stimulating the need to appear good in a person of power or authority. This reveals a peculiarly Machiavellian taste for tactics, which Jonson, a careful student of Machiavelli, is pleased to indulge. He has the dexterity of a conjuror coaxing acceptance of a carefully selected card. His subject's vanity is an important aspect of the question, and if this can be turned to positive account, all well and good. In Jonson's political poems (in particular the epistles he wrote to various well-placed friends and acquaintances), we see that the conflict between virtue and vice, prevalent in everything he wrote, takes the opportunistic form of attempting to promote virtue *in the world* via the agency of somebody in a position to influence events and their outcome. At the same time, Jonson's application of Machiavelli has its limits, as his very concern with virtue would suggest. Books should act primarily as counsellors, a point that Jonson makes in his shrewd, Senecan-styled analysis of Machiavelli's advice in *The Prince*:

> A *Prince* without Letters, is a Pilot without eyes. All his Government is groping. In *Soveraignity* it is a most happy thing, not to be compelled; but so it is the most miserable not to be counsell'd. And how can he be counsell'd that cannot see to read the best Counsellors (which are books.) for they neither flatter us, nor hide from us?[2]

Jonson is qualifying Machiavelli's argument about the dangers of flattery – that virtually no advice is offered a prince without a grain of sycophancy, which makes it unreliable.[3] It is shrewd of Jonson to confront Machiavelli, as it shows that he is unafraid of debating effective ways of ruling with the sceptical Italian statesman, who is hardly known for his sentimentality. Jonson manages to reinstate the life of the mind (the great humanist priority) to a discussion from which Machiavelli (at least in *The Prince*) had expelled most thinking that was not immediately and directly related to action, and often violent action at that. The humanist John Selden would certainly have approved. When we think of Jonson as a poet of straightforwardly material circumstance, seeking to advance his social position through his adroit manipulation of his writer's craft, we must also remember the Jonson of the larger, more contemplative view. As a consequence, Jonson would have said, in response to Auden's despairing cry that 'poetry makes nothing happen', that poetry is capable of influencing events considerably.[4]

   Jonson's response to Machiavelli does, however, acknowledge that some of what the latter says about life and circumstances is all too true: that they are precarious, and that everybody's situation, the poet's, the patron's whose attention he solicits, even that of the prince himself, is subject to chance and fortune. That is, Jonson flatters in order to bring out the best in his subjects, while occasionally acknowledging the difficulties under which they may labour, the result being a sympathetic – not sycophantic – piece of verse cajolery, such as the stylistically accomplished sonnet (a model of its kind)[5] to his friend William Roe, who is to depart (classically enough) on a voyage:

> Roe (and my joy to name) thou'rt now, to go
>   Countries and climes, manners, and men to know,

> To extract, and choose the best of all these known,
>   And those to turn to blood and make thine own.
> May winds as soft as breath of kissing friends,
>   Attend thee hence; and there may all thy ends,
> As the beginnings here, prove purely sweet,
>   And perfect in a circle always meet.
>
> (lines 1–8)

As Jonson might say to Selden, here is a good example of flattering verses, illustrated specifically in the image of the winds as kissing friends, which at the same time apply discreet pressure on their recipient to behave appropriately, and not let himself or his friends down. The trick is all in the anticipation: using the idea of the circle, Jonson is able to detail and record all of Roe's achievements, his successes in outwitting the vagaries of fortune, as if already completed, when in fact everything is at its uncertain beginning.[6] Roe has no option but to play it the way Jonson tells it. The flattery lies in the classical, heroic model of voyaging, which Jonson subtly explicates. There is something of the chanciness of Ulysses in the anticipation of the voyage as set forth in the octave, which then concentrates into the energy and purpose of Aeneas, so named, in the sestet:

> So when we, blest with thy return, shall see
>   Thyself, with thy first thoughts, brought home by thee,
> We each to other may this voice inspire:
>   This is that good Aeneas, passed through fire,
> Through seas, storms, tempests; and embarked for hell,
>   Came back untouched. This man hath travailed well.
>
> (lines 9–14)

Richard S. Peterson, along with other commentators, refers the reader to the specific, contemporary meaning of 'hell', which does indeed seem placed to effect at the turn of the penultimate line.[7] Roe had a reputation for profligacy, and was involved in a lawsuit against a certain Walter Garland whom he accused of swindling him out of property. 'Hell' was an old term for debtor's prison.[8] This is doubtless relevant, but there is more to say. Both Peterson and David Riggs remark how the poem elides with Jonson's longer, scurrilous poem – a kind of antitype – 'The Famous Voyage', which for Riggs alludes to the poet's own reputation for 'wenching'.[9] What the sestet in the sonnet in praise of William Roe carefully omits, while hardly failing to raise the question in the mind of the reader, is the knowledge that one of the key moments of recollection, served by Aeneas' descent into Hades, concerns the poignant encounter with the

reproachful Dido, whom in order to complete his voyage 'untouch'd' the
Trojan hero had felt compelled to abandon, as he tries to explain:

> infelix Dido, verus mihi nuntius ergo
> venerat exstinctam, ferroque extrema secutam?
> funeris heu! tibi causa fui? per sidera iuro,
> per superos, et si qua fides tellure sub ima est,
> invitus, regina, tuo de litore cessi.

> (Unhappy Dido! Was the tale true then that came to me, that
> you were dead and had sought your doom with the sword?
> Was I, alas! the cause of your death? By the stars I swear, by
> the world above, and whatever is sacred in the grave below,
> unwillingly, queen, I parted from your shores.)[10]

How much of this is Jonson silently alluding to in the Roe sonnet? As far
as his subject's conduct goes, there seems to be nothing to connect him to an
unsavoury incident such as the desertion of an ill-treated 'wench'. However,
particulars in this instance may cede to the general. Jonson may be compli-
menting William Roe on having been 'untouch'd' by the disorderly passion,
to which Aeneas was temporarily prey in his love affair with the Carthagi-
nian queen, and which led ultimately, as he recognizes in the encounter, to
her bloody suicide. In that respect, Jonson's friend would be a better Aeneas
than the 'good Aeneas' himself, who admits to his guilt even while trying to
excuse his transgression ('the gods compelled me', *Aeneid*, line 461).

   We are reminded that passion sits ill with Jonson's approach to lyric
poetry. There are few effusive, tormented outpourings among the *Epigrams*,
The Forest, and *The Underwood*, and certainly no sonnet sequences. Though
the sonnet as a genre was beginning to be outmoded by James' reign, there
would have been nothing to deter Jonson from trying his hand as late as
1600, say (when he would have been a maturing 28-year-old), had he
been so inclined. Yet Jonson proves circumspect regarding amorous
passion. In *Volpone*, for example, what effectively exposes the protagonist
is the passion he feels for Celia, a passion that produces sensations which
are voluptuous, colourful, and Ovidian, but which lead quickly to derange-
ment and loss of control, as he indulges fantasies of erotic fulfilment:

> Whilst we, in changèd shapes, act Ovid's tales,
> Thou like Europa now, and I like Jove,
> Then I like Mars, and thou like Erycine;
> So of the rest, till we have quite run through,
> And wearied all the fables of the gods.
> Then will I have thee in more modern forms,

Attirèd like some sprightly dame of France,
Brave Tuscan lady, or proud Spanish beauty;
Sometimes unto the Persian Sophy's wife,
Or the Grand Signior's mistress; and for change,
To one of our most artful courtesans,
Or some quick Negro, or cold Russian.

(*Volpone*, 3.7.221–32)

The similarity of this description to what was performed more decorously in the court masque may be Jonson's way of indicating how any stage representation of the erotic, no matter how subdued in content, may lead to or signal loss of control on the part of the player – a warning perhaps to his employers against the dangers of assuming mythological identities. More generally, Jonson frequently registers the erotic as dangerous to the individual's power of discrimination, and experiences an evident, sardonic satisfaction in showing characters losing their minds under the assault of instinct masquerading as argument, as all too palpably occurs to Volpone in this scene with Celia. Jonson, in short, is happier with the Horatian mode, with its insistence on friendship; it is fitting therefore that the passionate Dido, and all that she entails, should be excised from a poem which, though it invokes Aeneas in one of his supremely agonizing moments, deliberately misrepresents him as a man taking good care not to dally in an affair of the heart.

Along with more obvious things, such as Jonson's adept appropriation and deployment of classical voices, the sonnet to William Roe brings out his preference for form over utterance, to invoke a classical distinction. Form is what holds the unruliness of emotions at bay, and nowhere is this more cunningly demonstrated than in that love poem which renounces and repudiates love, 'My Picture Left in Scotland'. This is a poem that at first glance might seem to argue that the repudiating, such as it is, belongs to the lady:

I now think Love is rather deaf than blind,
For else it could not be
That she
Whom I adore so much should so slight me,
And cast my love behind.

(lines 1–5)

Yet, as with the non-appearance of Dido in the triumphantly, fluidly sententious sestet ending the sonnet to William Roe, the absence of

the mistress enables the poet to foreground the art of persuasion as its
own end:

> I'm sure my language to her was as sweet,
>   And every close did meet
>   In sentence of as subtle feet
>   As hath the youngest he,
>   That sits in shadow of Apollo's tree.
>
> (lines 6–10)

Jonson emphasizes what poetry accomplishes in terms of style, even though,
in this instance, it has accomplished nothing with *her*. He has his own
rueful, yet strangely confident answer to this; beauty is heedless and undiscriminating, and contents herself with finding her mirror image in a lover's
youthful, handsome bearing. The art not the intention of saying, however, is
what matters. The poet turns his physical defects to account, demonstrating
that mastery of line is all, and thus gives an Aristotelian answer to the Platonic objection to the inferiority of art. The very process and performance
of writing discovers a universal law: art transcends the deficiencies of
material circumstances, and in a more principled way than the mistress
could ever envisage – the case is put with due irony – leaves them behind:

> Oh, but my conscious fears
>   That fly my thoughts between,
>   Tell me that she hath seene
>   My hundred of grey hairs,
>   Told seven-and-forty years,
>   Read so much waste, as she cannot embrace
>   My mountain belly, and my rocky face;
> And all these through her eyes have stopped her ears.
>
> (lines 11–18)

For those who *can* hear, and for that matter *see*, in the sense of discriminate,
then in the very fluency of manner in which he rehearses the objections to
himself as lover, the poet cancels them out.

When we consider the political aspect of Jonson's poems, particularly the
epistles, then we need to take into account his extraordinary capacity for
transforming the subject and enabling it to enlist different values all at
once. Both the poem to William Roe, and in a more specific way 'My
Picture Left in Scotland', use the occasion to sound an idea that belongs
generally to the dominant theme but which expresses itself unobtrusively.
The particular, combined idea we have been looking at is a humanist

preference for friendship (among equals, subsequently among men) and harmony, the enemies of which are passion (associated with, or occasioned by, women) and discord. In turn, such considerations form part of a larger theme that runs through much of Jonson's work in the first two decades of the seventeenth century, and this is his concern for peace, shaped very much according to James' particular ideology, and evident in a number of the court masques on which Jonson collaborated.

Take, for example, Jonson's famous address, 'To Sir Robert Wroth', which, as it belongs to the country house genre, in part cultivates a form of reflective satire. Jonson observes the usual division of court (bad) and country (good) but solves the problem of where to place the monarch in such a scheme by having James remake his court in the pastoral retreat that Wroth thoughtfully and sympathetically supplies:

> Or, if thou list the night in watch to break,
>   A-bed canst hear the loud stag speak,
> In spring oft roused for thy master's sport,
>   Who for it makes thy house his court.
>
> (lines 21–4)[11]

Jonson applies the stratagem that he had described to Selden (see above) of gently urging his subject to undertake an appropriate conduct by depicting him as already doing it. His method here (as also in the opening to the companion poem, 'To Penshurst') is to disguise negative imperatives as if they were invocations of accomplishments admirably and discriminatingly achieved: 'art no ambitious guest . . . / Nor com'st to view the better cloth of state . . . / Nor throng'st, when masking is, to have a sight', etc. (5–9). Whatever ambition may drive a frustrated or dissatisfied Wroth to compete in the world of luxury and grandeur, Jonson seeks to curtail by reminding him of the 'riches' he already possesses, the trick being to combine a vision of paradise possessed (the golden age no less) with a lesson in being content with one's lot, however modest. Both Wroth and the Sidneys at Penshurst appear to have been in need of such instruction.[12]

The subtlety with which Jonson manages internal references, a characteristic of all his poetry, makes it difficult for the reader to say conclusively where or at whom he may be pointing an incidental finger. As in the poem to William Roe, the thorough absorption of the classical model makes the experience of reading already so complete that it is not easy to decide whether a further particular signpost exists or not. Nonetheless, it is possible to pick up trails here and there. Invariably the golden age model brings up the subject of peace, which Jonson duly shapes to James'

ideology, and which finds recurrent expression in the masques. As David
Riggs shows, Jonson found himself in something of a bind when James'
young war-like son commissioned him to write *The Speeches at Prince
Henries Barriers* for performance on Twelfth Night, 1610.[13] It was clear
that Henry was determined to turn his father's policy of appeasement on
its head, and had he lived he would very likely have taken England into
fresh military skirmishes with Spain. In fact, Graham Parry argues, James
did himself for once take the military initiative, helping out at the Siege
of Juliers, during the dispute over the succession of the Duchy of Cleves.
Such a manoeuvre would certainly complicate Jonson's footwork as he
tried to maintain a balance between the various interests of father and
son.[14] Jonson's diplomatic nervousness at being compelled to distance
himself from James' generally held peace strategy, and his personal uneasiness at promoting a warmongering movement with which he was tempera-
mentally and idealistically out of sympathy, reveals itself in the close of the
Barriers, where in a rather desperately temporizing move, Jonson has the
prophet Merlin point out that even the most heroic kings of English
history promoted the peaceful arts of 'trade and tillage'.[15]

Turning back to Jonson's address to Sir Robert Wroth, we find an
answering chord in these lines:

> Let others watch in guilty arms, and stand
>   The fury of a rash command,
> Goe enter breaches, meet the cannon's rage,
>   That they may sleep with scars in age,
> And show their feathers shot, and colours torn,
>   And brag that they were therefore born.
>
> (lines 67–72)

True to the classicizing principle active throughout a poem constructed
along pastoral lines, echoes of anti-war statements as provided by ancient
poets abound.[16] Yet the passage inserts itself rather oddly within the
eulogy, and seems called upon to serve a larger argument, concerning the
unscrupulousness of the legal profession, which encloses the anti-war
protest. Just before the lines quoted, the poet says:

> The jolly wassail walks the often round,
>   And in their cups their cares are drowned;
> They think not then which side the cause shall leese,
>   Nor how to get the lawyer fees.
>
> (lines 59–62)

Similarly, Jonson picks up the legal motif as soon as he ends his anti-militarism statement, as follows:

> Let this man sweat and wrangle at the bar,
>   For every price, in every jar,
> And change possessions, oftner with his breath,
>   Then either money, war or death:
> Let him than hardest sires more disinherit,
>   And each-where boast it as his merit
> To blow up orphans, widows, and their states;
>   And think his power doth equal fate's.
>
> (lines 73–80)

Echoes of the anti-war imagery can be heard in the passage, particularly effective being the verb 'blow up', which idiomatically means 'ruin' but which carries the force of a battlefield explosion. Yet the lines protesting war are secondary within the overall argument, and have less obvious point in a poem such as this than the anti-lawyer satire, itself an ancient convention, and one that is apt for an attack on civic corruption, while carrying for the owner of an estate, always fearful of mounting debt, a sympathetic understanding of the kind of enemy he is most likely to fear. Where else should we look, then, for an explanation of the anti-war passage's intrusion?

Notwithstanding the clear classical overtones, Jonson's diction in the lines denouncing war more immediately echoes words that Shakespeare gives to Henry V in his famous exhortation to the troops before the Battle of Agincourt:

> He that shall live this day, and see old age,
> Will yearly on the vigil feast his neighbours,
> And say, Tomorrow is Saint Crispian:
> Then will he strip his sleeve and show his scars,
> And say, These wounds I had on Crispin's day.
> Old men forget; yet all shall be forgot,
> But he'll remember with advantages
> What feats he did that day.
>
> (*Henry V*, 4.3.44–51)

In terms of influence, this example differs from the classics in that, whereas Jonson merely rehearses Virgil's protest in an English voice, in repeating Shakespeare he opposes him; recollection of the earlier play strikes a discordant, sceptical note. Consider how his caustic 'sleep with scars in age / And show their feathers shot' parodies the buoyant, 'Then will he strip his sleeve and show his scars'. In response to Shakespeare's heroic validation of military combat (and combat on a foreign soil at that), the acerbic Jonson puts the pacifist case. But if he is sounding a caution against what he sees as a dangerously confident endorsement of militant nationalism, why is he doing it here in this poem?

The answer may lie in the compulsion he felt to promote a more militant line in the conclusion to *The Speeches at Prince Henries Barriers*, discussed above. Perhaps rankling at that obligation, which had exposed Jonson in the all too uncomfortable role of court lackey, called upon to vary his penmanship as the political wind shifted, the poet now finds a quiet opportunity to settle one or two scores. It is all the more ironic that he should find his moment in a poem dedicated to the Sidney family, given that Sir Robert's wife, Lady Mary Wroth, was niece to the most celebrated member of them all, Philip Sidney, who met his death in precisely the way Prince Henry was bound to approve, fighting the Spanish on the foreign field of Zutphen. That, however, was a generation or more ago in 1586, during the build-up to the Armada attempt at invasion, which Shakespeare is recalling as his Second Tetralogy approaches its climax, especially in Henry V's speeches, such as the St Crispin one, emphasizing the achievements of 'we happy few'. Now the Sidneys are to be celebrated for their purposeful withdrawal from the political front line, and from the factionalism that was exercising court politics. Martin Butler sees Jonson endorsing the 'ideal economy', as practised at Penshurst:

> The Sidneys are presented as stewards of their domain, landlords whose ownership is justified by the life of exemplary discipline which they lead. They are neither self-aggrandizing courtiers nor an oppositional 'country' party, but channels of influence between centre and periphery.[17]

This pursuit of a responsible middle way, avoiding extremes, while offering both the construction of the house and the conduct of its management as a normative model, naturally reflects Jonson's own ambition regarding how he would like to be seen as a poet. In this respect he writes himself into the country house ideal that he claims to see realized both in Penshurst and in the Wroth estate at Durants. As for Shakespeare, Jonson's uneasiness at the former's superior reputation can never be wholly detached from any of the various celebrated comments he is recorded as having made on him. To insert a brief parody of Shakespeare's invocation of post-Armada triumphalism, as a deferred response to Prince Henry's aim at its revival, would be for Jonson too enticing an opportunity to miss, in a poem that overall perhaps strains to justify such a manoeuvre.

Not the least compelling feature of the fascinating 'An Epistle to Sir Edward Sackville, now Earl of Dorset' (*Underwood 13*) is its resumption of the satirical tone. It stands immediately before the epistle to Selden in *The Underwood*, while that poem is succeeded by the even more virulent 'Epistle . . . to the . . . Wars', as if the calmer, temperate Selden poem, with its accent on craft and moderation, is being asked to provide a solid bridge between two outbreaks of angry expostulation, the first vehement, the second barely controlled. It is not easy to date the Sackville epistle precisely but it was probably composed, as the title indicates, shortly after Sir Edward succeeded to the earldom in 1624.[18] In writing such an epistle, then, Jonson is choosing a sympathetic, masculine ear in which to pour his anger, very much as John Donne had done two to three decades previously in his satires and elegies. Ben proves to be emphatically sealed of the Tribe of Jack. The complexities of the epistle, in which one genre bends to accommodate another, involve the characteristic self-disgust of the suitor who is compelled to abase himself, no matter how obliging his patron proves; notwithstanding, Jonson succeeds in turning his frustration inside out and finding external objects on which to displace his self-contempt.

Gift-giving remains forever a ticklish subject, with the 'donee' (Jonson's word, 'Sackville', line 163) feeling the further obligation of thanks, even though he is rewarded for services already rendered, and the freedom that accompanies mutual respect remains compromised by inescapable material interest.[19] This is enough to account for the peculiarly uneasy, impatient, even impetuous tone, which sees Jonson hurrying away from his own obligations to his donor and towards an assault on the various objects of his contempt. Seneca, as was long ago discovered, frames the process with his usual acumen;[20] for example, Jonson's observation,

> For benefits are owed with the same mind
> As they are done, and such returns they find

(lines 5–6),

is a pointed, epigrammatic adaptation of Seneca's,

> Reddit enim beneficium qui libenter debet . . . Eodem
> animo beneficium debetur, quo datur
> (For he who freely acknowledges a favour is doing a
> favour . . . A favour is owed in the same spirit in which it is given).[21]

Invoking Seneca enables Jonson to establish the desired relationship between himself and his patron, that is, a relationship of equals. The presence of the classical author who mixes irony with psychological perceptiveness brings patron and poet closer together, and it ought to be enough to establish their relationship on the proper footing. It is not quite so straightforward as that, however, as the world that exploits gift-giving, and wilfully disregards the relationship of mutual respect that Jonson is eager to promote, obtrudes all too harshly. Indeed, violently, as in the lines depicting the swordsman ready to hire himself out ('Now dam'mee, Sir, if you shall not command / My sword', lines 53–4), which progressively, and dexterously, metamorphose into 'blade' meaning knighthood. To those that have, it shall be given. 'Names' attract 'bounties' (lines 62–3), as benefactors fall over each other to bestow their favour on those who have most recently been 'made' (i.e. knighted, line 63), and who therefore stand to be exploited in their turn.

This is not, therefore, just to pit sword against pen, for it wryly under-scores the point that the world of letters and patronage is itself a cut-throat one. The example fits the steadily rising anger the speaker registers at the viciousness of the world in which he is compelled to operate. Those who dazzle with their eminence command more than those who genuinely, and so more modestly, express a need. Is there no way out? Stanley Fish makes the challenging claim that Jonson, in poems such as the 'Epistle to Sackville', foregoes the practice of satire as such, and seeks a retreat from the public theatre of the court into a private world of shared values, the emphasis being more on protection than exposure: 'by and large the body of the poetry lacks something essential to satire, the intention to indict or reform. *The verse is not projected outward into a world it would shape, but inward into a world it would protect*' (my italics).[22]

The example just given from the poem would in my view belie this con-tention. Fish's argument applies itself more convincingly to the famous invi-tation to a friend to supper (*Epigrams 101*), where in the safety of the poet's 'poor house', away from prying eyes or listening ears ('And we will have no Poley or Parrot by'), the two friends can recreate the Horatian ideal of friendship and hospitality. Jonson's offer of 'cates' whose tastiness depends on the willingness of the friend to suspend the more delicate or dis-criminating operations of his palate mirrors the argument concerning the reciprocity of gift-giving in the Sackville epistle: 'It is the fair acceptance, sir, creates / The entertainment perfect, not the cates' (lines 7–8). Similarly, 'Gifts and thanks should have one cheerful face, / So each that's done and ta'en becomes a brace' ('Sackville', lines 39–40); that is, the distinction between giver and receiver dissolves in mutually generous recognition. However, there is a striking difference between the two poems, not only in terms of the material of which they treat (i.e. there are more objects of satire in 'Sackville' than Fish allows) but also in their verse manner. 'Inviting a friend' deploys its repeated enjambment and caesura carefully to maintain a rhythmic equilibrium suited to the poem's easy, conversational intimacy. The constant refusal of the couplets to 'close' the subject indicates not an anxiety but a relaxed dwelling in uncertainty: some dishes 'may' arrive, others are guaranteed; a diverting lack of clarity as to detail only serves a larger sense that the experience, with its last-line emphasis on 'liberty', will be worthwhile. Although the 'Epistle to Sackville' begins quietly enough, with this shared sense of understanding, its rhythm soon becomes agitated, inducing a sense of thematic disquiet. The starting point for this is a further piece of Senecan axiomatic thinking:

> They are the noblest benefits and sink
> Deepest in man, of which, when he doth think,
> The memory delights him more from whom
> Then what he hath received.
>
> (lines 19–22)[23]

So far all well and good, the rhythm enacting that steady ruminative measure so familiar from 'Inviting a friend', the theme announcing itself as the pleasure to be found in contemplating the generosity of spirit of the giver rather than the thing given. Everything suddenly changes mid-line:

> Gifts stink from some,
> They are so long a-coming, and so hard;
> Where any deed is forced, the grace is marred.
>
> (lines 22–4)

The effect is achieved by the irruption of 'stink', a strong word in itself but also internally both perpetuating and undermining the comfortable rhyme, 'sink . . . / . . . think' just above. The subversion of this rhyme, occurring the more unexpectedly as an internal echo, precipitates the angry ripostes to those who, in the poet's imagination, calculate and distort the character and value of gift-giving. As the poem gathers momentum, we see that courtliness, so carefully defined by Castiglione, has descended to the level of the street (the place of promiscuity and indiscriminateness) and bravery has been substituted by brutishness:

> I only am allowed
> My wonder why the taking a clown's purse,
> Or robbing the poor market-folks should nurse
> Such a religious horror in the breasts
> Of our town gallantry! Or why there rests
> Such worship due to kicking of a punk.
>
> (lines 88–93)

Street scenes are characteristic of Donne's satires (as in Donne's likely source, Horace, *Satires* I.9):

> Now we are in the street; he first of all
> Improvidently proud, creeps to the wall,
> And so imprison'd, and hem'd in by me
>   Sells for a little state his liberty;
> Yet though he cannot skip forth now to greet
>   Every fine silken painted fool we meet,
> He them to him with amorous smiles allures,
> And grins, smacks, shrugs, and such an itch endures,
>   As prentices, or schoolboys which do know
>   Of some gay sport abroad, yet dare not go.
>
>   (*Satire* I, 67–76)

Each poem is characterized by anger at the prevalence of false or superficial values, whether reflected in the behaviour of Jonson's town bully or of Donne's town fop. Animating the disgust is an uneasy and claustrophobic feeling, typical of such satire, that the speaker cannot extricate himself from the conduct he deplores. This is especially true of Donne's relation to his creeping, horribly *companionable* 'changling motley humorist' *Satire* I, 1.1), and gives rise to the fear that the poet may indeed share some of the cringing motivation that inspires his despised 'friend'. Arthur Marotti, examining the social conditions of writing, has expressed the view that the satiric impulse, when you get right down to it, is uncomfortably compounded of envy as much as it is of disinterested, savage indignation: 'satire was less a way of expressing one's devotion to moral ideals or one's condemnation of worldly vice than it was the literary form practiced by those whose ambitions were frustrated and who yearned to involve themselves more deeply in the social environments they pretended to scorn'.[24]

This is as much as to say that there is no escape for poets such as Donne and Jonson, and that Fish's claim, that Jonson withdraws into a world which he must do his utmost to protect, yields to the harsh truth that that world is undermined from within. The greatest threat to Jonson's equanimity comes not so much from envy (though that can be discerned with a little searching) as from humiliation. The reception of a gift that can never be matched in the same currency (no matter how valid the plea that poetry is superior to money) leaves the poet discomforted, and even friendship that does its best to guarantee equality is never quite enough to overcome the sensation of inferiority, as the close of the Sackville epistle seems ruefully to admit.

We might follow such examples to the supreme level. King Lear turns himself voluntarily and ironically, by his ill-considered act of patronage, from donor to donee, and then rues the consequences as his ungrateful daughters humiliatingly reduce the size of his retinue:

> GONERIL Hear me, my lord:
> What need you five and twenty? Ten? or five?
> To follow in a house where twice so many
> Have a command to tend you?
> REGAN What need one?
> LEAR O reason not the need! Our basest beggars
> Are in the poorest things superfluous.
>
> (*King Lear* 2.4.253–8)

All is relative according to the scale of nature, a truth which has its dark corollary, as the behaviour of Lear's daughters indicates: moral value can be emptied out entirely without effective protest. Lear rages impotently:

> No, you unnatural hags,
> I will have such revenges on you both
> That all the world shall — I will do such things —
> What they are, yet I know not, but they shall be
> The terrors of the earth!
>
> (271–5)

What finally saves Lear is the conversion of humiliation into humility, which becomes evident as the play wears on, nowhere more so than in the reconciliation with Cordelia in the fourth act. Meanwhile he delivers some time-honoured, disinterested truths, which are the very meat of satire:

> Plate sin with gold,
> And the strong lance of justice hurtless breaks;
> Arm it in rags, a pygmy's straw does pierce it.
>
> (4.5.157–9)

Like Lear, Jonson knows how to rage pointedly. If we accept Fish's view, which sees him as protecting rather than assailing a particular situation, then we have to concede the futility of the exercise, as everything is prone to crumble. If with Marotti we insist on the materiality of the circumstances underlying the satire, then we have to recognize in turn that humiliation, as Lear's example makes clear, is a greater goad than envy, even though the latter has its place.

King Lear's unhappy relations with his daughters may serve to introduce
the theme of Jonson and his patronesses, fortunately for Jonson characterized by a much greater mutual understanding and appreciation. Despite
what we have observed about Jonson's uneasiness on the subject of love,
he is happy enough to engage some women in his discourses on morality,
especially if these women are well born, well educated, and can claim nobility of mind as well as of person. Jonson's characteristic practice of raising a
separate topic, or introducing a secondary figure, whilst writing a poem to a
particular person, shows itself clearly in 'To Elizabeth, Countess of Rutland'
(Sir Philip Sidney's daughter), where he alludes both to another poet and to
another patron(ess) in the course of his address. This poem, dated 1600,
comes relatively early in Jonson's career, and shows him jockeying for
position among his rivals.[25] A governing image in the epistle is that of
gold (noted already in terms of ancient pastoral), which Jonson famously
draws upon repeatedly throughout his writings, and which serves as a
means of uniting the material world, where political transactions take
place, with the ideal world. The most ironic example of this is Volpone's
invocation of gold at the beginning of that play:

> Good morning to the day; and next, my gold!
> Open the shrine, that I may see my saint.
>
> (*Volpone*, 1.1.1–2)

Jonson opens his address to the countess of course more quietly, as if in a
spirit of rational repudiation of Volpone's excessive zeal, and in a lengthy
first paragraph details the ways in which the commodity infiltrates and
corrupts:

> Whilst that for which all vertue now is sold
> And almost every vice, almighty gold;[26]
> That which, to boot with hell, is thought worth heaven,
> And, for it life, conscience, yea, souls are given;
> Toils, by grave custome, up and downe the court.
>
> (lines 1–5)

The paragraph ends somewhat surprisingly, Jonson's main clause, when it
finally arrives, bringing an apologetic admission to the countess that he
has none of this paradoxically unwanted substance to give her:

> whilst gold bears all this sway,
> I, that have none to send you, send you verse.
>
> (lines 19–20)

It is hard to imagine a more ingenious, more elegant way of crafting a request than this, in which first the speaker demonstrates the worthlessness of the thing sought, and then pretends that the obligation to bestow it lies with him and not with the patron whose favour he seeks. Jonson might well have added, in that epistle to Selden with which this chapter began, that the obligation to be virtuous carries with it a further obligation to act charitably. Nowhere does the spiritual find expression so satisfactorily as in the act of giving to the needy.

Not that Jonson presents himself with cap in hand; on the contrary we have just seen him turning the tables, in his unilateral dialogue with the countess, by appropriating the role of benefactor. She, the poem will argue, has the more to gain. As in all of Jonson's contentions, what he claims is not just clever but also true. The metaphoric value of gold means that the commodity can be made to work two ways at once, the spiritual and the material being interchangeable. This, John Barrell argues, is what Shakespeare is up to in Sonnet 29, 'When in disgrace with fortune and men's eyes', where the poet seeks more than a spiritual recompense from his powerful young friend. The sonnet's closing couplet performs one of those perlocutionary actions whereby what is said urges a response in kind:

> For thy sweet love remember'd such wealth brings,
> That then I scorn to change my state with kings.
>
> (Son. 29, lines 13–14)

While put diplomatically, and with all due grace, this is not – contends Barrell – just a statement about restoring one's morale with comforting thoughts, but more pertinently (and cleverly not impertinently) a request for a hand-out.[27] If this is so, then Jonson's ploy is even more intricate and far-reaching than Shakespeare's, for gold has more conceptual resonance in Jonson's treatment of it than 'wealth', say, has in Sonnet 29. The idea of the Golden Age subdivides, as we have seen, into categories such as peace, repose, perfection, and the pastoral life. Gold is reward, and that too can take different forms, such as the one Jonson offers the countess, which is lasting reputation, equally solid and irreducible. In the poem's long middle stretch, Jonson demonstrates the perishable nature of all rival substances, such as marble or brass, employed unsuccessfully to perpetuate the memory of vanished heroes and their deeds. Only the words of the poet can guarantee a lasting name:

> But, madam, think what store
> The world hath seen, which all these had in trust
> And now lie lost in their forgotten dust.

It is the muse alone can raise to heaven,
And, at her strong arm's end, hold up and even
The souls she loves. Those other glorious notes,
Inscribed in touch or marble, or the coats
Painted, or carved upon our great men's tombs,
Or in their windows, do but prove the wombs
That bred them, graves; when they were born, they died
That had no muse to make their fame abide.

(lines 38–48)

Whereas the most durable of substances must perish, poetry, whose light and airy medium is language, proves permanent and enduring. Gold itself has undergone a metamorphosis: true gold is in the imagination. This is the promise Jonson holds out to the countess, assuring her that the achievements of even an Achilles would be forgotten were it not for the poet (51–7). The idea of course is Horatian, but finds comparable, and contemporary, expression in another Shakespearean sonnet, 'Not marble nor the gilded monuments' (no. 55). We can be fairly sure that Jonson would have been one of those private friends to whom Francis Meres refers in speaking of the circulation of Shakespeare's sonnets prior to their publication in 1609. What better way, then, of demonstrating the continuing life of the classics than alluding discreetly to Shakespeare's revival of them? Yet the moment brings its own awkwardness, especially when it comes to reading the intentions behind Jonson's glorious apology. For Jonson seems to be borrowing Shakespeare's idea of the rival poet, and applying it in a way that is both more professional and more self-interested than it appears in the sonnets to the Young Man (Sonnet 29 notwithstanding). Even as he concedes the activity of rival versifiers in the field, Jonson pointedly reminds the countess that she has a rival muse (most likely the Countess of Bedford). Consider then:

You, and that other star, that purest light,
Of all Lucina's train, Lucy the bright;
Than which a nobler, heaven itself knows not.
Who, though she have a better verser got,
(Or 'poet', in the court account) than I,
And who doth me, though I not him, envy
Yet, for the timely favours she hath done
To my less sanguine muse, wherein she hath won
My grateful soul, the subject of her powers,
I have already used some happy hours,
To her remembrance.

(lines 65–75)

The Countess of Rutland may be flattered to find herself keeping company with the Countess of Bedford, or she may not. How tactful is it of Jonson to train his eye so patently on opportunities elsewhere, while paying court to his supposedly preferred patron? The happy coincidence that she and Bedford are sister stars in the constellation of Elizabeth (Lucina) does not alter the fact that Jonson is jostling for position in Lucy's court with the likes of such rivals as Samuel Daniel, to whom as late as 1603 Bedford was assigning commissions for writing masques. (Jonson gained the ascendancy in 1604.)[28] While Jonson elevates his muse above earthly, temporal concerns, he himself engages in the cut-and-thrust of poetic rivalry. Meanwhile, circumstances, which present no bar to the countess's ultimate triumph (the muse confers longevity), are about to trap the poet in a snare from which he can only escape with a certain indignity. Jonson's polished praise comes to an abrupt end with the stark words, 'The rest is lost'. In fact, the ending of the poem was suppressed not missing: it had carried a conventional hope (preserved in manuscript) that the countess's union would be blessed with a son, only for the earl to prove impotent.

In various ways, Jonson contradicts the declaration with which he underwrites his epistle, and so betrays his promise. Speaking confidently about the eternizing capacity of poetry, which preserves its subject in that golden realm from which all earthly blemishes are dispelled, and which – another artful allusion – the countess's father had famously elevated above the world of ordinary nature,[29] he notwithstanding pursues worldly concerns to a degree which finally undoes him. Think back to Jonson's poem to William Roe, where the poet casts himself in the role of spectator, waiting with a group of friends to welcome the hero home in triumph, and where he deploys the circle as a symbol of perfection, impermeable to material disruption. By entering directly into the epistle to Rutland, he has a much harder task concealing the self-interest that has caused him to put himself there; but he might still have succeeded, had not events, which ought to have yielded to eternity, outmanoeuvred him shortly beyond the poem's temporal conclusion.

It is a seasoned, somewhat bruised and rueful Jonson, then, who writes to Katherine, Lady Aubigny that complex and absorbing verse letter which immediately follows the epistle to the Countess of Rutland in *The Forest*.[30] Jonson's opening address turns characteristically on the difference between good and bad, but he has substituted for the golden world of the imagination a more prosaic – but no less valuable – entity, the mind:

> 'Tis grown almost a danger to speak true
> Of any good mind now, there are so few.

> The bad, by number, are so fortified,
> As, what they've lost to expect, they dare deride.
>
> (lines 1–4)

Jonson proceeds cautiously in this poem, more carefully than in the address to Rutland, and the adroit use of enjambment, which he deploys repeatedly and variously throughout his poetry, enacts not a steady, confident stride from line to line but rather the movements of a man who fears losing his step at any moment. The epistle shows a particular, syntactical penchant for withholding or delaying the sense, in order to complete it in an unexpected manner:

> I, therefore, who profess myself in love
> With every vertue, wheresoe'er it move,
> And howsoever; as I am at feud
> With sin and vice, though with a throne endued;
> And, in this name, am given out dangerous
> By arts and practice of the vicious.
>
> (lines 7–12)

The concessive 'though with a throne endued' hovers tantalizingly between two meanings. Is it that sin *might* strengthen itself were it to gain the backing of the throne, or is it indeed a fact that the monarchy is so compromised? Jonson portrays himself at risk as he defends virtue in a world of vice, and demonstrates the point by taking further risks as he makes his protest.

This in turn brings us to his relationship with his addressee. He congratulates Lady Aubigny foremost on her possession of a 'good mind', the word 'mind' recurring three times in the poem, once, as we have seen, at the beginning (line 2), and then twice as the rhyme word. For example,

> My mirror is more subtle, clear, refined,
> And takes and gives the beauties of the mind.
>
> (lines 43–4)

And in conclusion:

> Madame, be bold to use this truest glass,
> Wherein your form you still the same shall find,
> Because nor it can change, nor such a mind.
>
> (lines 122–4)

Any number of commentators have seized upon the difficulty Jonson may have made for himself in promoting the intellect as the 'greatest' of qualities, as if this were to challenge the validity of the aristocratic order, rule by birth, etc. Greatness lies in status; let the scholar know his place.[31] Yet one wonders if he or his patron would have seen it that way. The Platonic tradition of the mind as ultimate repository of all that is valuable would surely hold sway over anxieties about threats to the hierarchical order, and, hegemony notwithstanding, no aristocrat would have any illusion as to the permanence of his or her position in a world subject to princely whim or to the larger, unpredictable treachery of circumstance.[32] *The Mirror for Magistrates*, published at the beginning of Elizabeth's reign, and still going strong in the early years of James', presented a constant reminder of the fall of great ones. That, more than any imaginary conflict between aristocrat and cleric, or scholar, as representing opposing forces across a class divide, would be what his reader primarily understood when Jonson spoke of the 'practice of the vicious'. On the contrary, the poet and patron are on the same side, the discriminating noblewoman being encouraged to see the mind as the only sure refuge in adversity.

All things must decline; yet in referring Lady Aubigny to the spirit of vanity which impels women to look in the mirror ('No lady but, at some time, loves her glass', line 26), Jonson establishes a convention whereby a poet pays a woman the supreme compliment of braving self-knowledge. Followers in this tradition include the Earl of Rochester, in his poem 'A Letter from Artemisia in the Town to Chloe in the Country', and Alexander Pope in 'On the Characters of Women', in each of which a woman does not hesitate to recognize the defects common to her sex. Consider, especially in relation to the Jonsonian theme of the primacy of discrimination, Jonathan Swift's elevation of mind over body in the birthday poems to Stella:

> Now, this is Stella's case in fact;
> An angel's face, a little cracked
> (Could poets or could painters fix
> How angels look at thirty-six);
> This drew us in at first to find
> In such a form an angel's mind,
> And every virtue now supplies
> The fainting rays of Stella's eyes.
>
> ('To Stella on her Birthday, 1721')

Jonson shows up in his verse epistles as a poet in need of securing his position. As these examples make clear, however, that position, and what it further implies, may modify itself as circumstances alter. A confident Jonson, as he declares himself in some of his poems, is capable of urging

good behaviour on his patrons, or well-placed friends, as if he were truly
bestowing gifts on them and not looking for something in return. In
other poems the picture alters, and often to gloomy effect; but hardly any-
where do we find a Jonson who is not capable of developing a separate, if
related, line of thought, in a poem that is ostensibly devoted to a particular
idea. That versatility proves salvationary in poetic terms. Poetic rivalry is a
significant sub-theme, and takes a variety of forms: attempting to edge out a
contender in the race for preferment (Daniel); chafing at the arbitrariness of
fortune, which has given the ascendancy to a rival whose values he deplores
(Inigo Jones); reflections on the change in political temper, as one monarchy gives way to another (which marks the rivalry with Shakespeare). Under
a single heading Jonson is able to sound both selfish and selfless at the same
time. While he writes invariably with an eye to the main chance, he can with
justice claim to strike an ideal note, and often in the midst of the most
material and personal of circumstances. What he inspired in poets who
came after him is sufficient proof. The examples of satiric genius, which
derive from him through the later seventeenth century and beyond, show
that the lineage of the Tribe of Ben, like that of Katherine, Lady
Aubigny, is of long duration.

NOTES

1. 'An Epistle to Master John Selden', *Underwood* 14, 20–2; in *Ben Jonson: Poems*,
   ed. Ian Donaldson (Oxford University Press, 1975), 153. References to the
   poems are to this edition.
2. *Timber: or, Discoveries, 1641*; in *Ben Jonson*, ed. C. H. Herford and
   Percy and Evelyn Simpson, 11 vols. (Oxford: Clarendon Press, 1925–52),
   VIII, 601.
3. See Machiavelli, *The Prince*, Ch. 23, 'How Flatterers must be Shunned'
   (New York: The Modern Library, 1950): 87–9.
4.   Now Ireland has her madness and her weather still,
                    For poetry makes nothing happen: it survives
                 In the valley of its saying where executives
                    Would never want to tamper.
                         (W. H. Auden, *In Memory of W. B. Yeats*, lines 35–8).

   Jonson, like his hero Sidney, would group various kinds of writing
   under 'poetry'.
5. Jonson makes the poem rhyme in couplets throughout, as opposed to
   employing more orthodox quatrain and tercet divisions. He is showing how
   the sonnet can be adapted to the rhyming scheme characteristic of
   epigrammatic expression; in other respects, notably the balance of octave to
   sestet, and the use of the 'turn', the poem observes pure sonnet form.

6. Anthony Mortimer writes discerningly on Jonson's use of the circle as a structural principle in several poems, including that to Selden. See 'The Feigned Commonwealth in the Poetry of Ben Jonson', *Studies in English Literature* 13.1 (1973): 69–79.

7. For a detailed account of the classical texts present in the sonnet, see Richard S. Peterson, *Imitation and Praise in the Poems of Ben Jonson* (New Haven: Yale University Press, 1981), 33–43.

8. Peterson, *Imitation and Praise*, 42–3. The case is recorded by Herford and Simpson (*Ben Jonson*, I, 223–30).

9. David Riggs, *Ben Jonson: A Life* (Cambridge, MA and London: Harvard University Press, 1989), 233.

10. Virgil, *Aeneid*, trans. H. R. Fairclough, 2 vols., Loeb Classical Library (Cambridge, MA and London: Harvard University Press, 1918; rev. edn 2000), I, Bk VI, lines 456–60.

11. Riggs, *Ben Jonson* (183) notes a comparably ingenious piece of manipulation in the masque 'Love Restored'.

12. See J. C. A. Rathmell, 'Jonson, Lord Lisle, and Penshurst', *English Literary Renaissance* 1 (1971): 250–60.

13. See Riggs, *Ben Jonson*, 164–7.

14. Graham Parry, 'The Politics of the Jacobean Masque', in *Theatre and Government under the Early Stuarts*, ed. J. R. Mulryne and Margaret Shewring (Cambridge University Press, 1993): 94–6, and Roy Strong, *Henry Prince of Wales and England's Lost Renaissance* (London: Thames and Hudson, 1986), 76–7 and 151.

15. See *The Speeches at Prince Henries Barriers* (Herford and Simpson, *Ben Jonson*, VII, 328–9); Riggs, *Ben Jonson*, 167.

16. Principally Virgil, *Georgics* II, 503 ff. Donaldson further cites Tibullus, Martial, and Horace (Donaldson, *Ben Jonson: Poems*, 93).

17. Martin Butler, '"Servant But Not Slave": Ben Jonson at the Jacobean Court', *Proceedings of the British Academy* 90 (1996): 82.

18. Jonson appended the 'Epistle to Selden' to the latter's *Titles of Honour* (1614). 'To the Wars' was probably written in 1620 when English volunteers were being recruited to aid Frederick of the Palatinate (Donaldson, *Ben Jonson: Poems*, 155, citing Herford and Simpson).

19. See Alison V. Scott, *Selfish Gifts: The Politics of Exchange and English Courtly Literature, 1580–1628* (Madison: Fairleigh Dickinson University Press, 2006), 141–4.

20. The extensive borrowings from the *De Beneficiis* were first documented by William Dinsmore Briggs, in 'Ben Jonson: Notes on "Underwoods XXX" and on the "New Inn"', *Modern Philology* 10 (1913): 573–85.

21. See *De Beneficiis* I. Translation provided by George Parfitt, ed., *Ben Jonson: The Complete Poems* (Harmondsworth: Penguin, 1975; rev. rpt, 1982), 521.

22. Stanley Fish, 'Authors-Readers: Jonson's Community of the Same', *Representations* 7 (Summer 1984), 56.

23. See *De Beneficiis* I.xv, 4.

24. Arthur F. Marotti, *John Donne, Coterie Poet* (Madison: University of Wisconsin Press, 1986); in *John Donne's Poetry*, ed. Donald R. Dickson (New York and London: Norton, 2007), 233.

25. It was sent to the countess on New Year's Day, 1600.

26. Riggs' observation is worth quoting: 'In the course of conducting his feud with vice and his love affair with virtue, Jonson retells the story of his poetic career' (Riggs, *Ben Jonson*, 229).

27. See John Barrell, *Poetry, Language and Politics* (Manchester and New York: Saint Martin's Press, 1988), Ch. 2, 'Editing Out', 30.

28. This time the rival poet is not Shakespeare but most likely Daniel, whom Jonson particularly disliked. See J. R. Barker, 'A Pendant to Drummond of Hawthornden's Conversations', *Review of English Studies* n.s. 16 (1965), 287.

29. 'Nature never set forth the earth in so rich tapestry as divers poets have done . . . Her word is brazen, the poets only deliver a golden'. Sir Philip Sidney, *An Apology for Poetry*, ed. G. Shepherd (1965, 1973); third rev. edn by R. W. Maslen, Manchester University Press, 2002), 85.

30. In terms of composition the two poems were about a dozen years apart.

31. 'If praising Lady Katherine for true greatness implies the possibility that she (and her peers) may not possess it, then praise on these terms comes perilously close to blame, radically calling into question the whole class system founded on the assumption that members of the aristocracy are the true *aristoi*, those who possess *areté*'. Michael McCanles, Ch. 2: 'Jonson and "Vera Nobilitas"', in his *Jonsonian Discriminations: The Humanist Poet and the Praise of True Nobility* (University of Toronto Press, 1992), 73.

32. See my argument on Jonson and Machiavelli, above p. 91.

CHAPTER 5

Jonson's politics of gender and genre: Mary Wroth and 'Charis'

Marea Mitchell

'Your spacious thoughts with choice inventiones free, Show passiones power, affections severall straines.'[1]

Critics have commented on various connections between Ben Jonson and Mary, Lady Wroth. We know, for example, that Wroth performed in Jonson's 'Masque of Blackness', that Jonson wrote commendatory verses to her[2] and dedicated *The Alchemist*, the only one of the first folio plays to be dedicated to a woman, to her. We know he described her as 'most aequall with virtue and her Blood: The Grace and Glory of Women'.[3] We know, too, that he is reported to have criticized the behaviour of the man to whom she was married. According to Drummond, Jonson felt that 'my Lady Wroth is unworthily married on a Jealous husband'.[4] Josephine A. Roberts has also argued for the direct influence of Jonson's masques on various scenes within Wroth's *Urania*.[5]

Critics, too, have specifically connected Jonson and Lady Mary Wroth with Jonson's poetic sequence 'A Celebration of Charis in Ten Lyric Pieces'. W. David Kay suggested that Cupid's description of Charis echoes the praise of Wroth in *Epigram 105*,[6] and Helen Ostovich extends and develops the connections between Wroth, Charis, and Frances Fitzdotterel in *The Devil is an Ass*, focusing on the transfer of verses from 'Charis' to the play.[7]

Aside from arguing for specific connections between Jonson and Wroth that can be deduced from their work, critics have also commented on similarities in approaches adopted by the two writers. While Kay writes of Jonson's 'conflicted attitudes towards women', Ostovich suggests that he has a more sympathetic understanding of the women he knew, and in particular some of the women in the Sidney family.[8] Barbara Smith suggests that Jonson's attitude towards Wroth also escapes some of the stereotypes that mark traditional commendatory work in that 'conspicuously absent from Jonson's praise . . . is the mention of chastity, which is so ubiquitous in his praise of women':[9] a position no doubt partly necessitated by the acknowledgement that Wroth bore two children out of wedlock to her cousin William Herbert. Linking Jonson with Wroth, Smith also suggests that they 'agree on the nature of feminine virtue and both have used (with great variance in frequency) a female persona to express feminine points of view including one on the injustice of the double standard requiring only women to be monogamous'.[10] And it has been persuasively argued that Jonson's reputation for misogyny has deserved more sceptical treatment than it has received in recent years. As Michael G. Brennan suggests, 'Jonson was one of the few dominant male poets of the period to attempt a convincing poetic representation of the woman's perspective on such topics of love.'[11]

If these similarities or points of connection between Wroth and Jonson can be observed, then it is also obvious that they occur within a sea of difference. Most notable, of course, is their difference in social rank or class. Shored up by birth in the Sidney family and marriage into the Wroth family, Mary experienced, as Maureen Quilligan puts it, 'a social legitimacy even her uncle did not possess'.[12] Jonson, son of a minister, stepson of a bricklayer, enjoyed no similar social standing, a fact that many critics acknowledge in their emphasis on Jonson's interest in self-creation.[13] Jonson has to establish an alternative to the pedigree that preceded Wroth as a matter of course.

How and in what ways sex and gender work as authorizing markers in the seventeenth century are important questions. How gender interacts with or offsets relations of class is also a moot point. While these issues are, at a general level, beyond the scope of this chapter, it is apposite to wonder what kinds of commonality might exist between a woman of Wroth's background and a man of Jonson's, each of whom has literary talents and aspirations. How class and gender interact or offset each other in terms of the privileges they might enable would merit further discussion.

Setting aside individual circumstances, it is also relevant to examine the broader cultural contexts in which both Jonson and Wroth wrote, in particular in relation to significant changes at the top of the social and political hierarchies. Leeds Barroll has suggested that while 1603 saw the replacement of an English queen with a Scottish king, nevertheless the ascension of King James and Queen Anne brought about new possibilities for women. If Elizabeth had 'operated as a monarch, a rôle essentially patriarchal'[14] and worked hard to ensure that her sex did not limit her power or her position as a monarch, then this was not something that Anne had to consider. While she did not have the power in her own right enjoyed by Elizabeth, neither was she subject to the same kind of political necessities nor did she need to justify her role in relation to her sex. Barroll points out the potential for increased opportunities for women with Anne as queen that is at first blush counter-intuitive:

Paradoxically, then, the accession of James in 1603 could activate, for the first time in decades, the political aspirations not only of some men, but more importantly of a number of ambitious and talented women.[15]

Barbara Kiefer Lewalski extends this kind of argument in her examination of women's active participation in court masques by Jonson and others:

Their very presence as performers makes the female body the locus of action and meaning – in striking contrast to the public theatre, where boy actors took the women's parts. Here the ladies are the spectacular center of attention.[16]

If women were literally the 'spectacular' centre of attention in masques, in the sense of being deliberately set up to be looked at, then it is possible to argue that a cognate kind of attention is turned to women in other forms of cultural production of the period. While Wroth was never one of the intimates in Anne's court, it is not necessary to argue direct connections between Anne and Wroth to suggest that the latter may have benefited to some extent from shifts in attitudes to women's abilities that were developing in the seventeenth century.[17] As Lewalski suggests, 'If we can move beyond formulas of confinement and control, we will hear these new voices sounding new themes'.[18] And these new voices might then include different male registers. If women as a group of potential writers, readers, and patrons were expanding, then the implications of this are significant for men as well as women. We might also expect to find the acknowledgement by male writers of new expectations about and from women.

Wroth and Jonson, for different reasons and with different levels of intensity and directness (related to their own experiences and understandings of gendered behaviour), experiment with models of feminine behaviour that escape conventional models. Both use satire to purge romance of its traditionally gendered binary oppositions,[19] and through that purging create a space for images of desiring women that escape a negative stereotype. In particular Jonson's 'A Celebration of Charis in Ten Lyric Pieces' constructs a dialogue that allows not one but two women to speak, and also gives them the last word. This sequence also conjures a desirable male body that is not the speaker's, and creates an image of female sexuality that is neither driven by irrational, fleshly desires nor asexually and chastely dependent on the masculine libido. If, as Clare R. Kinney rightly says, 'the male body is not, officially, culturally imaginable as an object of female desire',[20] then there are nevertheless examples within early modern culture that are exceptions to the general rule. Shakespeare's long narrative poem *Venus and Adonis* is a case in point. Yet in this example and in others where women are portrayed as sexually active, even voracious, that behaviour is marked as predatory and inappropriate.

'Charis', on the other hand, redefines notions of female desire as an active rather than a negative virtue. Two women express their opinions concerning desirable features in men, and part of their power over the speaker lies in the fact that the hypothetical ability to say yes or no to the poetic lover seems to have a material force absent from so many other poetic and sonnet sequences. Rather than being silent, absent, or passive, the woman who chooses not to make a choice in 'Charis' is exercising the power not to do something in particular, in this case, not to settle for second best. Overall, one of the significant things about this sequence is its interest in new patterns of female constancy that can be seen as actively engaging with desire rather than expressing no interest or disinterest in it. Furthermore, it is particularly significant that this effect is achieved through the construction of a male speaker/persona whose voice and position are continuously undercut by the conversation that he allows. The irony is that the speaker is silenced by the voice he enabled to speak, and that the dialogue is one that is ultimately not safely within the control of the male participant. Indeed, the butt of the satire is the narcissistic male lover unable to control the object of his endeavours. The rest of this chapter explores a couple of examples of encounters between men and women in Jonson's 'Charis' and Wroth's *Urania* to show how they 'complicat[e] critical commonplaces'[21] concerning attitudes towards women's behaviour in the early modern period.

Wroth directly takes romance and works within its familiar structures to pursue new lines of interest in female protagonists. Most spectacularly she takes the starting point of her uncle's *Arcadia* and its antecedents not to repeat the motif of an absent idealized female beloved, Urania, but to instantiate a heroine concerned with her own self-fulfilment and identity. Her Urania is not the source of elevation in others ('Hath not the only love o her made us, being silly ignorant shepherds, raise up our thoughts above the ordinary level of the world, so as great clerks do not disdain our conference?' Claius asks Strephon rhetorically in Sidney's text),[22] but of significance and value in herself. The sheer scope and narrative complications of romance enable multiple perspectives that can be unfolded successfully to suggest complexity rather than simple truths and certainties. Female perspectives in Wroth's version of romance provide satirical filters that upset traditional hierarchies of understanding.

For Jonson, the occasional step into explorations of love and romance suggests not so much a lack of interest as perhaps a different angle on common themes. While 'Charis' does sound an erotic note not dominant in Jonson's work,[23] its tone is consistent with the ironic quality that colours so much of his work.[24] The edginess that can be linked to Jonson's struggle for commercial and intellectual success[25] also attends his portraits of heterosexual relationships. The politics of sexual relationships and the relationships of power between men and women are often to the forefront of Jonson's work. *Epicoene* and *The Devil is an Ass* are obvious examples of this interest, but love and its manifestations in broad and micropolitical terms ('the power relations between people in everyday life')[26] are frequent players in Jonson's work.[27]

From the outset of 'A Celebration of Charis in Ten Lyric Pieces', the reader is invited into an intimate and unusual relationship with the speaker, a relationship where we are invited not to laugh in a poem whose hallmarks are satire and irony. In a move that critics have seen as inviting autobiographical identification, Jonson personalizes the speaker by referring to his age and profession. The lines 'Though I now write fifty years', 'it is not always face, / Clothes, or fortune gives the grace: / Or the feature, or the youth; / With the ardor and the passion, / Gives the lover weight, and fashion' (311) have been taken as relevant to Jonson's age, appearance, and size in ways that separate him from the stereotype of the lean, wasting, handsome, and young lover of many love sequences. Jonson establishes images that remind readers of January and May of fabliaux familiar from comic tales based on sexual and gender incongruities but less at home in poetic forms. There may even be an echo of Philip Sidney's ridiculous Basilius from *New Arcadia* in the line 'And let nothing high decay'.[28] But the main effect is the creation of a material and identifiable lover who draws attention to his inauspicious position.

In the second verse the speaker again calls attention to his physical frailties in turning a conventional image of being unexpectedly struck by love into an image that mocks appearance and abilities. Seeking to control Cupid, who runs away from him, the speaker picks up the bow and arrow, only to be struck by the Lady's look, which literally stops him in his tracks. Just as the readers were acknowledged as part of the audience in the first stanza, here too a sense of public commentary is involved as the speaker acknowledges the judgment of others, all of whom mocked him 'and call'd of one / (Which with grief and wrath I heard) / Cupid's Statue with a beard, / Or else one that plaid his ape, / In a Hercules's shape' (312). This range of images again associates the figure of the

speaker with old age (having a beard) and indignity (aping Cupid inappropriately in a form more associated with Hercules). The third 'piece' sees
the speaker undergo a reprieve from the indignity of scurrilous comments
only to be shot by Cupid, leaving him bleeding on his knees, with the
arrow sticking from his heart.

These first three pieces, then, have been the speaker's description of the
situation to an audience implicitly sceptical, instructed not to laugh, but
supplied with images of indignity and foolhardiness that encourage such
condescension. The end of the third piece 'What he suffered' seems to
introduce a turning point that will reassert some control over the situation
by the speaker. Here the audience is invited to hear how he will 'revenge me
with my tongue', and 'dexterously . . . make example too' in a promise the
rest of the sequence fails to supply (312–13). The verses that follow ('Her
Triumph') were perhaps the best known, appearing not only in *The Devil is
an Ass* but also in other manuscripts.[29] In many ways they are highly conventional, and we see an idealizing blazon that anatomizes the female body
while simultaneously demonstrating the male poet's verbal skills of description and celebration. Yet each verse in this piece also includes ideas and
expressions that undermine the serenity of the female beauty that they explicitly announce. In the first stanza, would-be lovers are prepared, it seems, to
run through swords and seas to maintain sight of her, but the images of
drowned and penetrated male bodies are not consistent with the images
of revenge that the speaker previously promised. The second stanza, while
explicitly praising the lady's eyes and hair, does so by invoking images of
wrinkled foreheads and the impact of time and the elements. The third
stanza emphasizes the whiteness, softness, and sweetness of the lady, but
conspicuously does so through images that depend on their negative. So,
for example, we are encouraged to think of the lily before it has been man-
handled, the snow before it has been contaminated. We are invited, as it
were, not to think of the elephant.

In the more condensed imagery of the final lines, each positive attribute
has its opposite: the bud has its briar, the 'nard' its fire, and the 'bag' has a
bee with a sting (313–14). The lady portrayed throughout 'Her Triumph'
has a density and colour that is not unequivocally appreciated by her lover.
Far from being a pale shadow or an idealized absence she has an energy
associated with an experienced woman of the world ('a flesh and blood
woman, functioning in the realm of the real')[30] even if she is younger
than the speaker.

This sense of the character of the lady is further developed in the sixth
verse that directly compares her with Venus, through a supposed confusion

by Cupid between his mother and the lady. Again we have the conventional imagery of a woman's physical description: hair, eyes, breath, breasts, and so on. Where the poem steps away from commonplace, however, is in the final three lines in which the speaker proposes a new triumvirate to put in place of the three Graces whose presence has been implied in naming the lady Charis. In place of the battle between Venus, Juno, and Minerva for the judgment of Paris, the narrator establishes Charis as the combination of all three in three lines whose freshness and energy is reinforced by breaking up the regular 'aa/bb' rhyming pattern and forcing the emphasis onto three lines rather than the rhyming couplets that have dominated the bulk of the poem:

> She is Venus, when she smiles,
> But she's Juno, when she walks,
> And Minerva, when she talks.
>
> (315)

Relying on conventions and imagery that are familiar and accessible Jonson creates an image of femininity that has a physicality and immediacy that go far beyond the stereotypes with which he begins.

Verse six, 'Claiming a Second Kiss by Desert', exploits an ambiguity raised in verse five. Line 42 in 'His Discourse with Cupid' compares and then distinguishes between Charis and Cupid through a semantic ambiguity. To Cupid's claims that Charis is identical with his mother, the speaker initially confirms the resemblance and adds details of his own, only to throw a spanner in the works in the final clause:

> I confess all, I replied,
> And the glass hangs by her side,
> And the girdle 'bout her waist:
> All is Venus, save unchaste.
>
> (315)

It may be taken here that the comparison between Charis and Venus falls down with Charis' implied chastity, but the terminating clause leaves a sense of ambiguity hanging in the air.[31] In the following verse another comparison is made for Charis to inhabit. This time the comparator is a bride and here the chastity comparison leaves Charis in the negative. Nevertheless, the speaker asserts, she is more admired than a bride. The speaker's gamble is:

> That the bride, allowed a maid,
> Looked not half so fresh and fair,
> With the advantage of her hair

> And her jewels, to the view
> Of the assembly, as did you!

(315)

With a breathtakingly back-handed compliment the speaker acknowledges both the woman's sexual experience and the admiration she commands.

The cumulative effect of the pieces is to suggest that Charis is more chaste than Venus but less chaste than a bride, a situation not uncommon for mortal women, and the rest of verse six suggests a knowing playfulness about the hyperbole of amatory verse that is recognized by both its subject and its object. Guess, says the speaker, which of his extravagant claims about her effect on others is true, and surely all this extensive praise deserves another kiss.

The tendency of the poem to steer a path between the extreme representations of women is then trumped when the woman is allowed to speak for herself. Though reluctant to describe an ideal man, Charis eventually does so in fifty-four lines that form the longest single section of the sequence, effectively silencing the speaker with a portrait that bears no resemblance to what the reader knows about him. It is the peak of the humour of the verses that all the praise lavished on the woman and the invitation to her to speak result in the disenfranchisement of the male speaker. Liberated from the commonplaces, Charis uses her voice to express her preference and the right not to exercise it. The female beloved, invited to speak, then expresses her opinion about an ideal man and her commitment to that ideal. The kind of constancy or chastity that she embodies is not the most conventional kind, desireless or passionless, but one that sets its own standards and sticks to them.

'Her Man Described by Her Own Dictamen' is an idealized impossibility. Young, fashionable, masculine, sensitive, well dressed, valiant, and honest, Charis' ideal is as impossible as Ben's portrait of her. Fantasy woman's fantasy man silences 'loser-like' lover, who now does not even have 'leave to speak' (318–19). The pill of satire has so purged romance as to leave a vacuum. Charis, caught between ideal and reality, chooses nothing but does so as a positive act of discrimination, even if it is one that leaves Ben nothing to say.

Yet that, of course, is not the end of the sequence, and it would be to underplay the wit of the verse to neglect the final lines. The second lady who speaks shifts the tone into mock-sophistication where looks, mind, youth, and breeding are important but secondary to sexual prowess. The final lines of the sequence, then, compound the sense of female independence by mischievously suggesting that a woman can be as undiscriminating about sexual partners as any man: 'What you please you parts may call, / 'Tis one good part I'd lie withal' (310). In a sense these lines also exacerbate the idea that while the 'pieces' originate from a male subject and speaker it is men throughout the sequence who become the objects. First, Ben the speaker becomes the object of criticism through his pursuit of Charis. Second, we have Charis' hypothetical ideal man, anatomized in some detail. Third, we hear the lady's reduction of masculinity to sexual performance.

Perhaps more than anything else, however, the sound of the second lady's voice reminds the reader that what has seemed to be a private conversation is actually public. The sequence has always had public dimensions, implied in the notion of 'celebration', manifested in the criticism of those observing 'Ben's' behaviour. The second lady pulls us back into the social arena that frames the understandings of what can be said and done. Ben's courtship of Charis and her reaction have never been private matters. They have always occurred within social and political domains, subject to criticism, influenced by the view of others.

At the broader level of the sequence itself, Jonson the poet demonstrates his skill by writing his character Ben out of the narrative. While, as Donaldson argues,[32] the loss of erotic control is followed by loss of narrative control for Ben, this mapping of female superiority over male insufficiency is produced by Jonson's preferment of female voices. It may be, as Orgel suggests, that this is part of a fantasy of 'heroic self-sufficiency [that] is fed by a parallel fantasy of the misanthropic self-sufficiency of beautiful women',[33] and it may also be that Jonson in 'Charis' addresses the contradictions between 'poetic ideals and social realities',[34] acknowledging both the power and the sensibilities of women in his time.

In this way, Jonson's sequence is of a piece with the exploration of women's position that is a consistent concern of Lady Mary Wroth's *Urania*. Here, we could acknowledge that to come at 'Charis' with *Urania* is rather like hitting a nut with a sledgehammer in the sense of relative densities. *Urania* is also the kind of text that can be said to be capable of proving just about anything because of its length and variety. A comparison between them does, however, suggest points on the spectrum of representations of desiring women. If Jonson edges towards an ironically sympathetic exploration of women's positions in 'Charis',[35] then this kind of examination is central to Wroth.[36] Her literary work is embedded with images of women who stick to their feelings and desires in spite of parental inducement and social pressures. Pamphilia, the heroine of both sprawling volumes of *Urania* and the sonnet sequence 'From Pamphilia to Amphilanthus', repeatedly asserts her fidelity to the wandering Amphilanthus, even when both of them are married to someone else.[37] Pamphilia demonstrates the ability to exercise choice and stick to it that 'Charis' imagines.

The first story, with which *Urania* opens, is symptomatic of the shift of focus from male to female that occurs throughout its many pages. We begin with the lamentations of Urania herself, bewailing her lack of identity, and ignorance of her own origins. Most obviously demarcating its difference from Sidney's *Arcadia*, Wroth's text begins not with two shepherds lamenting the absence of the idealized beloved but with the woman herself. Her first encounter, then, is with the apparently near dead Perissus who tells her the story of his love for Limena who is married to a jealous and abusive husband.[38] While this incident may mimic Pyrocles' discovery of Gynecia's verses in *Arcadia*,[39] the tone and significance produce sharp divergence. The most striking thing about this narrative is the way that it is focalized through Urania. Her responses to Perissus' sad story frame his behaviour as self-indulgent when counterpointed with and understood through Urania's often sceptical comments and questions. Overhearing his laments, poetic and prosaic, Urania is confronted with abject despair:

> Hateful all thought of comfort is to me,
> Despised day, let me still night possesse;
> Let me all torments feele in their excesse,
> And but this light allow my state to see.
> Which still doth wast, and wasting as this light,
> Are my sad dayes unto eternall night.
>
> (*Urania*, 3)

While Urania has initially been sympathetic ('How well doe these words, this place, and all agree with thy fortune' (3)), interaction with Perissus provokes criticism:

'Sir', she said, 'having heard some part of your sorrowes, they have not only made me truly pitie you, but wonder at you; since if you have lost so great a treasure, you should not lie thus leaving her and your love unrevenged, suffering her murderers to live while you lie here complaining'. (4)

To this palpable hit and others like it, Perissus has few answers. As he provides more information about Limena's ill treatment at her husband's hands, Urania and the readers learn that Perissus does not even know if she is actually dead, provoking Urania to question further his acts of despair:

how idle, and unprofitable indeed are these courses, since if shee be dead, what good can they bring to her? And not being certaine of her death, how unfit are they for so brave a Prince, who will as it were, by will without reason wilfully lose himselfe? (14)

Then, finally, Urania delivers the *coup de grâce*. Invoking him to take action, Urania reminds Perissus of his obligations and reputation:

Thus shall you approve your selfe, a brave and worthie Lover, deserving her, who best deserv'd: but let it never be said, Perissus ended unrevenged of Philargus, and concluded his dayes like a fly in the corner. (15)

The desperation of unrequited male love looks very different when it is recounted to a female listener embedded in the text who flags a sceptical response for the reader. The spectacle of male lament looks far from illuminating when it is contrasted with the possibility of action. From this perspective Perissus looks less afflicted than derelict, content to wallow in assumed misery when he does not even know the facts of the situation. The practical woman is clearly more impressive than the narcissistic man.

To take one more example from many, deep in the first part of *Urania*, book three, Pamphilia tells the story of Nicholarus.[40] The audience includes the Queen of Naples, Pamphilia's aunt, and mother of Amphilanthus, who has been taken to shadow the real-life figure of Mary Sidney, Countess of Pembroke, mother of Mary Wroth's lover and cousin, William Herbert. Nicholarus' romantic problem is that he loves where he is not loved in return, so suffers 'love of one, who for his misery loved another' (366). As so often in *Urania*, the lady in question is married but it is not her husband whom she loves. When Nicholarus threatens to take by the sword what she will not willingly surrender she 'wished her love, or husband, the worse of the two by much, had been present' and is indeed saved by her 'servant' (367) and lover. Forced to leave, Nicholarus continues to importune her with verses that commend 'varitie in love' (368), copies of which Pamphilia does not have, though she does have the lady's replies to him, provided by Amphilanthus.

Silenced again, the male lover is denied the chance to present his arguments. *Urania* provides only the rebuttal. The lady continues the theme within *Urania* of promoting a constancy that relies not on marriage vows but on a choice freely bestowed and maintained by the female lover:

> And much I wonder you will highly rate
> The brutish love of Nature, from which state
> Reason doth guide us, and doth difference make
> From sensuall will, true reason lawes to take.

Wer't not for reason, we but brutish were,
Nor from the beasts did we at all differ;
Yet these you praise, the true stile opinion,
By which truths government is shroudly gon.

                                                              (369–70)

Many of the ideas and themes here would be at home in Sir Philip Sidney's *Arcadia*, particularly the correlation between reason and humanity, between sensuality, nature, and brutish bestiality. Yet these lines in favour of constancy in love are spoken by a married woman about someone other than her husband, raising implications peculiar to Wroth and *Urania*. Inconstancy and variation in love are criticized in favour of a union of true minds that is not necessarily or inherently sanctified by legal or religious ritual. Wroth has taken much further than Jonson the idea of a woman exercising her own judgment. Time and time again she satirizes inconstant and infatuated men who fail to match the standards and practices of their female counterparts.

Throughout *Urania* episodes involving romantic or erotic relationships between men and women are presented from the woman's point of view, altering the perspective on familiar scenarios. In the case of Nicholarus the reason why the lover is scorned is more important that the fact that he is, and the description highlights the conscious choice and preference of the woman.

Two more poems by Jonson will serve to illustrate his interest in a female perspective that is cognate with Wroth's. 'In the Person of Womankind: A Song Apologetic'[41] turns the tables on the singing of women's praises when the female speaker declares 'We have both wits and fancie too, /And if we must, let's sing of you'. The female speaker here also attacks the self-serving pictures of women that men make for their own ends. She goes on to describe the paucity of male virtue that entails that to draw from life the speaker must build a composite of parts taken from many sources to produce 'One good enough for a song's sake'. It is the difficulty of the process, says the speaker, that demonstrates the art of the maker, not the end product. The pleasure to be gained is from the artistry in the making. The impersonation of a woman produces a perspective that both criticizes male practice and identifies the pleasure in making that is traditionally proscribed for women.

The poem that immediately follows this makes a point frequently seen in *Urania* that it is futile for women to be constant given the inconstancy of men. It traces a line of ambiguity between misogynist notions of women's inherent infidelity ('Our proper virtue is to range') and an idea that restriction of movement and intellect limits female capacity: 'We are not bred to sit on stools . . . / We are no women then, but wives'. This resonates with what Quilligan represents as Wroth's interest in 'a woman's social experience that is specifically not that of a wife, the one role upon which all discussion of female experience focussed in the seventeenth century'.[42] The poem goes on to advocate trial and error as the precursor to perfection in love, and to argue that good only has merit when its difference from bad is understood and appreciated. While the sophistry in these arguments is clear, the sting is in the final lines that throw male inconstancy back as the reason why women are inconstant: 'For were the worthiest woman cursed / To love one man, he'd leave her first'. The slam-dunk effect of the rhyming couplet suggests a witty turning of the tables against sexual double standards. The preceding arguments may be flawed but that male conduct is no better than female conduct is the defence of the inconstant woman.[43]

That Wroth takes the discussion of female inconstancy further again is evident in *Urania*. In Book III, Urania and Pamphilia canvass definitions of constancy that go beyond simple formulations. Encountering a Pamphilia in distress, Urania lectures her with advice that if her lover is inconstant 'which is a thing familiar with men' (*Urania*, 468) her constancy should be to her beauty, which is jeopardized by her ill health. Constancy to love should be replaced by constancy to virtue and male constancy. While there is no sense that readers expect Pamphilia to abstain from loving Amphilanthus, which would be the outcome of Urania's advice, nevertheless that advice contains its own wisdom. Urania's redefinition of constancy indites men as its chief defaulters.

The silencing of male voices and the amplification of female voices also has significance in the new kinds of poetic model it suggests. Lewalski insightfully points out that Wroth's empowerment of women does not simply proceed from a straightforward role reversal, giving the female lover all the power that attended the male lover:

A female lover's overt, passionate solicitation of her male beloved would violate cultural norms too egregiously; but also her assumption of the Petrarchan lover's subservient posture would approximate contemporary structures all too closely, and could not empower her to construct her own identity and story.[44]

The space for a female voice is one that has to be carefully negotiated, and cannot simply be achieved by inverting expectations of masculine and feminine behaviour or by women taking on the positions that men have found productive. If no female character cross-dresses in *Urania*[45] then this might suggest Wroth's awareness of the limitations of gender inversion, and that aping masculinity carries its own dangers. It might also suggest the desire to create alternative models of femininity not underscored by notions of masculinity.

Jonson, as we know, said that reading Wroth's poetry had made him 'A better lover, and much better poet'.[46] While we might take both aspects of this compliment with a grain of salt, Jonson in praising Wroth and other women acknowledges what could not be denied: that women were forming an increasingly important part of literary culture, as readers, patrons, and writers. It is not then surprising that, while Wroth's incursions into what might be described as sexual politics are more extensive than Jonson's, both writers experiment with different kinds of perspective on 'affections severall straines'. With 'choice inventions', irony, wit, and satire, each explores the areas beyond literary and social commonplaces about gendered behaviour. The imagining of a female point of view with which both engage illuminates the corners and shadows of seventeenth-century sexual conventions.[47]

That this exploration was not without risks that were recognized by both Wroth and Jonson is evident in a return to Jonson's dedication of *The Alchemist* to Wroth, to which I referred at the beginning of this chapter. In the 1616 Folio the dedication to Wroth begins with a standard compliment: 'To the Lady Most Deserving Her Name and Blood, Mary La[dy] Wroth'. The praise is relatively bland, linking Mary with the Wroth and Sidney families and locating them as the source of her merit. The first edition of 1612, however, was rather more forthcoming in its praise, and it is in this version that Mary was 'most aequall with virtue, and her Blood: The Grace and Glory of women'.[48] Also dropped from the 1616 Folio were these lines:

Or how, yet, might a grateful minde be furnishe'd against the iniquitie of Fortune; except, when she failed it, it had power to impart it selfe? A way found out, to overcome even those, whom Fortune hath enabled to returne most, since they, yet leave themselves more.

What prompted Jonson to effect what looks like an editorial toning down from 1612 to 1616 can only be the subject of speculation. In 1614 Wroth's husband died, leaving her with financial debts, and in 1616 their son James died, apparently compounding her problems. In February 1616 Jonson was granted a royal pension, and in the same year there seems to have been a considerable upheaval in the court of Queen Anne. From the first to the second decade of the seventeenth century Wroth seems to have lost favour with Anne, and Roberts also draws attention to a rumour that Anne favoured Wroth's cousin and later lover William Herbert.[49] It is undoubtedly foolhardy to argue causes from what might be coincidences, but a few connections come to mind. Wroth, no longer at court, sans husband, in 1616 might have seemed to Jonson a less attractive and a less likely patron. Praising with superlatives someone out of favour at court might also have seemed unwise to one accepting the royal coin. It might well be, too, that the reference to Fortune's iniquities and resilience in experiencing them seemed a less than tactful remark to make in the public forum of the 1616 folio.[50]

As many critics have argued, the path to success for Jonson was one that he travelled with considerable self-consciousness and with careful attention to self-presentation.[51] Lewalski has also argued that Wroth was not only the most prolific female writer of the time but also the 'most self-conscious'.[52] This tendency to self-consciousness is yet another factor in the relationship between Jonson's and Wroth's writing. In this light it is possible to see the irony, wit, and ambiguities characteristic of 'Charis' as strategically designed to negotiate the troubled waters of gendered relationships in the seventeenth century.

At this point we might also consider the question of the style and structure of 'Charis', as Ian Donaldson does when he suggests that 'whether the apparently fragmentary nature of these "pieces" is accidental or the product of a considered aesthetic is open to question'.[53] If we cannot be certain as to intention or purpose, it is possible to suggest that the fragmentation allows more free play than a more structured model might. The form of 'Charis' also militates against a fixed or uniform perspective, leaving the reader without a stable point of interpretation. On a larger canvas Wroth also manipulates conventions to explore the dynamics of gendered and erotic relationships while refusing the reader a position from which the whole may be overseen.

Whatever the considerable differences between Jonson and Wroth, Jonson's work, like Wroth's, can be read as influenced by encounters with strong-minded and intelligent women, some of whom were patrons, some of whom were fellow writers, some of whom were audience. While it is possible to overplay the sense that Jonson's work demonstrates a coherent or sustained commitment to sexual politics and women in particular, attention to his work alongside Wroth's is suggestive of the ways in which the work of each writer engages with some of the social dynamics of their times. It is not necessary to argue a direct relationship between

'Charis' and Wroth (nor Charis and Wroth) to suggest their common interests in the politics of gender and genre.

NOTES

1. From William Drummond's ode to Wroth, in *The Poetical Works of William Drummond of Hawthornden*, ed. L. E. Kastner, 2 vols. (Manchester University Press, 1913), II, 271.
2. *Epigrams 103* and *105*, and Sonnet 28 in *Underwood* identify her by name. All quotations are from *Ben Jonson*, ed. Ian Donaldson, Oxford Authors (Oxford University Press, 1985). See also Josephine A. Roberts' edition *The Poems of Lady Mary Wroth* (Baton Rouge: Louisiana State University Press, 1983), 16.
3. See Roberts, *Poems*, 16.
4. Donaldson, *Ben Jonson*, 603.
5. Mary Wroth, *The First Part of the Countess of Mongomery's 'Urania'*, ed. Josephine A. Roberts (Binghamton, NY: Center for Medieval and Early Renaissance Studies, 1995). All references are to this edition and are included in parentheses in the text.
6. W. David Kay, *Ben Jonson: A Literary Life* (Basingstoke: Macmillan, 1995), 134.
7. Helen Ostovich, 'Hell for Lovers: Shades of Adultery in *The Devil is an Ass*', in *Refashioning Ben Jonson: Gender, Politics and the Jonsonian Canon*, ed. Julie Sanders with Kate Chedgzoy and Susan Wiseman (Basingstoke: Macmillan, 1998), 155–82. Prior to this there had been arguments that a model for Charis and Mrs Fitzdotterel was Elizabeth, Lady Hatton, see Ian Donaldson's discussion of Fleay's work in his *Ben Jonson* (1985), 682. Ostovich's arguments are the more extensive, but the fact it is possible to conceive of more than one real-life model attests to the general relevance of the ideas.
8. Kay, *Ben Jonson*, 132; Ostovich, 'Hell for Lovers', 155.
9. Barbara Smith, *The Women of Ben Jonson's Poetry: Female Representations in the Non-Dramatic Verse* (Aldershot: Scolar Press, 1995), 62.
10. *Ibid.*, 68.
11. Michael G. Brennan, 'Creating Female Authorship in the Early Seventeenth Century: Ben Jonson and Lady Mary Wroth', in *Women's Writing and the Circulation of Ideas: Manuscript Publication in England 1550–1800*, ed. George L. Justice and Nathan Tinker (Cambridge University Press, 2002), 81–2.
12. Maureen Quilligan, 'The Constant Subject: Instability and Female Authority in Wroth's *Urania* poems', in *Soliciting Interpretation: Literary Theory and Seventeenth-Century English Poetry*, ed. Elizabeth D. Harvey and Katharine Eisaman Maus (University of Chicago Press, 1990), 307.
13. See, for example, Richard Helgerson, *Self-Crowned Laureates: Spenser, Jonson, Milton and the Literary System* (Berkeley: University of California Press, 1983); Robert C. Evans, *Ben Jonson and the Poetics of Patronage* (Lewisburg: Bucknell

University Press, 1989); Lawrence Lipking, *Life of the Poet: Beginning and Ending Poetic Careers* (University of Chicago Press, 1981); Richard Dutton 'Jonson's Satiric Styles', in *The Cambridge Companion to Ben Jonson*, ed. Richard Harp and Stanley Stewart (Cambridge University Press, 2000), 58–71.

14. Leeds Barroll, 'The Court of the First Stuart Queen', in *The Mental World of the Jacobean Court*, ed. Linda Levy Peck (Cambridge University Press, 1991), 191.

15. *Ibid.*

16. Barbara Kiefer Lewalski, *Writing Women in Jacobean England* (Cambridge, MA: Harvard University Press, 1994), 30.

17. This is not to ignore the controversy that *Urania* encountered when various figures in it were identified as pertaining to real people. See Roberts, *Poems*, 31–7.

18. Lewalski, *Writing Women*, 315.

19. Helgerson, *Self-Crowned Laureates*, 126.

20. Clare R. Kinney, 'Mary Wroth's Guilty "Secrett Art": The Poetics of Jealousy in *Pamphilia to Amphilanthus*', in *Write or Be Written: Early Modern Women Poets and Cultural Constraints*, ed. Barbara Smith and Ursula Appelt (Aldershot: Ashgate, 2001), 69.

21. Steve Mentz, *Romance for Sale in Early Modern England* (Aldershot: Ashgate, 2006), 5. Gordon McMullan's edition of essays *Renaissance Configurations: Voices/Bodies/Spaces 1580–1690* (London: Macmillan, 1998) also tackles critical commonplaces that associate women's reading habits with privacy, domesticity, and constraint.

22. Philip Sidney, *Arcadia,* ed. Maurice Evans (Harmondsworth: Penguin, 1977), 63.

23. Ian Donaldson, *Jonson's Magic Houses: Essays in Interpretation* (Oxford: Clarendon Press, 1997), 147.

24. Lesley Mickel, *Ben Jonson's Antimasques: A History of Growth and Decline* (Aldershot: Ashgate, 1999), 101.

25. See Helgerson, *Self-Crowned Laureates*, 184.

26. See Evans, *Patronage*, 36.

27. See also Ian Donaldson, 'Jonson's Poetry', in *The Cambridge Companion to Ben Jonson*, ed. Harp and Stewart, 119–39, 132.

28. 'Let not old age disgrace my high desire', Sidney, *Arcadia*, 217.

29. See Donaldson, *Jonson's Magic Houses*, 145.

30. Smith, *The Women of Ben Jonson's Poetry*, 10.

31. Kay suggests that the 'claim that she [Charis] corresponds exactly to Venus except for her chastity . . . relieves any doubts about her character' (*Ben Jonson*, 134), but it can also be argued that such doubts, once raised, are not so easily dispelled.

32. Donaldson, *Jonson's Magic Houses*, 61.

33. Stephen Orgel, 'Jonson and the Amazons', in *Soliciting Interpretation*, ed. Harvey and Maus, 131.

34. Evans, *Patronage*, 68.

35. Obviously, 'Charis' is not on its own here, and *Epicoene* and *The Devil is an Ass* are two other texts that can immediately be seen as containing sympathetic representations of women.

36. Josephine A. Roberts' work has been the foundation of Wroth studies. For important contributions to this burgeoning field see also, for example, *Reading Mary Wroth: Representing Alternatives in Early Modern England*, ed. Naomi J. Miller and Gary Waller (Knoxville: University of Tennessee Press, 1991); Helen Hackett, *Women and Romance Fiction in the English Renaissance* (Cambridge University Press, 2000); *Writing and the English Renaissance*, ed. William Zunder and Suzanne Trill (London: Longman, 1996); *Early Women Writers 1600–1720*, ed. Anita Pachecho (London: Longman, 1998); Wendy Wall, *The Imprint of Gender: Authorship and Publication in the English Renaissance* (Ithaca, NY: Cornell University Press, 1993); *Women and Literature in Britain 1500–1700*, ed. Helen Wilcox (Cambridge University Press, 1996); *Voicing Women: Gender and Sexuality in Early Modern Writing*, ed. Kate Chedgzoy, Melanie Hansen, and Suzanne Trill (Keele University Press, 1996).

37. In Amphilanthus' case he marries because he (falsely) believes that Pamphilia is married elsewhere, while Pamphilia marries because she knows he is married elsewhere and out of duty to her country. As so often in *Urania* these different circumstances are a mark of character.

38. While we do not need to read every similar episode as directly autobiographical the prevalence of women unhappily married in *Urania* cannot be ignored. This episode is briefly referred to in Marea Mitchell and Dianne Osland's *Representing Women and Female Desire* (New York: Palgrave, 2005), 208, fn. 32.

39. Quilligan, 'The Constant Subject', 315.

40. The aspersions on Nicholarus' amatory status are mirrored in his political status as a usurper to Albania.

41. Jonson, *Underwood*, 5. Donaldson, *Ben Jonson*, 321.

42. Quilligan, 'The Constant Subject', 321.

43. Jonson, *Underwood*, 5. Donaldson, *Ben Jonson*, 322.

44. Lewalski, *Writing Women*, 253.

45. Quilligan, 'The Constant Subject', 331.

46. Jonson, *Underwood*, 28. Donaldson, *Ben Jonson*, 349.

47. Drummond's ode to Wroth, *The Poetical Works of William Drummond*, II, 271. It should be noted that this interest in a female point of view was being explored by other writers too. Examples can be found in the work of two men close to Wroth, her father Robert and her uncle Philip Sidney. See, for example, Robert Sidney's Song 6, in *The Poems of Robert Sidney edited from the Poet's Autograph Notebook*, ed. P. J. Croft (Oxford: Clarendon Press, 1984), 62, and in prose Philip Sidney's representation of Philoclea's feelings for Pyrocles/Zelmane (*Arcadia*, 237–40).

48. Roberts points this out in *Poems*, 16.

49. Roberts, *Urania*, liii.

50. I am grateful to Alison Scott for discussion on this point, though I do not implicate her in the suggestions here.
51. See, for example, Helgerson, *Self-Crowned Laureates*; Lipking, *Life of the Poet*; Evans, *Patronage*; David Norbrook, *Poetry and Politics in the English Renaissance* (Oxford University Press, 2002); and Ian Donaldson, 'Jonson's Poetry'.
52. Lewalski, *Writing Women*, 243.
53. Donaldson, 'Jonson's Poetry', 134.

CHAPTER 6

Jonson's metempsychosis revisited: patronage and religious controversy

Richard Dutton

Readers of my *Ben Jonson, 'Volpone' and the Gunpowder Plot* (Cambridge, 2008) will recognize a good deal of the material in this chapter. It was drafted before that material came together in book form, but has only found its way into print subsequently. Such are the vagaries of academic publishing. For all the inevitable repetitions there are, I believe, two major differences between the chapter and the book, which makes the chapter worth publishing in its own right. The chapter traces the long gestation of my thinking about *Volpone* and its context, from my doctoral dissertation (1971) and the book that flowed from it (1983), through occasional, unrelated revisitations of aspects of the play (1998ff), to my belated appreciation of the significance of its 'metempsychosis' material, the last piece of the puzzle to fall into place. In doing so the chapter also traces a long and sometimes painful journey from being a Cambridge New Critic, through the famous 'return to history' of early modern studies in the 1980s and 1990s, to my current critical mode. I should describe that as one of a revisionist cultural historian, sufficiently comfortable with poststructural thinking to be able to approach the play from the perspective of its first readers rather than that of the text per se. *Ben Jonson, 'Volpone' and the Gunpowder Plot* is not concerned with that journey. It is built consistently around reading the 1607 Quarto of *Volpone* as it might have been read by initiate readers when it first appeared, those with some knowledge of Jonson's stormy relationship with authority and of the currents of religio-political controversy in the wake of the Gunpowder Plot. I hope those differences justify the inevitable overlap.

With this chapter I come full circle on a subject which has been with me all my published life. I first addressed *Volpone* in the context of the Gunpowder Plot and Jonson's relationship with Robert Cecil, Earl of Salisbury, in *Ben Jonson: To the First Folio* (Cambridge, 1983). I have returned to it in four essays since then and address it now for the last time (as I expect), in relation to editing *Volpone* for the new Cambridge *Ben Jonson*. I have been at it so long, in fact, that I am embarrassed to find myself quoted as an authority on the issue by others who have visited the subject since, and whom I have consulted in the hope of finding new information on this most slippery of subjects.[1]

Here I intend particularly to examine the 'show' of the metempsychosis of the soul of Pythagoras, performed for Volpone by Nano, Androgyno, and Castrone early in the play (1.2.1–62). I intend to link it to John Donne's tantalizingly obscure poem on the same subject ('Metempsychosis, or the Progress of the Soul'), and beyond that to reflect more widely on the religious dimension of *Volpone* and how this makes the play so uncomfortable as a comedy. I also want to emphasize how much more accessible these readings are in the 1607 Quarto of the play than they are in the more familiar 1616 Folio version. But what I have to say rides on the back of my earlier publications on the subject; first, I want to recapitulate their main points.

(i) In *To the First Folio* I noted the relationship of *Volpone* to the Gunpowder Plot in November 1605; how Jonson is careful within the text and paratext to spell out a timetable of the play's writing which has it devised, composed, and performed before 25 March 1606, on a schedule which parallels Sir Politic Would-Be's journey to Venice; how Sir Pol's chatter of 'intelligences' and 'plots' clearly, if inanely, echoes the political climate in England after the discovery the Plot; how this intersects with the Catholic Jonson's known involvement with the Plot – he dined with many of the conspirators a month before its discovery, and was called in by the Privy Council in its wake to try to track down a Catholic priest with information – and with his prosecution, together with his wife, for recusancy in the early months of 1606, while the surviving Plotters were being executed and he was writing the play. I also pointed out elements within the text which potentially alluded to Robert Cecil, who as the king's chief minister was crucial to the discovery of the Plot and who (in the eyes of many Catholics) was its chief political beneficiary – some would even say instigator. Chief among these are the subtitle of the play, 'The Fox' (a common nickname for Cecil, as it had been for his father, Lord Burleigh), and the role of the dwarf, Nano, who declares himself to be 'a pretty little ape', praised for 'pleasing imitation / Of greater men's action, in a ridiculous fashion' (3.3.12–14) – Cecil was a short, hunch-backed man – and Jonson very ostentatiously contrives to get him on stage with Sir Pol, but gives him nothing to say (see 3.5.29 and 4.2. passim). Sir Pol's ludicrous disquisitions on 'intelligences' and cyphers could not but bring to mind the fact that Cecil controlled the most sophisticated espionage network in the country. I considered this in relation to what else we know about Jonson's

relations with Cecil, who patronized him a good deal in the early years of
James I's reign. It is clear that, after Cecil's death in 1612, Jonson had a
poor opinion of him: in the 1616 arrangement of the *Epigrams* two poems
praising Cecil (nos. 63 and 64) are immediately followed by 65, 'To My
Muse', which begins: 'Away, and leave me, thou thing most abhorred, /
That hast betrayed me to a worthless lord' (1–2).[2] But it is much less clear
how much of this we should read back into 1605/6, when Cecil's patronage
was critical to securing Jonson's place as a court poet.

About what all this added up to in respect of the play, I was at best tentative: 'it may well be that Sir Pol's real significance in *Volpone* lies in his irrel-
evance, the fact that his talk of plots and cyphers obfuscates the simple truth
that the state of Venice is in far more danger from the cancer within itself
than it is from his "politic" scheming'. Reflecting on the strict and
not-entirely-poetic justice meted out by the play, I concluded: 'We are left
to wonder, from *Volpone*, what real justice awaits the politicians and plotters
of Jacobean London, and how many of their own plots were only "drawn out
of play-books"', as Sir Pol's had been (5.4.42). I also conceded that there 'is
room for a good deal of debate about some of what I have claimed here as
"glancings" and what they add up to'.[3] This came in a chapter devoted to
'Covert Allusions' in Jonson's works, written as the re-historicization of
early modern literary studies with which we are now so familiar was only
just getting under way. Such forays for meaning outside the strict parameters
of the text were not then common, partly because the kinds of political
reference I was proposing were thought to be precluded by the censorship
of the stage conducted by the Master of the Revels.[4]

So my own study then focused on that censorship, resulting in *Mastering
the Revels: The Regulation and Censorship of Early Modern Drama* (1991),
in which a key conclusion was that the Masters of the Revels were far less
repressive than had been supposed, as long as matters were handled
discreetly and with adequate fictional veiling: what we should now call
deniability was critical. Ironically, *Volpone* was one of the few early plays
by Jonson that did *not* figure in this study, because it was one of the few
for which no evidence survives that it offended anyone or was subject to
special scrutiny. After *Sejanus* and *Eastward Ho!*, in particular, this was
some achievement, as Jonson indirectly acknowledges in the Epistle prefac-
ing the play: 'and not my youngest infant but hath come into the world with
all his teeth' (lines 45–6).[5]

(ii) I next returned to *Volpone* to write specifically on the Epistle 'To . . .
the Two Famous Universities', a key document in Jonson's literary criticism.
This was in an essay called 'The Lone Wolf: Jonson's Epistle to *Volpone*'.[6]

That Epistle has long been seen as a pivotal moment in Jonson's career, redefining his critical bearings in relation to the classical precedents towards Aristotelian, Horatian, and New Comedy norms, and eschewing the personal satire often suspected in the 'comicall satyres'.[7] My point was to emphasize just how clearly, to an alert reader, the essay spells out less an Olympian change of critical philosophy than Jonson's strategy as a writer at that particular moment, in the light of extraordinary circumstances. His insistence, for example, on 'the impossibility of any man's being a good poet without first being a good man. He that is said to be able to inform young men to all good disciplines' (lines 20–2) is a direct retort to the fact that, as well as recusancy, he stood charged with being 'by fame a seducer of youth to the Popish religion'.[8] Elsewhere he contrives to remind those who know him of his repeated brushes with the authorities – over *The Isle of Dogs, Every Man Out of His Humour, Poetaster*, and *Sejanus*, which brought charges of 'popery and treason' from the Earl of Northampton ('Conversations with Drummond', line 273). Perhaps most critically, his closing promise 'to spout ink' in the faces of his detractors, 'and not Cinnamus the barber with his art shall be able to take out the brands' (lines 127–9), inevitably evokes his own public branding as a felon after reading 'neck verse' to avoid hanging for the killing of Gabriel Spencer; it was while imprisoned for that offence that he converted to Roman Catholicism. The Epistle also alludes quite strikingly to his most recent brush with the authorities, over the co-authored *Eastward Ho!* Not only does the phrasing 'My works are read, allowed (I speak of those that are entirely mine)' refer to the fact that one problem with the play was that it was performed unlicensed, but Jonson also contrives to weave into the Epistle passages from one of the urgent letters that he wrote to senior figures at court, soliciting release both from prison and from the threat of judicial mutilation. It was the letter he wrote to Robert Cecil.

The passages are: 'My noble Lord, they deal not charitably, who are too witty in another man's works, and utter, sometimes, their own malicious meanings, under our words'.[9] This reappears in the Epistle as: 'there are that profess to have a key for the deciphering of everything; but let wise and noble persons take heed how they be too credulous, or give leave to these invading interpreters to be over-familiar with their fames, who cunningly, and often, utter their own virulent malice under other men's simplest meanings' (61–4). The second passage is this:

let me be examined, both all my works past, and this present . . . whether, I have ever (in any thing I have written private, or public) given offence to a nation, to any public order or state, or any person of honour, or authority, but have equally laboured to keep their dignity, as mine own person safe.   (221)

This reappears in the Epistle as:

howsoever I cannot escape from some the imputation of sharpness . . . I would ask of these supercilious politics, what nation, society, or general order, or state I have provoked? what public person? whether I have not, in all these preserved their dignity, as mine own person, safe?   (43–9)

In both these instances Jonson was quoting from famous defences of satire, in Martial and Erasmus (*The Letter to Martin Dorp*), but the specific phrasing clearly echoes that of the letter from prison. This is the only indisputable link between *Volpone* and Cecil, and would have been apparent to very few people beyond Jonson and Cecil themselves – possibly Chapman (who shared the *Eastward Ho!* imprisonment) and a few others who were close to Jonson at this time, like those who wrote commendatory verses for the play's publication. So this is a subtext in a play of subtexts (or in the paratextual material around the play) which points a very privileged readership to Jonson's troubled history in the autumn of 1605. Shortly after writing those letters Jonson was in fact released unharmed – and then seen dining with the Gunpowder Plotters. Whether Cecil had a hand in Jonson's release we do not know, but he was certainly the person who as Chief Secretary to the Privy Council called upon Jonson in the wake of the Plot to seek out a Roman Catholic priest.[10]

The Epistle to *Volpone* is formally a letter of thanks to the Universities of Oxford and Cambridge 'for their love and acceptance shown to his poem in the presentation' and as such invokes impeccable classical precedents and deploys them towards unimpeachable Christian humanist ends. At the same time, however, it alerts readers who are looking for it to a history of confrontation with authority – and celebrates the fact that *Volpone* itself has escaped such a confrontation. In the quarto version it is signed breezily 'From my house in the Blackfriars' – a very fashionable address for a convicted felon. Like several of the commendatory poems it hints that Jonson has eluded his pursuers, just as the Fox traditionally does.

(iii) My next piece on *Volpone* appeared as '*Volpone* and Beast Fable: Early Modern Analogic Reading'.[11] This addressed a question I had nowhere seen addressed directly: what are we to make of the fact that the play – uniquely, as far as I can see, among the plays of the period – in effect takes the form of a beast fable. Purists might argue that the essence of a beast fable is to have animals behaving as humans, whereas in *Volpone* what we have is humans behaving like animals. But in the play this is a distinction without a difference, given the fluid conditions of stage impersonation: what distinguishes an actor pretending to be an animal performing the role of a human being from one pretending to be a human being acting like an animal? Volpone *is* a fox, Mosca a fly, Sir Politic a parrot, and so on. At all events, the play indubitably draws heavily on beast-fable lore, including Æsop and Caxton's *Reynard the Fox*.[12]

I therefore examined what we know of Jonson's acquaintance with beast fables, and found there were two he certainly knew. One of these relates to the Cecils, and the other probably does too. We can in fact only date Jonson's knowledge of these fables from after the publication of *Volpone*, but there are reasonable grounds for assuming that he knew both of them earlier. One is Spenser's *Mother Hubberds Tale*, which in some respects is a striking analogue to the play; it also has significant affinities with Donne's 'Metempsychosis', as we shall see. We know that Jonson possessed a copy of Spenser's 1617 *Works*, with annotations to the *Tale*.[13] The 1591 volume of *Complaints* in which it first appeared had officially been withdrawn from sale, but it does seem that copies could be bought as late as 1596, at inflated prices, and it was widely circulated in manuscript.[14] Given its notoriety (which I discuss below), it seems inconceivable that Jonson did not know of *Mother Hubberds Tale*, at least in general terms. It is a poem of 'personation', of disguisings carried to the point where identities themselves change, which is an essential feature of Jonson's play.[15] It tells the tale of two shape-shifting social climbers, the Ape and the Foxe, who come to court:

> Where the fond Ape himselfe uprearing hy
> Upon his tiptoes, stalketh stately by,
> As if he were some great *Magnifico*,
> And boldlie doth amongst the boldest go.
> And his man Reynold with fine counterfesaunce
> Supports his credite and his countenaunce.
>
> (lines 663–8)

This passage strikingly parallels the situation in the play when, with Volpone's support, Mosca plays 'some great *Magnifico*'. But it was probably other passages which incurred official wrath, such as:

> Justice he solde injustice for to buy,
> And for to purchase for his progeny
> . . . .
> He fed his cubbes with fat of all the soyle,
> And with the sweete of others sweating toyle,
> And crammed them with crumbs of Benefices.
>
> (lines 1147–53)

This relates to the Foxe, now Chief Minister to the Ape, who is impersonating the Lion-King. It could easily be construed as commenting on Lord Burghley's efforts in the early 1590s to acquire positions of power and patronage for his sons, and very probably was. As William Oram summarizes: 'Modern commentators agree that the picture of the Fox as courtier in the last two episodes of the poem glances at Lord Burghley, and the topical satire may have caused Spenser trouble... It was not reprinted with the rest of the *Complaints* in the 1611 edition of Spenser's works, probably for fear of antagonizing Robert Cecil, earl of Salisbury, Burghley's son'.[16]

By the time of *Volpone*, Burghley was long dead, but as Pauline Croft puts it: 'By 1601, when Essex went to the block, Robert Cecil had succeeded his father as secretary of state and Master of the Court of Wards', perpetuating what had been characterized since at least 1585 as the *regnum Cecilianum*.[17] Resentment at this was common across the political spectrum, but had a particular edge among Roman Catholics who saw their treatment as part of this wider process of familial aggrandisement.[18] With the Gunpowder Plot, from which Cecil emerged more powerful than ever, all the opprobrium that had formerly attached to the father now firmly attached to the son. It was, apparently, about this time that Richard Niccols composed a sequel of sorts to *Mother Hubberds Tale*, *Beggars Ape* (not published until 1627), which plays cruelly on Cecil's deformity.[19] Jonson's long-term view of all this is perhaps indicated by the notation against line 1148 of *Mother Hubberds Tale* ('And for to purchase for his progeny'), where 'the words "Lord Tresorors" have been written'.[20] The plural 'Tresorors' is particularly telling. Cecil became Lord Treasurer in 1608, so attaining the highest office achieved by his father: they were the only father and son ever to hold the post. Spenser's lines had prophesied the entrenching of the Cecil dynasty.

The other beast fable which I suggest may relate to *Volpone* is today almost unknown. But Jonson's own *Epicene* suggests that it made *something* of a mark in the first decade of the seventeenth century:

> LA FOOLE Ay, and there's an excellent book of moral philosophy, madam, of Reynard the Fox and all the beasts, called *Doni's Philosophy*.
> CENTAURE There is indeed, Sir Amorous La Foole.
> LA FOOLE I have read it, my Lady Centaure, all over to my cousin here.
> MISTRESS OTTER Ay, and 'tis a very good book as any is of the moderns.[21]

This clearly shows that Jonson knew of the tale of Reynard the Fox. But the most striking feature of this passage is that La Foole and Mistress Otter are quite wrong about that tale appearing in Doni's *Moral*

Philosophy. This is an oddly laboured and thus foregrounded joke, one that – to be effective – requires an unusually specific awareness on the part of the audience. Does it point to anything more than La Foole's empty-headedness?

The work known as Doni's *Moral Philosophy* has a long and complex history. Originally written by an Indian author, Bidpai, it was translated into Italian by Anton Francesco Doni, and latterly translated into English by Sir Thomas North (better known to posterity as the translator of *Plutarch's Lives*). His version was first printed in 1570 and reprinted in 1601.[22] The oriental origins of the work explain why it does not overlap with the Western *Reynard the Fox* tale. But Jonson's contemporaries were more interested in it as a work of the Italian translator, Doni. Like Pietro Aretino ('But, for a desperate wit, there's Aretine!' enthuses Lady Would-Be in the play: 3.4.96), Doni had been attracted to Venice by its relatively relaxed censorship and flourishing book-trade – a feature of the city which contrasts markedly with the English climate of suspicion and 'construction' outlined by Jonson for his own writing in the Epistle. Jonson's friend, John Florio, categorized Doni's work (of which the *Moral Philosophy* was the best known) as 'fantasticall, & so strange'.[23]

The *Moral Philosophy* is a long and involved beast fable narrative, frequently interrupted by shorter, self-contained fables that comment in some way on the wider narrative. North, in his 1570 dedication of the work to the Earl of Leicester, stressed that these were indeed not 'ryding tales, spoken to no purpose', and presented them, like his Plutarch, as repositories of moral truths and maxims, particularly relevant to courtiers. He commended

this noble and pleasant Treatise, which at first sight will seeme to manye a vaine thing, treating only of Beastes: but better advised, they shall find it within full of Moralitie, examples, and government . . . Wherein you may my Lord, see into the Court, looke into the common wealth, beholde the more part of all estates and degrees: and the inferiour and common sort also maye learne, discerne, and judge what way is to be taken in the trade of their life: but Courtyers above all others attending on the Princes presence. A Glasse it is for them to looke into, and also a meete schoole to reform such schollers as by any maner of devise, practise, or subtiltie, unjustly seeke to aspire, or otherwise abuse the Prince.[24]   (sig. A3v–A4v)

For all the faux-naive charm of the beast fable, it is clearly what we should today call a political work, but too labyrinthine to summarize here. The precise parallels between it and *Volpone* are very few. Yet features of the closing sequence, suddenly involving a Foxe who has not figured in the story before and who turns out to be the king's 'chiefe Secretarie in Court and out of court' (108v), are close enough to be intriguing.

The central figure of the Moyle (mule) confesses his past treachery to the Foxe and designates him as his heir; the Foxe then betrays him, which inevitably reminds us of Mosca's double-crossing of Volpone, once the inheritance is in his grasp; the truth only emerges in the courtroom (with mordant irony) because it suits the self-interest of parties there; the Moyle's carcass is symbolically displayed, suggesting a moral closure to the tale but glibly glossing over the dangerous survival of the Foxe, just as the 'mortifying' of Volpone (5.12.125) fulfils the letter of Jonson's promise in the Epistle 'to put the snaffle in their mouths that cry out we never punish vice in our interludes' but leaves open far more complex issues of justice and accountability.

The *Moral Philosophy* is a compendium of political wisdom, rehearsing endless permutations on the relationship between a monarch and his advisers, and on matters of trust, loyalty, and deceit. Sooner or later, something in it was almost bound to parallel real events. But it also has the great virtue of being 'fantasticall, & . . . strange': no one could argue (as someone clearly did with *Mother Hubberds Tale*) that North had made it up, intending particular 'applications' to be inferred from it. Yet these tales of politic executions, treacherous alliances, threatened torture on the rack, and hoodwinked justice read like a history of Tudor-Stuart times, and their dedication to Leicester locates them in the factional politics of Elizabethan England. In such a context, the main tale of a mule who was 'Secretarie to the King of all us unreasonable beasts' must in 1570 have brought to mind Mr Secretary (William) Cecil.

By 1601 Burghley and Leicester were both dead. It is difficult to resist the suspicion that the tale of the Moyle's original treachery, betraying the Bull, 'so wyse a subject, and so grave a counseller', to his royal master, who then executed him, now brought to mind what had happened to the Earl of Essex earlier that year.[25] This would explain why someone felt there might be a new market for the old volume. And the downfall of Essex was widely blamed on his arch-enemy and the chief beneficiary of his demise, Robert Cecil. Mr Secretary Cecil may thus have seemed an even more appropriate embodiment of the treacherous mule than his father had been in the 1570s. Only a Sir Amorous La Foole would merely find the tale of 'Reynard the Fox and all the beasts' in '*Doni's Philosophy*'.

Beast fable was widely recognized as a form of coded political satire. Richard S. Peterson even suggests that 'to advise their betters and patrons in matters of conscience' in satirical works of this kind 'was a manifesto of independence and of the right of the greatest poets and writers of the land'.[26] Given the reaction of his 'betters and patrons' to his previous plays Jonson may well have felt that the form would suit his purposes if it simply afforded him deniability, fictional room within which his targets need not take offence. These two beast fables gave him different precedents in this regard: *Mother Hubberds Tale* clearly did cause offence, *Doni's Philosophy* apparently not, though it registered sufficiently to warrant an insider-joke in *Epicene*. And both were read as attacks on the Cecils (the Spenser almost certainly, Doni probably), which is hardly surprising, given the unprecedented influence they wielded in the last decades of Elizabeth's reign and the first of James'. It seems not unreasonable to read *Volpone*, the unique beast-fable play, in their light.

(iv) I next turned to consider one of the more obvious impediments to the assumption that, in *Volpone*, Jonson might be glancing at affairs in contemporary England: the fact that he had set it, with unprecedented detail and specificity, in Venice.[27] This is vouched for by reference to contemporary accounts from visitors to the city, Thomas Coryat and Fynes Moryson.[28] Jonson had read Gaspare Contarini's *The Commonwealth and Government of Venice*, as translated by Lewis Lewkenor (1599), which is cited by Sir Politic Would-Be in the play itself (4.1.40). He had also doubtless consulted Italian friends, such as the Ferrabosco brother musicians, and John Florio, whose Italian–English dictionary he used and to whom he presented a copy of the 1607 Quarto of the play, now in the British Library. The Venetian detail is, in fact, just as impressive and accurate as the Roman sources so painstakingly cited in the 1605 Quarto of *Sejanus* – and just as misleading. Something of that ambiguity is apparent, in the 1607 Quarto text at least, in the length of time Jonson delays revealing that we are in Venice at all. The folio text announces 'The Scene: Venice' on a preliminary page, but there is no such clue in the quarto. Its readers (and early audiences) had to wait until the beginning of the second act, when conversation between Peregrine and Sir Pol clarifies where they are. So we absorb the reality of the Venetian setting just as the time frame is being spelled out by Sir Pol in relation to topical events in London.

The characters clearly have Italianate names, but this may follow plays like *Every Man in His Humour*, where characters also have Italianate names, but the action is in fact set in London. Much of *Volpone*'s Venetian detail appears strategically late in the play, and is paradoxically associated with the English Would-Bes, contributing to a degree of ambiguity. This is furthered by certain features of the text which are strangely out of place in the apparent effort to produce an authentic and plausible Venice. When Volpone describes the noise made by Lady Would-Be, he says: 'The bells in time of pestilence ne'er made / Like noise, or were in

that perpetual motion; / The cockpit comes not near it' (3.5.5–7). For
Jonson's audience, *London* was the city crowded with churches whose
bells tolled ceaselessly during heavy plagues, such as that which passed in
1603/4, and its cockpits were the scene of noisy sport – not least the
Cockpit-at-court, much frequented since his accession by the king
himself. Indeed, in his very next play, *Epicene*, Jonson was to single out precisely these items as representative of the extremes of sound faced by the
noise-afflicted Morose (1.1.179–83, 4.4.13–14). That implication is all
the stronger if we detect in the phrase 'perpetual motion' an allusion
to the famous supposed perpetual motion machine devised by the Dutch
scientist Cornelius Drebbel, which was on display in the royal park at
Eltham Palace, and noisily attracting many visitors: that too is mentioned
by Morose (5.3.62–3).

   But it is the avocatori in the court scenes, of all the Venetian detail in the
play, which have caused most comment.[29] As Brian Parker puts it, in
the Introduction to his edition, Jonson was perhaps 'misled...about
the nature of the *Avocatori*, who actually functioned as prosecuting
attorneys, not as the sentencing magistrates that Jonson misrepresents'.[30]
The *Avocatori di Commun* (of whom there were three, and not four as
Jonson has it) were in fact prosecutors, not justices who handed down judgments. They would normally examine the accused, and if they found there
was no charge to answer, they could dismiss the case. But if they suspected
the accused were guilty, they would pass the case to a higher court, where
they themselves would prosecute. In their early scenes, Jonson seems to
follow the spirit of this; at the beginning of 4.5, for instance, they imply
that they are going to refer the case to the Senate:

> FIRST AVOCATORE The like of this the Senate never heard of.
> SECOND AVOCATORE 'Twill come most strange to them when
>   we report it.   (4.5.1–2)

Yet by the next scene it seems clear that judgment lies in their own hands
('You shall hear ere night / What punishment the court decrees upon 'em',
4.6.61–2), and that is certainly how it is played out in the final scenes. What
Jonson depicts there – with the avocatori both examining the case and
handing down judgments – is just such a bench of magistrates as he
himself faced while he was writing the play, in the Consistory Court on
trial for recusancy. This is an irony which would not have been lost, for
example, on Edmund Bolton (see below) and other members of the initiate
audience, such as those who wrote commendatory verses for the play.

It is commonplace to observe that Jonson located *Volpone* in Venice because of the city's associations with luxurious trade and money-making. But the Venice that Jonson in fact evokes is a place with relatively relaxed censorship laws, a key battleground in the Counter-Reformation (Sir Henry Wotton, who had recently taken up residence there as English ambassador, entertained hopes that it would turn Protestant, so robustly did it stand up to the Papacy), a place known 'for liberty of conscience' (4.2.61) – a verbal slip on the part of Lady Would-Be which in fact is very much to the point. The Venice of the play in fact mirrors the recusant Jonson's post-Gunpowder-Plot England in a striking number of ways.

(v) I have completed one other piece on *Volpone*: 'Jonson, Shakespeare, and the Exorcists' examines the climactic scene of Voltore's supposed 'possession' (5.12.21–35), Volpone's last stratagem to prevent the truth emerging in court.[31] My principal aim in this was to challenge some of the emphases in Stephen Greenblatt's widely influential 'Shakespeare and the Exorcists', arguing that Shakespeare, Jonson, and other early Jacobean dramatists were far from willing accomplices in efforts to identify the religious charisma of exorcism exclusively with theatrical deceit. Of course, Samuel Harsnett's campaigning volumes against both Puritan and Roman Catholic exorcisms, to which Greenblatt refers (*Discovery of the Fraudulent Practices of J. Darrel* (1599) and *A Declaration of Egregious Popish Impostures* (1603, reprinted 1604, 1605)), do stress quasi-theatrical fraud. But when Jonson depicts Voltore as possessed, the whole point is that there is never any doubt but that it is fraudulent, a patent attempt to prevent all of Volpone's frauds from being revealed. Jonson is not demystifying exorcism; he is demystifying the attempts of the Anglican Church to maintain its own supposed spiritual authority by 'revealing' the chicanery of other faiths.

In the end, this is of a piece with the allusions in the 1607 text to Jonson's status as a recusant, a man on trial for his faith by the Anglican authorities. As mentioned earlier, the religious policies of the era were commonly ascribed by Roman Catholics to the greed of the Cecils rather than to true conviction. The Puritan Walter Yonge records how these charges reappeared in force in the wake of the Gunpowder Plot: 'there were divers pasquils and libels cast about in London by a certain papist against the Earl of Sarum, Sir Robert Cicell, charging him to be the only match which kindled the King's displeasure against the Roman Catholics, wishing him to desist if he tendered his own life and safety. One of which he himself answered, and is extant in print'.[32] I suggest that

Volpone as a whole, from its blasphemous opening invocation to gold to its final mock-possession, reflects on a spiritual malaise that grips the whole society. And it lays the blame for it squarely at Cecil's door.

METEMPSYCHOSIS

We are now in a position to add one last argument, one last dimension, to this case. This revolves around John Donne's association with *Volpone*. He contributed the second commendatory poem in the 1607 quarto and, as I shall suggest, his poem 'Metempsychosis, or the Progress of the Soul' contributes significantly to the 'metempsychosis' entertainment in the play (1.2.1–61), a play-within-a-play which resonates throughout the wider drama. It seems clear that Donne and Jonson were particularly close in the early years of James I's reign, and that religious politics was one issue which drove them together.[33] Donne was an Anglican convert from a Catholic family that had shown conspicuous witness for its faith: on his mother's side he traced descent from the More and Heywood families, two of his uncles became Jesuits, and his brother Henry died in prison, having been caught harbouring a priest.[34] Jonson converted to Catholicism while he was in prison for killing the actor, Gabriel Spencer: 'Then took he his religion by trust of a priest who visited him in prison. Thereafter he was twelve years a papist' ('Conversations with Drummond', 204–5). Though they moved in opposite directions, they were both victims of the religious oppression of the era and very probably had similar views on the forms it took.

Donne's endorsement of *Volpone* in his Latin commendatory poem 'Amicissimo et meritissimo BEN. JONSON' (signed 'I. D'.) is thus a telling gesture. Nothing in the poem is inflammatory as such, but the phrasing is highly suggestive: 'If counsellors in the law[s] of men and God would dare follow and emulate what you have dared here in your art, Poet, O, we should all have the wisdom needed for salvation'.[35] The 'wisdom needed for salvation' is, of course, a very moot commodity, given the religious politics of the day, while the 'counsellors in the law[s] of men and God' must presumably be the politicians, lawyers, and priests who have dogged Jonson's career and recently brought him to the Consistory Court (the charges there had been 'stayed' during the summer of 1606 but never dismissed). Donne goes on to hail Jonson as one who 'hearken[s] as an innovator after those whom you will follow', that is as a classicist who nevertheless does new things with the models he imitates. This picks up on Jonson's own formulae in the Epistle and the Prologue, where he insists that 'From no needful rule

he swerveth' (Prologue, 32) and justifies the severity of the ending by appeal
to classical precedent, but suggests that the issue is not merely one of
copying the ancients. It is also one of putting their example to creative
modern uses. The poem ends: 'Genius and toil put you on a level with
the ancients; excel them, so that you may raise a new race from our
wickedness, in which we surpass both past and future ages.' Donne thus
characterizes the present age as uniquely vicious, but points to Jonson's
art as a vehicle for delivering people from it. This might, of course,
apply – with a little metaphorical licence – simply to the artistic challenge
which Jonson faces in rendering classically correct the drama of the age,
where 'nothing but ribaldry, profanation, blasphemy, all licence of offence
to God and man is practised' (Epistle, lines 34–50), in 'miscellane interludes' (line 80). But Donne strongly suggests that it is the age itself, and
not merely its drama, that Jonson may transform. If we look to see what
Donne implies is uniquely vicious about the modern age, we need also to
trace the influence of his poem, 'Metempsychosis', on Jonson's own
'metempsychosis' entertainment.

Donne's poem is a bafflingly learned and arcane work, which has tempted
critic after critic to attempt to define its genre, the circumstances of its composition, and its subject.[36] I do not intend to rehearse much of that here, but
to focus on the suggestion first made by M. van Wyk Smith, in the second
part of a two-part article, and roundly endorsed by Brian Blackley in his
doctoral dissertation on the poem, that the object of its elusive satire is
Robert Cecil.[37] Smith comes to this conclusion partly by routes that will
already seem familiar to readers of this chapter, though in fact he never
mentions Jonson or *Volpone*, and I reached my own conclusions on them
before discovering his work on Donne: 'The use of the beast fable is in
itself a clue to Donne's intentions since in 1601, the date of the poem, alle-
gorical beast satires were almost all political satires, and at least two works of
the period throw some light on Donne's poem, namely Spenser's *Mother
Hubberd's Tale* (1591) and Richard Niccol's *Beggar's Ape* (?1607)'.[38] As
we have seen, both of these poems satirize the Cecils.

Smith moves on to the tantalizing clues within 'Metempsychosis' itself
about the current identity of 'the great soule' whose transformations the
poem will relate. These are primarily found: in the Epistle which, having
declared its subject a neuter 'it', suddenly switches to the female gender,
and at the very end to the male, promising 'all her passages from her first
making when she was that aple which Eve eate, to this time when shee is
hee, whose life you shall find in the end of this booke'; in stanza 6 where
we are told that he/she has progressed from Mesopotamia (the supposed

site of Eden) to 'Thames' (line 60) or London; and in stanza 7, which is worth quoting in full:

> For the great soule which here amongst us now
> Doth dwell, and moves that hand, and tongue, and brow,
>   Which as the Moone the sea, moves us, to heare
>   Whose story, with long patience you will long;
>   (For 'tis the crowne, and last straine of my song)
>   This soule to whom *Luther*, and *Mahomet* were
>   Prisons of flesh; this soule which oft did teare,
> And mend the wracks of th'Empire, and late Rome,
>   And liv'd when every great change did come,
>   Had first in paradise, a low, but fatall roome.
>
> (lines 61–70)

Smith observes: 'This rather too obvious reference to the common idealization of the Queen as the moon (Cynthia, Diana), coupled with the sly pun on "crowne", has led most earlier critics like Gosse and Grierson to believe that the poem is an attack on Elizabeth'.[39] As he recognizes, the key ambiguity lies in 'moves'. It might imply that 'the great soule' now inhabits and animates the queen. But it might equally suggest that 'the great soule' is actually a separate force, manipulating that which manipulates us – literally, the power behind the throne, which in the wake of Essex's demise could only be Robert Cecil. This would give a very particular sense to the Epistle's 'this time when shee is hee'.

Smith goes on to outline Donne's possible reasons for animosity towards Cecil, which concur with many we have already noted in respect of Jonson – though his supposed part in Essex's downfall looms much larger and Donne never had the patron/client relationship with him that Jonson did. He describes the work as 'a series of beast satires, some referring directly to Cecil, others only glancing at him'.[40] Brian Blackley endorses all of this: 'Who better to subject to satiric scorn than the clever manipulator behind the crown?'[41] He devotes some time to examining Donne's possible politics in all of this, since Donne had never been a particular adherent of Essex's, though he had served with him on his military expedition in 1596–7; he had been more attached to Ralegh. Blackley argues that during 1599/1600 Donne and Essex were in close proximity in York House, where the earl was kept under virtual house arrest after the failure of the Irish expedition, while Donne was secretary to Sir Thomas Egerton, the Lord Keeper, whose official quarters were there (32 ff). Donne might well have developed a degree of sympathy through such close contact, and it is certain that he had at least one close friend – Henry Wotton, another interesting connection with *Volpone* – in the Essex faction.

Blackley also draws on the work of Dennis Flynn to argue that Donne's antagonism towards Cecil was not only a matter of sympathy for Essex, nor was it confined solely to 'Metempsychosis'.[42] Flynn has argued that such works as *The Courtier's Library* and *Ignatius His Conclave* are also coded libels on Cecil, both written long after Essex was dead.[43] He ascribes some of Donne's animus to his particular friendship with Henry Percy, ninth Earl of Northumberland. As Blackley summarizes: 'Building on Donne's relationship with the Earl of Northumberland, Flynn places Donne politically in direct opposition to Cecil on the basis of religious persecution and imprisonment of Northumberland for his involvement in the conspiracy behind the Gunpowder Plot'.[44] The 'Wizard Earl' of Northumberland stood in high favour at the beginning of James' reign, becoming a member of the Privy Council. Although a conforming Anglican himself, he forwarded a petition from English Catholics for toleration to James at one of his earliest meetings with the king. Unfortunately, Thomas Percy, one of the five central Gunpowder Plotters, was his kinsman and employee. He dined with Northumberland the night before the Plot was discovered, and since Percy was killed outright when government forces moved against the Plotters he could not exonerate the earl. The association was sufficient in itself to have the earl confined to the Tower of London for the next sixteen years, apparently suspected of having been the senior aristocrat whom the Plotters intended to install as Lord Protector during the minority of Princess Elizabeth, who was to be their puppet monarch.

Given Donne's attachment to Northumberland, it would be entirely logical that he should associate himself with Jonson's attack in *Volpone* on the government-inspired paranoia surrounding the Gunpowder Plot. 'Amicissimo et Meritissimo BEN. JONSON' tactfully aligns him with the play's resistance to the repression of Roman Catholics in general, such as Jonson himself and Edmund Bolton (the historian, who contributed the first of the commendatory poems), and their supposed supporters like Northumberland. Flynn, in a later article, uses the poem to associate Donne with Jonson's audacity in his dealing with these issues: 'what stands out most prominently in the poem is how much Donne admired Jonson's daring as a writer. Donne's repetition of this Latin root *aude-* in the opening lines shows, first of all, that the daring of *Volpone* is his focus, and daring is a quality we would expect him to discern'.[45]

In this article Flynn gets as close as anyone has to spelling out that Donne's presence in *Volpone* is not confined to the commendatory poem but extends to 'Metempsychosis': *and that the key point of connection is Cecil*. But he does so while his real attention is elsewhere: 'Along with several other writings by Donne, his "Metempsychosis" (mentioned by Levin in this context, but not by Tulip) also expressed an animus against Cecil, the powerful Elizabethan Privy Councilor lampooned as the latest, current repository of the serially transmigratory soul'.[46] As his parenthesis indicates, the idea that Jonson's play may draw on Donne's 'Metempsycho-sis' is not new. It goes back at least as far as an influential 1943 essay by Harry Levin.[47] But Levin's attention also was only half engaged with the borrowing from Donne. For him, metempsychosis was a resonant metaphor for a turning point in Jonson's career, which he makes the closing point of the essay: 'After *Volpone*, it may be said that Jonson's genius underwent a metempsychosis of its own and, having died with a stern satirist, was reborn in a genial observer'.[48]

In as much as Levin was interested in Jonson's specific debt to Donne, he muddied the water by following the then orthodoxy that the 'great soule' of 'Metempsychosis' has come to rest in the person of the queen: 'they darkly intimate that the soul's final destination is to be the body of Queen Elizabeth'.[49] And since Elizabeth was three years dead by the time of *Volpone* such topical allusiveness had died with her. Levin therefore assumed that Jonson's interest in Donne's poem lay in its broader themes and in helping to define his satirical mind-set: 'Donne, in choosing religion, chose the idealistic extreme of satire ... Jonson chose realism, and *Volpone* marks this crucial phase of his development . . . Jonson's animus against the Puritans had extended to the professions of medicine and law, and the whole world of finance'.[50]

No one (apart, fleetingly, from Flynn) has revisited this compelling formulation since van Wyk Smith proposed that the 'great soule' of Donne's poem resided not in Elizabeth but in Cecil, who was not only not dead but, in the wake of the Gunpowder Plot, more powerful than ever. Once we see Cecil as the key topical link between the two works, we can see that the connections are in fact much more specific than those between 'idealistic' and 'realistic' objects of satire. The issue is the perverse exploitation of religion by Cecil in pursuit of wealth and power: this parody of religion, the bare-faced worship of gold that we see in the opening moments of the play, has in fact subsumed all the institutions which normally contribute to a society's health, including politics, marriage, family, medicine, law, and trade.

Before going further we need to confront an obvious objection to this reading of the relationship between *Volpone* and Donne's poem, which is Jonson's discussion of 'Metempsychosis' with William Drummond of Hawthornden in 1618/19: 'The conceit of Donne's "Transformation" or μετεμψυοσις was that he sought the soul of that apple which Eva pulled, and thereafter made it the soul of a bitch, then of a she-wolf, and so of a woman. His general purpose was to have brought in all the bodies of the heretics from the soul of Cain, and at last left it in the body of Calvin. Of this he never wrote but one sheet, and now, since he was made doctor, repenteth highly, and seeketh to destroy all his poems' ('Conversations with Drummond', lines 97–103). As with much in the record left by the Scots laird/poet of his conversation with Jonson, we wish we knew more: what is the tone here? Just how serious was Jonson being? Did Drummond actually know the poem, which had only circulated in limited circles in manuscript, so that Donne felt able to use 'The Progress of the Soul' as the title of a very different work, the second of his 'Anniversaries' for Elizabeth Drury (published 1612)? Is it significant that this is the longest discussion of any single work in the record Drummond left?

At all events, several scholars have pointed out that Calvin will hardly do as the latest repository of 'the great soule'. For one thing, he is neither alive nor 'among us'; for another, the poem explicitly mentions Luther (1483–1546) as one embodiment of the soul, and Calvin's life (1509–64) overlapped with his, which would make literal metempsychosis impossible (the same objection would, incidentally, also preclude the erstwhile favourite candidate, Elizabeth I, born 1533; but not Cecil, born 1563). Of course there was no compulsion on Donne to be literal, nor on Jonson to remember accurately – though if I am right about the significance of Donne's poem to his own *Volpone*, it is a curious lapse. Cecil was dead and Jonson clearly felt free to disparage him to Drummond in other contexts: 'Salisbury never cared for any man longer nor he could make use of him' ('Conversations with Drummond', 297–8), and he told the tale of protesting at being seated too low on his table (264–7). All in all, I am inclined to think this was a joke at the expense of the rather earnest Drummond, perhaps prompted by some merriment at the thought of his 'daring' old friend, Donne, now a most respectable Doctor of Divinity (1614) and Reader in Divinity at Lincoln's Inn (1617). In this context a purely religious version of Donne's poem was of more currency with Jonson's host than a topical satire whose subject was six years dead.

But in 1606/7 Cecil was far from dead. And this requires us to address a point made forcefully by the historian Pauline Croft, who has done more than anyone in recent years to give proper weight to Cecil's historical standing: 'In 1606 Salisbury was still giving Jonson occasional commissions, so the likelihood that the dramatist would deliberately offend his patron seems remote. However, Jonson's intentions and the public's reading of

Volpone may well have varied. The frequent use of fox imagery in the post-humous libels [against Cecil] strengthen the view that the play was seen by the theatre-going populace as referring, however obliquely, to Salisbury'.[51] I think this slightly misses the point. Jonson doubtless had no deliberate intention of offending Cecil: the whole point of a beast-lore fable is to satirize the great and powerful while retaining deniability. And it should be said that the play *in itself* handles this quite deftly. Without the Epistle, without the commendatory poems, without even the running headers which remind us that 'Volpone' means 'The Fox', the pointers are minimal and ambiguous. When Peregrine turns to the audience, and says of Sir Politic Would-Be:

> O, this knight,
> Were he well known, would be a precious thing
> To fit our English stage: he that should write
> But such a fellow, should be thought to feign
> Extremely, if not maliciously.
>
>   (2.1.56–60)

he is playing at least one double bluff. Sir Pol does, of course, focus much of the material associated with Cecil, with his talk of plots, intelligence, concealed statesmen, spies, and so on.[52] But at the same time he is credited with features which are strongly reminiscent of Sir Henry Wotton, the ambassador in Venice, a friend of Jonson's and even closer friend of Donne's; and yet other features which point towards the colourful adventurer, Sir Anthony Shirley. As R. B. Parker puts it: 'Jonson may well have borrowed such details as the fact that Wotton had been in Venice a little over "fourteen months" (IV.i.36), was an inveterate gossip and diarist... collected ingenious "engines" and inventions (including one for preventing fire in powder magazines), and was notoriously in debt to Venetian Jews for furnishing his palazzo (cf. IV.i.40–1). Other details, however, seem closer to the career of the adventurer Sir Anthony Shirley, who tried to get the Venetians to employ him by proposing new devices of war (cf. IV.i.70ff.), then ran into trouble at Zante and Aleppo..., was kept under surveillance (and, he claimed, attacked) by agents of the English government for intriguing against the Turks' and so on.[53]

The signals are multiple, and so deniable. The target does not stand still. And it confuses matters significantly that the most obvious target, Wotton, was a friend. But it is apparent elsewhere that Jonson was prepared to subject his friends to a rough guying, as much as his enemies – and even his patrons. In *Epicene* it seems inescapable that the Collegiate Ladies are identified to a degree with the circle of powerful ladies who surrounded Queen Anne and performed with her in masques that Jonson wrote, such as *Blackness, Beauty,* and *Queens.* When Jonson has Morose exclaim 'She is my regent already! I have married a Penthesilea' (3.4.53–4), he could hardly have forgotten that he wrote the role of Penthesilea for Lucy, Countess of Bedford, in *The Masque of Queens,* barely a year earlier. Since Lucy Bedford was a serious patron of writers, and courted as such by both Donne and Jonson, one has to assume that Jonson would have expected this to be taken in good part – as indeed he expected King James to appreciate the joke of Justice Overdo in *Bartholomew Fair* railing against tobacco and seeking out enormities in disguise. These were the kind of familiarities which went with being the court poet which, in 1606, Jonson was in the process of becoming. And he must have known that he owed much of that opportunity to Cecil, who individually patronized him several times.

But the situation with Cecil and *Volpone* is different in kind and degree from this 'rough guying': if Sir Pol's conversation inevitably sometimes puts us in mind of Cecil, his association with the play by no means ends with Sir Pol (as does that of Wotton and Shirley). In the most sophisticated analysis we have of Cecil's patronage of Jonson, James Knowles argues that it was the specific nature of the patronage relationship there that irked Jonson: 'In short, Cecilian patronage operated precisely the type of arrangement which infringed Jonson's sense of the poet's demesne, and although Jonson was designated "the Poett" in several of the Hatfield bills, Cecil's "device", "conceit", and "invention" of his entertainments usurped the poetic function, which lay in the creation of the "soul" of the masque'.[54] This seems more than likely, but it does not preclude the possibility that there was also a level of political/religious resentment in Jonson's relations with Cecil (which dated back to his imprisonment over the lost *Isle of Dogs* in 1597), compounding his grievances as a poet, though it would have been necessary to keep any hint of this out of their face-to-face dealings. Indeed, the Epistle to *Volpone,* insisting on both the integrity and the independence of the poet, while simultaneously acknowledging his submission both to classical precedents in writing and to the state's judgment of what was fit, seems to reflect just such a mind-set.

If we may allow ourselves some moments of pure speculation, it is surely reasonable to reflect that the play as a whole is about patron/client relations, albeit very different ones from those involved in Jonson's employment as a poet. Volpone is patron to a string of suitor clients, who seek to please him. If there is a sense in which Volpone represents Cecil, there must also be a

sense in which Voltore, Corbaccio, and Corvino represent Jonson himself,
prepared to prostitute himself in any way to gain an advantage. It has
become quite commonplace to regard Volpone's performance as Scoto of
Mantua, a mountebank selling early modern equivalents of snake oil, as
Jonson's wry reflection on his own role as a popular dramatist, ingratiating
himself with another form of paying patron. But we need to recognize how
many forms of patronage are in play at this moment in Jonson's career, and
may manifest themselves in as charged a work as this. Thinking specifically
of Cecil/Jonson, the most intriguing relationship in the play is that of
Volpone and Mosca, patron and parasite/client. At the end of the 'metempsychosis' show, Volpone asks:

>   Now, very, very pretty! Mosca, this
> Was thy invention?
> MOSCA If it please my patron,
> Not else.
> VOLPONE It doth, good Mosca.
> MOSCA Then it was, sir.
>
>   (1.2.63–5)

Mosca is the playwright who only admits to authorship 'if it please my
patron'. From that point on, it is difficult not to read the emerging struggle
between them as Jonson's imaginary turning on the patron he undoubtedly
resented, even as he recognized the need he had of him.

    Jonson told Drummond that 'He hath consumed a whole night in lying
looking at his great toe, about which he had seen Tartars and Turks,
Romans and Carthaginians, fight in his imagination' ('Conversations
with Drummond', lines 268–70). For some reason this appears between
the anecdote about resenting being sat at the lower end of Cecil's table
and that about Northampton accusing him of popery and treason over
Sejanus. I can't help feeling that Jonson's imagination played in that way
about what he would do with the patrons he resented, if he had the
chance, and that in *Volpone* he got as close to it as he ever would. The
next anecdote but one is: 'He hath a mind to be a churchman, and so he
might have favour to make one sermon to the king. He careth not what
th[e]r[e]after should befall him; for he would not flatter, though he saw
death' (lines 276–8). The dream of unmediated, uncensored speech is
one which must have haunted a man like Jonson, trapped in a world of
patronage compromise. Ironically, by the time Jonson spoke to Drummond,
his old friend Donne, a royal chaplain, had every opportunity to deliver
sermons to the king, but never used the opportunity in quite that way: in

his own way, he was just as trapped within the patronage bind. Jonson himself certainly never escaped it. But in *Volpone* he subjected it to every imaginary indignity he could muster.

CONCLUSIONS

We may conclude, therefore, that Jonson's use of a 'metempsychosis' show in *Volpone* is a conscious allusion to Donne's poem on this theme, that he expects his initiate readers to recognize as much (the numbers of those with knowledge of Donne's poem would always have been limited), and that he further expects them to recognize Cecil as the key linking feature. When we look at the 'show' itself, there is little verbal overlap with Donne's poem, beyond the Pythagorean argot, which in both instances acts as a mystifying smoke-screen, a necessary gesture towards deniability. But it is possible that Donne's poem explains one specific feature: the soul of Pythagoras comes to rest not in Nano, who recites the show and who (as the 'pretty little ape') may himself remind people of Cecil, nor in Volpone himself, but in Androgyno, another of Volpone's reputed 'bastards'. It is widely understood that this downward trajectory encapsulates the whole theme of moral and physical degeneration so central to the play, but why specifically does the 'soul' come to rest in a hermaphrodite? Mystic hermaphroditism had a role in Pythagorean numerology (odd numbers were male, even female) so it is not entirely unexpected. But is it also an allusion to the gender play, 'this time when shee is hee', in Donne's poem?

Be that as it may, the show itself is based on Lucian's parody of Pythagorean thought in his *Dream, or The Cock*, with some details from Diogenes Laertius' account of Pythagoras. But there are moments when it veers into unmistakably modern reference:

[NANO.]   but I
    Would ask how of late thou hast suffered translation,
    And shifted thy coat in these days of reformation?
ANDROGYNO. Like one of the reformed, a fool, as you see,
    Counting all old doctrine heresy.

and   (28–32)

[ANDROGYNO.] Into a very strange beast, by some writers called an ass;
By others a precise, pure, illuminate brother
Of those devour flesh, and sometimes one another,
And will drop you forth a libel, or a sanctified lie,
Betwixt every spoonful of a Nativity Pie.

                                                          (42–6)

This puts us squarely in the world of post-Reformation religious controversy, in which the transmigratory soul inhabits firstly a Protestant, 'Count-
ing all old doctrine heresy' (a line which presumably amused the Catholic
Jonson and his confidants), and latterly a strict Puritan ('a precise, pure,
illuminate brother'), who is clearly parodied for his self-righteous conviction
of his own election, and for his prissy refusal to say 'Christmas' (with its
resonance of the Catholic 'mass').

But it is the reference to 'those devour flesh, and sometimes one
another' that lifts this above conventional Puritan-baiting and extends
the Pythagorean ban on eating 'forbid meats' (33) into a metaphor of
cannibalism, a theme which pervades the play.[55] In terms of Christian doctrine, 'forbid meats' and 'devouring flesh' clearly refers to the Eucharist –
consuming the bread and wine in commemoration of Christ's body
and blood, as enjoined in the Last Supper.[56] But the significance of that
act – whether it involved the transubstantiation of the body and blood
or not – had been central points of contention in the Reformation.
Jonson, as a Roman Catholic, was not legally permitted to take the Mass
of his own church (distinctive from that of the Anglican because ordinary
communicants only took it in one kind: i.e. the wine, but not the bread;
Anglicans took it in both kinds). Conversely, he was required to take
Anglican communion at least once a month – his failure to do that since
James' accession is what led to his arraignment (along with Edmund
Bolton and eighteen others) in the Consistory Court.

As R. B. Parker points out, the lines on devouring flesh do not only bring
to mind the Eucharist; they also echo St Paul's warning to the Galatians:
'But if ye bite and consume one another, take heed that ye be not consumed
one of another'.[57] These lines thus invoke the post-Reformation situation in
which Christians consumed one another in the name of their respective
faiths, a situation that the Gunpowder Plot seemed bound to seal in
place in England for generations to come. And the man that most Catholics
blamed for that was Robert Cecil.

Tracing topical allusions of this kind in early modern plays is often like
chasing a will-o-the-wisp: we glance them fleetingly, with what seems perfect
conviction, only to have them disappear and leave us incapable of convincing others of their existence. Given their authors' need for deniability,
this is inevitable. But the quarto of *Volpone* gives the initiate reader better
access to such a reading than any other text of the era: the Epistle, with
Jonson's coded *apologia* for his life so far, as both poet and Catholic
(coupled with the unmistakable note of triumph that this play had received
wide approbation, including that of the universities, rather than censorship

and official scrutiny); the commendatory poems, which remind us of his recusant status as they celebrate Jonson's audacious use of classical forms and his fox-like escape from his enemies; the constant reminders in the page-headers that Volpone is 'The Foxe' (something the play on-stage only really stresses in the final act). All of these alert us to the significance of those elements of the play-in-performance we have already discussed, including its beast-fable format, Sir Pol, and Nano, and the emphasis on a world of diseased spirituality: possession, exorcism, and religious cannibalism. And they all point in the same direction: at Robert Cecil and the ongoing *regnum Cecilianum*, the apparent architect and beneficiary of the parlous state of English Catholics in the wake of the Gunpowder Plot.

The presence of Donne's commendatory poem, which alerts us to Jonson's debt to Donne in his own 'metempsychosis' text, is thus a last link in a very solid chain. The malignant 'great soule' whom Donne so obliquely satirized in 1601 has been reincarnated on the stage in 1606, more powerful and more spiritually dangerous than ever – not in a single character, but refracted through so many facets of the text. In reaching this conclusion, I am tempted to one further speculation: that this target at the heart of the play helps to explain the bleakness and severity of the play's ending. As early as 1668 Dryden complained in *An Essay of Dramatick Poesie* that 'there appears two actions in the Play; the first, naturally ending with the fourth Act; the second forc'd from it in the fifth'.[58] Later commentators have asked why Volpone and Mosca do not simply quit at the end of Act 4, or again when Volpone agrees to share the wealth with Mosca (5.12.67), allowing for a relatively genial New Comedy ending (more akin to that of *The Alchemist*) in which justice of a sort is done and the tricksters get to enjoy some of the spoils.

Instead we get a remorseless, competitive drive towards self-destruction, with an outcome about which Jonson is quite emphatic in the Epistle: 'And though my catastrophe may in the strict rigour of comic law meet with censure as turning back to my promise, I desire the learned and charitable critic to have so much faith in me to think it was done of industry . . . my special aim being to put the snaffle in their mouths that cry out we never punish vice in our interludes &c.' (lines 100–7). As a true classicist he claims models for this among the ancients, though in fact he significantly exaggerates – and must know he exaggerates – the precedents. And he produces a conclusion in which the Avocatori impose strict Venetian justice (laced with personal pique at having been deceived) on all those who have erred. He does not even, as Coleridge famously lamented, engineer a romance between Celia and Bonario. It was for these reasons that Northrop Frye described the play as 'a kind of comic imitation of a tragedy', pushing the bounds of comedy to the very limits.[59] Yet that is appropriate if what is at issue in the play is not merely swindling, or greed, or perjury, but the perversion of a society's soul. When Jonson condemned Volpone to the Hospital for the Incurabili 'to lie in prison, cramped with irons / Till thou be'st sick and lame indeed' (5.12.123–4) there must have been a deep psychological satisfaction in 'mortifying' this particular fox – even as the realist in him knows that foxes in beast fables are never finally vanquished, and indeed Volpone will rise again to speak the Epilogue, with all its ironies:

> Now, though the Fox be punished by the laws,
>   He yet doth hope there is no suff'ring due
>   For any fact which he hath done 'gainst you.

(lines 2–4)

NOTES

1. See, for example, Pauline Croft, 'The Reputation of Robert Cecil: Libels, Political Opinion and Popular Awareness in the Early Seventeenth Century', *Transactions of the Royal Historical Society* 1 (1991): 43–68; James Knowles, '"To raise a house of better frame": Jonson's Cecilian Entertainments', in *Patronage, Culture and Power: The Early Cecils*, ed. Pauline Croft, Studies in British Art 8 (New Haven: Yale Center for British Art and Yale University Press; London: Paul Mellon Centre for Studies in British Art, 2002), 181–95; Dennis Flynn, 'Donne's "*Amicissimo, et Meritissimo Ben: Jonson*" and the Daring of *Volpone*', *The Literary Imagination* 6 (2004): 368–89.
2. References to Jonson's poems and to the 'Conversations with William Drummond of Hawthornden' are to the editions in *Ben Jonson*, ed. Ian Donaldson, The Oxford Authors (Oxford University Press, 1985).
3. Richard Dutton, *Ben Jonson: To the First Folio* (Cambridge University Press, 1983), all quotations 152.
4. I wish to acknowledge here the work of James Tulip in 'Comedy as Equivocation: An Approach to the Reference of *Volpone*', *Southern Review* 5 (1972): 91–101, and 'The Contexts of *Volpone*', in *Imperfect Apprehensions: Essays in English Literature in Honour of G. A. Wilkes*, ed. Geoffrey Little (Sydney: Challis Press, 1996), 74–87. His early essay covers some of the same territory as my chapter in *Ben Jonson: To the First Folio* (which in fact was first drafted in my doctoral dissertation, 1971), but I did not know of it until long after my book was published – a consequence, I fear, of separate hemispheres in the days before the Internet. It adds a distinctive emphasis on 'equivocation', a key issue in suspicion of Jesuits at the time, to some of the points I had raised. Like my own chapter, however, a good deal of it is inevitably speculative.

5. References to *Volpone* and its paratextual matter are to the Revels Plays edition by R. B. Parker, rev. edn (Manchester University Press, 1999).

6. In *Refashioning Ben Jonson: Gender, Politics, and the Jonsonian canon*, edited by Julie Sanders, with Kate Chedgzoy and Susan Wiseman (Basingstoke: MacMillan, 1998), 114–33.

7. See, for example, James D. Redwine Jr, *Ben Jonson's Literary Criticism* (Lincoln: University of Nebraska Press, 1971).

8. See *Ben Jonson*, ed. C. H. Herford and P. and E. Simpson, 11 vols. (Oxford: Clarendon Press, 1925–52), I, 220–2.

9. Quoted from the Revels Plays *Eastward Ho!*, edited by R. W. Van Fossen (Manchester University Press, 1979), Appendix 2, 218–25, 221.

10. It is often thought that Jonson's patron, Esmé Stuart, Lord D'Aubigny (possibly the 'E. S.' of one of *Volpone*'s commendatory poems), or the Lord Treasurer, the Earl of Dorset, who sent Jonson wine after his release, eased his way out of prison. But we do not know the details.

11. Richard Dutton, '*Volpone* and Beast Fable: Early Modern Analogic Reading', *Huntington Library Quarterly* 67 (2004): 347–70.

12. See R. B. Parker, '*Volpone* and *Reynard the Fox*', *Renaissance Drama* 7 (1976): 3–42.

13. See James A. Riddell and Stanley Stewart, *Jonson's Spenser: Evidence and Historical Criticism* (Pittsburgh: Duquesne University Press, 1995).

14. See Richard S. Peterson, 'Laurel Crown and Ape's Tail: New Light on Spenser's Career from Sir Thomas Tresham', *Spenser Studies* 12 (1998): 1–31: 10–12 and notes 14 and 15; also Peter Beal, *Index of English Literary Manuscripts*, 4 vols. (London and New York: Mansell, 1980), I, pt 2, 527–8.

15. On this theme, see Stephen J. Greenblatt, 'The False Ending in *Volpone*', *Journal of English and Germanic Philology* 75 (1976): 90–104.

16. *Yale Edition of the Shorter Poems of Edmund Spenser*, ed. William Oram, Einar Bjorvand, and Ronald Bond (New Haven: Yale University Press, 1989), 327.

17. Croft, 'The Reputation of Robert Cecil', 48, 46.

18. See, for example, Richard Verstegen's *A Declaration of the True Cause of the Great Troubles, Presupposed to be Intended against the Realme of England* (Antwerp, 1592).

19. Richard Niccols, *Beggars Ape*, Scholars' Facsimiles and Reprints (New York, 1936), with a postscript by Brice Harris.

20. See Riddell and Stewart, *Jonson's Spenser*, 53.

21. Ben Jonson, *Epicene, or The Silent Woman*, ed. Richard Dutton, The Revels Plays (Manchester University Press, 2003), 4.4.80–8. All quotations from *Epicene* come from this edition.

22. The history of the work is very ably outlined by Joseph Jacobs in the introduction to his edition (the most recent) of the North translation, more accurately entitled *The Fables of Bidpai* (London, 1888).

23. John Florio, *Epistle Dedicatorie* to his *A Worlde of Wordes* (London, 1598), A45. The freedoms enjoyed by Aretino and Doni had been somewhat curtailed over the next half century, under various Counter-Reformation

pressures. But Venice, the last part of Italy not dominated by Austro-Spanish influence, and notoriously independent of the papacy, remained in practice one of the freest environments for writers in Europe.

24. Cited from the Huntington Library's copy of the 1570 edition (Doni, *Moral Philosophy*, trans. Thomas North (London, 1570)).

25. The rights to the book were assigned on 31 May 1594 to J. Roberts, who presumably employed S. Stafford to print the 1601 edition. According to the STC it is possible that there were two imprints of that edition (see #3054 and #3054.5).

26. Peterson, 'Laurel Crown and Ape's Tail', 19.

27. See my 'Venice in London, London in Venice', in *Mighty Europe 1400–1700: Writing an Early Modern Continent*, ed. Andrew Hiscock (Oxford, Bern and New York: Peter Lang, 2007): 133–51.

28. See, for example, R. B. Parker, 'Jonson's Venice', in *Theatre of the English and Italian Renaissance*, ed. J. R. Mulryne and M. Shewring (Basingstoke: Macmillan, 1991), 95–112; and David McPherson, *Shakespeare, Jonson, and the Myth of Venice* (Newark: University of Delaware Press, 1991). *Coryat's Crudities* was published in 1611, and based on travels after *Volpone* was written. Moryson travelled in the 1590s; much of his *Itinerary* was published in 1617, though the portion on Venice was not published until Charles Hughes brought out *Shakespeare's Europe* (London, 1903).

29. See Richard M. Perkinson, '*Volpone* and the Reputation of Venetian Justice', *Modern Language Review* 35 (1940): 11–18; Daniel C. Boughner, 'Lewkenor and *Volpone*', *Notes and Queries* n.s. 9 (1962): 124–30; G. J. Gianakaras, 'Jonson's Use of "Avocatori" in *Volpone*', *English Language Notes* 12 (1974): 8–14.

30. Parker, introduction to his edition of *Volpone*, 19.

31. Richard Dutton, 'Jonson, Shakespeare, and the Exorcists', *Shakespeare Survey* 58 (2005): 15–22.

32. *The Diary of Walter Yonge, Esq*, ed. George Roberts, Camden Society 41 (London, 1848), 2–3. Cecil's response to the libel is *An Answere to Certaine Scandalous Papers, Scattered abroad vnder Colour of a Catholicke Admonition* (London: imprinted by Robert Barker, 1606). Pauline Croft suggests that Cecil was not personally ill-disposed towards the Catholics: see 'The Religion of Robert Cecil', *Historical Journal* 34 (1991): 773–96; 783 ff. My point is about the perception of Cecil and his policies at the time, especially by recusant Catholics themselves.

33. See the Introduction to my edition of *Epicene*, cited above, 10–42.

34. See Dennis Flynn, *John Donne and the Ancient Catholic Nobility* (Bloomington and Indianapolis: Indiana University Press, 1995).

35. I follow the translation offered by R. B. Parker in the Revels edition of the play (72).

36. A select list of criticism on Donne's 'Metempsychosis' includes W. A. Murray, 'What Was the Soul of the Apple?', *Review of English Studies* 38 (1959): 141–55; Janel M. Mueller, 'Donne's Epic Venture in "Metempsychosis"', *Modern*

Philology 70 (1972): 109–37; Karl P. Wentersdorf, 'Symbol and Meaning in Donne's "Metempsychosis or the Progresse of the Soule"', *Studies in English Literature* 22 (1982): 69–90; Ronald J. Corthell, 'Donne's "Metempsychosis": An "Alarum to Truth"', *Studies in English Literature* 21 (1981): 97–110; John Klause, 'The Montaigneity of Donne's "Metempsychosis"', in *Renaissance Genres: Essays on Theory, History and Interpretation*, ed. Barbara Lewalski (Cambridge MA: Harvard University Press, 1986), 418–43; Kenneth Gross, 'John Donne's Lyric Skepticism: In Strange Way', *Modern Philology* 101 (2004): 371–99.

37. M. van Wyk Smith, 'John Donne's "Metempsychosis"', *Review of English Studies* 24 (1973): 17–25, 141–52; Brian M. Blackley, 'The Generic Play and Spenserian Parody of John Donne's "Metempsychosis"', unpublished dissertation, University of Kentucky, 1994.
38. Smith, 'John Donne's "Metempsychosis"', 141.
39. *Ibid.*, 143.
40. *Ibid.*, 148.
41. Blackley, 'Generic Play', 32.
42. See Dennis Flynn, 'Donne's *Ignatius His Conclave* and Other Libels on Sir Robert Cecil', *John Donne Journal* 6 (1987): 163–83.
43. *Ibid.*, 167; 177.
44. Blackley, *Generic Play*, 70.
45. Flynn, 'Donne's "*Amicissimo, et Meritissimo Ben: Jonson*"', 374.
46. *Ibid.*, 382. Flynn is actually discussing James Tulip's 'Comedy as Equivocation', cited above. Tulip proposes correspondences between Cecil and Sir Politic Would-Be, but does not mention 'Metempsychosis'.
47. Harry Levin, 'Jonson's Metempsychosis', *Philological Quarterly* 22 (1943): 231–9.
48. *Ibid.*, 239.
49. *Ibid.*, 236.
50. *Ibid.*, 237.
51. Croft, 'The Reputation of Robert Cecil', 57.
52. See Tulip, 'Comedy as Equivocation', passim.
53. Parker, Introduction to his edition of *Volpone*, 20–1.
54. Knowles, '"To Raise a House of Better Frame"', 188.
55. See E. B. Partridge, *The Broken Compass* (London: Chatto and Windus, 1958), 105–10.
56. Modern readers might assume that 'forbid meats' refers to the ban on eating meat on Fridays and during Lent, which is now strongly associated with Catholicism. But at the time Anglicans and Catholics both observed such fasts.
57. Galatians v. 14–15; Parker, Introduction to his edition of *Volpone*, 30.
58. Cited, with modern typography, from the 1668 edition of the *Essay* in the Stanley J. Kahrl Collection at Ohio State University, 42.
59. Northrop Frye, *An Anatomy of Criticism* (Princeton University Press, 1957), 165.

CHAPTER 7

Jonson's humanist tragedies

Tom Cain

The first plays that Jonson chose to preserve in the 1616 *Workes* were the comedies *Every Man In His Humour*, *Every Man Out of His Humour*, *Cynthia's Revels*, and *Poetaster*. Only after these four came his first extant tragedy, *Sejanus his Fall*. Another seven years, and three major comedies, passed before he wrote his second and last tragedy, *Catiline*. If one adds the plays published after 1616, the proportion of comedy to tragedy in Jonson's oeuvre is (ignoring the fragment *Mortimer*) fifteen to two. Such a figure seems decisive, and certainly reinforces statistically the consensus regarding Jonson's dramatic strengths and weaknesses.

And yet the picture it paints of the early part of Jonson's career at least is a false one. From the time of his first appearance as a dramatist sometime in the early 1590s, up to and beyond his success with *Every Man In* (1598) and *Every Man Out* (1599), Jonson was best known, and probably saw himself, as primarily a writer of tragedies. It was as a tragedian that he was praised in 1598 by Francis Meres:

[S]o these are our best for Tragedie, the Lord Buckhurst, Doctor Leg of Cambridge, Docter Edes of Oxford, master Edward Ferres, the Authour of the Mirrour for Magistrates, Marlow, Peele, Watson, Kid, Shakespeare, Drayton, Chapman, Decker, and Beniamin Iohnson.[1]

Of these names, only Shakespeare and Chapman recur where we would expect to find Jonson, in Meres' 'best for Comedy' category. Meres alone might be dismissed as poorly informed, were his classification not confirmed by John Weever's epigram, probably written at much the same date, 'late 1598 or 1599',[2] which praises Jonson's 'embuskin'd' (tragic) muse which 'doth retaine / So rich a stile, and wondrous gallant spirit'.[3]

It is impossible to say what plays Meres and Weever had in mind in this classification. Of the tragedies we can infer Jonson had written before 1598 not even the titles survive. Only an early version of a later-revised comedy, *The Case is Altered*, and the lost satire *The Isle of Dogs* (1597) are known from this period of his career. But a slightly later sequence of lost collaborative plays written between August 1598 and September 1599 is found in *Henslowe's Diary*: *Hot Anger Soon Cold*, a comedy, with Porter and Chettle (payment August 1598); *The Lamentable Tragedy of Page of Plymouth*, with Dekker (August/September 1599); and *Robert II, King of Scots*, with Dekker, Chettle, and an unnamed 'Jentellman' (September 1599). In October 1598 Henslowe also advanced £4 to Chapman for a 'play boocke & ij ectes of A tragedie of bengemens plotte' (100).[4] Given the dates, it is unlikely that Meres or Weever had any of these plays in mind. Their praise of Jonson, moreover, implies single authorship; there must, therefore, have been enough tragedies with Jonson's name as sole author before 1598 to have established his reputation as one of 'our best for Tragedie', an 'embuskin'd' playwright rather than one characterized by comedy's 'learned sock', as Milton was to remember him in the 1630s.[5]

September 1598, the month in which Meres' book was entered for publication, saw the first play in the sequence which was to change posterity's (though not, perhaps, his own) characterization of Jonson so fundamentally. At almost the same date as *Hot Anger* would have been ready for the Lord Admiral's Men, *Every Man In* was making a bigger impression on its first performances by the Lord Chamberlain's Men. In 1599, autumn performances of *Page of Plymouth* and/or *Robert II* may well have clashed with the first performances of *Every Man Out* at the new Globe. Jonson had begun writing tragedies for Alleyn and comedies for Burbage to perform simultaneously. One of the attractions of writing for the Lord Chamberlain's Men may have been that they were willing to take a risk with a new kind of satirical comedy. Another may have been Burbage's acting style, reputedly more sophisticated than that of Alleyn. There were, though, more fundamental reasons for the change of direction, reasons which ultimately led to the very different kind of Roman tragedies he was to write in 1603 and 1611. Within two days of the first performance of the successful but relatively conventional comedy *Every Man In*, Jonson was charged with the murder of an actor in the Lord Admiral's company. His narrow escape from the death penalty through pleading benefit of clergy left him, in October 1598, free, but a convicted felon, which meant not just that he had his thumb branded, but that his property was forfeit to the state. The episode is known to have prompted a reassessment of his spiritual position – he converted to Catholicism while in Newgate – but the brush with death seems also to have initiated a wider re-evaluation of his identity as a writer, and with it a programme of study in classical literature. When his books were burnt in 1623 he wrote with great specificity that among his lost papers were the fruits of 'twice-twelve-yeares' stor'd-up humanitie' ('Execration Upon Vulcan', *Underwood* 43, line 101), a calculation which takes us back to 1599, just after his trial. Such self-improvement does not figure in the lives of his collaborators at that time, Dekker and Chettle,[6] and it bespeaks an aspiration, following his escape from hanging, to refashion himself as a humanist writer who would hence-forth use the stage to 'raise the dispis'd head of Poetry againe . . . and render her worthy to be imbraced, and kist, of all the great and Maister Spirits of our World' (*Volpone*, 'Epistle'). Such a role entailed political as well as broadly moral reformist responsibilities.

The twin traumas of the murder conviction and the confiscation of his property were probably not the only incentives for this change of direction. The return to London in 1598 of his wealthy Westminster school-friend Robert Cotton, to rejoin his and Jonson's former teacher William Camden in the relaunch of the Society of Antiquaries, meant that Jonson had from the time of his murder trial onwards the support and stimulus of two authoritative scholars, and the resources of Cotton's growing library. Jonson had left Westminster around the age of fifteen, before his Latin (and certainly his Greek) education under Camden had been completed. By that stage he would have read, among others, Cicero, Plautus, Terence, Lucian, Ovid, and Horace, all of whom make an impact of some sort in the comical satires of 1599–1601.[7] By 1602–3, however, he had also read Tacitus (whose Latin can be difficult), Claudian, Livy, Juvenal, and (mainly in Latin translation) Dio Cassius, a Roman his-torian who wrote in Greek.[8] Tacitus was read in Lipsius' edition, and Jonson probably also read Lipsius' *Politicorum* at this time,[9] along with Machiavelli's *Principe* and *Discorsi* (neither then translated into English). It is reasonable to suppose that Camden and Cotton had advised on this choice of reading. Machiavelli influenced both men, and Camden had been in contact with Lipsius since sending him a copy of *Britannia* in 1586; Cotton probably also knew Lipsius, and certainly admired his work.[10] The triumvirate of Jonson, Camden, and Cotton is well known from the striking anecdote Jonson told Drummond of the vision of his dead son while staying with Cotton in 1603 ('Conversations with Drum-mond', lines 214–24; Herford and Simpson, *Ben Jonson*, I, 139–40); but the wider creative significance of their friendship throughout Jonson's early career has probably never been fully appreciated. Two small examples pertain to *Sejanus*: an undated letter to Cotton of 1602–3 asks for 'some book' on the geography of the Campania, presumably with reference to Tiberius' journey (*Sejanus*, 3.669–73).[11] As for Camden, a major source for *Sejanus* is Barnabé Brisson's *De formulis, et sollemnibus populi Romani verbis* (Paris, 1583) from which many references to classical sources are taken (and shamelessly cited by Jonson as if directly from the original). Brisson's book also transcribes Roman inscriptions, whose typography probably suggested the striking upper-case type used in the 1605 quarto of *Sejanus*. Brisson had contacted Camden, whom he much admired, a few years earlier, and it was probably through him that Jonson came to Brisson's work, as well as that of such antiquarians of Rome as Panvinius, Turnebus, Stuckius, and Rosinus. It may also have been Camden or Cotton who introduced Jonson to Henry Savile, the translator of Tacitus, and John Hayward, whose controversial *Henry IIII* (1599) was one of the first Tacitean treatments of English history.[12] In his Roman tragedies, Jonson saw himself as a historian like them, making 'truth of argument' the first requirement of tragedy in the prefatory epistle to *Sejanus*. These were not to be plays of great psychological complexity, nor would their protagonists be particularly heroic. Their profundity would lie in the questions they raised about the business of government and the dynamics of power, past and present. Jonson wished to treat in drama the subject matter he describes as the historian's in his poem to Savile, and to do so with the intellectual qualities of the ideal historian adumbrated there:[13]

> We need a man, can speake of the intents,
> The counsells, actions, orders, and events
> Of State, and censure them: we need his pen
> Can write the things, the causes, and the men.
> But most we need is faith (and all have you)
> That dares not write things false, nor hide things true.
>
> (lines 31–6)

Robert Cotton and another Westminster school friend, Hugh Holland, may have been the links to another, overlapping group who were equally important to Jonson's development, and his humanist literary ambitions. This was the coterie which centred on John Donne, Richard Martyn, and John Hoskyns, whom Jonson was later to acknowledge as the literary 'father' who 'polished' him.[14] For a young, ambitious writer who lacked both their education and social advantages, this group formed a demanding but creative audience, and it was them, and through them the wider Inns of Court audience, whom Jonson addressed in the sequence of comical satires that defined his new persona. They epitomized that élite audience to whom he continued to appeal for the rest of his career, often to the detriment of his theatrical success, since almost any dramatic longeurs could be justified by arguing that an intelligent and educated minority would appreciate 'a whole oration of Tacitus' (Jonson, 'Conversations with Drummond', line 528; Herford and Simpson, *Ben Jonson*, I, 149) or Cicero. They were also politically active: Donne, Martyn, Cotton, and John Davies were MPs by 1601, and Hoskyns and Christopher Brooke by 1604. Most spoke against what they saw as excessive use of prerogative powers in such matters as monopolies, and, under James I, against encroachments on the liberties of Parliament and the Common Law by king and church. As will be seen, Jonson's plays during this period show him moving towards a similar political position, involving freedom of speech and limit-ation of the absolute powers of the monarch.

By the end of *Poetaster* Jonson felt that his experiment in comic satire had failed, and that since comedy had 'proved so ominous' he would 'try / If Tragedy have a more kind aspect' (*Poetaster*, 'Apologetical Dialogue', 210–11). The result was *Sejanus*, whose bleak view of imperial Rome seems to follow on logically enough from the relatively optimistic, but much less historically accurate, picture of it in *Poetaster*. But Jonson did not turn to Rome immediately; instead he went back to the kind of tragedy he had probably been writing in the 1590s, with a series of additions to Kyd's *Spanish Tragedy*, then being dusted off for a revival by the Admiral's Men in their new Fortune Theatre. Work began almost as soon as *Poetaster* was finished, in September 1601. Henslowe paid for more 'additions' the following year, plus an advance for a new tragedy, *Richard Crookback*, now lost (if ever finished).[15] While it is difficult to see how the speeches written for Hieronimo could have fitted Jonson's new, sophisticated persona, *Richard Crookback* is another matter. Although at first sight it sounds like another product of the 1590s for Alleyn, Richard was the subject of serious attention from English humanists. It was probably in 1602, with *Richard Crookback* in mind, that Jonson read Thomas More's Latin *History of Richard III*,[16] while one of the university tragedians in Meres' list, Thomas Legge, is there because of his tragedy, *Richardus Tertius* (1579). Camden and Cotton were both committed to the writing of English history,[17] and would have regarded More (and probably Legge) as worthy models. More's history is heavily influenced by Tacitus, as was the work of his near-contemporary Machiavelli. Both the latter were major influences on *Sejanus*, but neither is found in *Poetaster*, or any earlier play of Jonson's. The inference must be that Jonson read them in 1601–2, perhaps inspired by his reading of More for *Richard Crookback*.

More and Machiavelli, like Lipsius, Camden, Cotton, and other huma-nist historians, compared 'ancient and modern events' so that readers could 'more easily draw those practical lessons (*quella utilità*) which one should seek to obtain from the study of history'.[18] In all three of his Roman plays Jonson was to attempt precisely that, dramatizing Rome in the crucial late republican and early imperial period, from 63 BC to AD 31, for the light it could shed on his own political and social milieu. In doing this, however, he did not turn to Rome, even in *Poetaster*, as a paragon to be imitated. For most of these humanist historians Rome, while it was a sophisticated and wealthy society whose 'women weare / The spoiles of nations, in an eare' (*Catiline*, 1.1.555–6), was also a deeply troubled one under constant threat of destruction from within itself, whether by civil war, conspiracy, or corruption. Lipsius had in fact first turned to Tacitus in order to help make sense of the Dutch wars of religion. Jonson had played a brief part in those wars, possibly because he sympathized with the liberties for which the Dutch rebels were fighting.[19] At home the armed conflict over ancient liberties (their doubtful existence ratified by such scholarly friends of Jonson as Cotton and Selden) did not come for another four decades, but Jonson saw close similarities between the corrupt Rome described by Tacitus and Sallust and the state of England under Elizabeth and, increasingly, James I.

Jonson's view of Elizabeth's regime, at least in its final years, was highly critical. Chettle noted that he failed to write anything on the queen's death.[20] He wrote instead in welcome of the new king, of whose learning and tolerance he, like Camden and Cotton, had high hopes. *The King's Entertainment* of March 1604 praised James for having 'made men see / Once more the face of welcome libertie' (lines 597–8; Herford and Simpson, *Ben Jonson*, VII, 102), the obvious implication being that such liberty had not been visible under Elizabeth. Jonson elaborates on 'the former age's stain' in language that is strongly reminiscent of *Sejanus*:

> Now innocence shall cease to be the spoyle
> Of ravenous greatnesse . . .
> No more shall rich men (for their little good)
> Suspect to be made guiltie, or vile spies
> Enioy the lust of their so murdring eyes.
> Men shall put off their yron minds, and hearts;
> The time forget his old malicious arts
> With this new minute, and no print remayne
> Of what was thought the former age's stayne.
>
> (lines 601–10)

The strategy of welcoming James by telling him how bad things had been was also employed by Richard Martyn, who had recently defended

Jonson to the Lord Chief Justice over *Poetaster*. Martyn, speaking on behalf of the Sheriffs of London and Middlesex, promised to show James 'the agues which keep low this great body' of England. Hugh Holland wrote to Cotton that Martyn 'with like liberty as eloquence was not afraid to tell the king the truth'. This whole circle, it appears, agreed on this critical view of late Elizabethan England.[21]

Contemporaries would have recognized in the language of both Jonson and Martyn a discourse that was, in contemporary terms, 'republican' in its emphasis on civil liberties, on the voluntary restraint placed on monarchic power, and on the well-being of the 'great body' of the commonwealth rather than that of the king.[22] Jonson's *Panegyre* on James' opening of Parliament in 1604 took things a little further. There he views the old liberties – similar to those he had fought for in the Netherlands – as having been crushed by a tyrant, in the shape of Elizabeth's father, Henry VIII, whose memory she had always honoured. Jonson described bitterly how Henry had established a new and unconstitutionally autocratic state, founded on 'bloody, base, and barbarous' statutes and 'lawes . . . made to serve the tyran' will',

> Where acts gave licence to impetuous lust
> To bury churches in forgotten dust
> And with their ruines raise the panders bowers:
> When publique justice borrow'd all her powers
> From private chambers; that could then create
> Laws, judges, counselors, yea prince, and state.
>   (98–106, Herford and Simpson, *Ben Jonson*, VII, 116)

This is a surprisingly bitter invective for a writer whom it has become usual to characterize as committed to the support of an authoritarian monarchy.[23] The alternative to such tyranny was, on the contrary, a monarchy with its powers limited, its virtuous aims dictated by the public, not the private good, advised by counsellors who were not the creatures of the prince, and a parliament whose legislation was independent of his private will, the whole supported by a church that was not 'buried', and a legal system independent of private pressures. This was the mixed state advocated by most northern humanist political theorists of the sixteenth century. It was also often in practice the political *status quo* in England, where Elizabeth governed what Patrick Collinson has called a 'monarchical republic'. This was not the oxymoron it now seems: classical republicanism does not appear in England until the Civil War, but *Poetaster*, *Sejanus*, and *Catiline* were written at a time of growing interest in Roman republicanism, and with it the development of quasi-republican modes of political thought applicable to the realities of contemporary England. These involved the concept of responsible citizenship, a notion perceived as fully compatible with a liberal form of monarchy.[24]

With such citizenship came a humanist agenda in which the intellectual has a responsibility to exert his influence on the ruler or his advisers for the public good. Jonson had already made tentative steps in this direction in *Cynthia's Revels*, where he experimented with 'new wayes to come to learned eares' ('Prologue', line 11). Cynthia, very clearly an idealized Elizabeth, recognizes the 'worth' (5.6.107) of Crites, the humanist poet who has succeeded the morally compromised Maciiente of *Every Man Out* as the voice of reform. Crites is granted power to purge the court, and to pass sentence on its endemic disease of 'self-love'. As this suggests, however, the problems of the court are those of personal rather than political morality, vices strongly reminiscent of those attacked by the verse satirists of the 1590s. But to satirize the prince's court while avoiding political issues and exonerating the prince from any responsibility for its corruption was, as Donne had also found in *Satire 5*, not a convincing strategy. As Donne, like Martyn using the 'ague' metaphor, cautiously implies in a letter to Wotton, the 'humors' of the court are those of the prince, and they spread to infect the state:

I am now free from an ague. Though I am afraid the state bee not so: for certainly the court hath in it much vnnaturall heate and the courts and seats of princes are the harts of all realms which taking forme from theyre humors are more or less corrupted as they confine or enlarge theyre owne wills: when I speak of the wills of princes I speak of verie vnlimited things.[25]

Jonson's solution to the problem of how to incorporate the prince into a more liberated moral and political discourse was to move the satirical scene to Augustan Rome, a setting which, as Envy finds in the prologue to *Poetaster*, can be presented as having nothing to do with contemporary England. 'O my vexed soul', she laments, 'How might I force this to the present state?'[26] Very easily, as many in the audience could have reassured her. Rome, though it contains the historical figures of Horace, Ovid, Virgil, and Augustus, also contains the very Elizabethan figures of the tradesman Albius and his wife Chloe, with their bay-windowed house (2.1.106–10, 122–5), in which Chloe wears her 'bum rolls' and 'whalebone bodice' (2.1.65), while her admirer the poetaster Crispinus sports an 'embroidered hat' with an 'ash coloured feather' (3.3.1–2), above 'ample velvet bases' (3.1.69–70). There was probably not a toga in sight: even a

historical figure like Maecenas has an Elizabethan flagon chain (5.3.38).
These and other details of costume and custom signal that the Rome
presented in *Poetaster* is, unlike that of the two tragedies, synchronic with
Jonson's London, and needs little 'force' to relate it to the 'present state'.
The focus on that state is, as with the earlier comical satires, partly on personal failings, in this case particularly those of the London literary world.
But the humanist view of the importance of literature in society is such
that literary vices cannot be sidelined as 'private' issues. Both Ovid's aban-
donment to love poetry, and Crispinus' willingness to use poetry to libel
Horace, are symptoms of the state's 'agues'. To combat them, the
poet-reformer Crites has metamorphosed into the immensely more powerful triumvirate of Horace, Virgil, and Maecenas, who act in the final scenes
as just the kinds of wise, disinterested adviser to the *princeps* that humanist
political theorists emphasized were essential. Lipsius, for example, insists
that no prince alone can bear the burden of rule, since

it is a hard thing for man, to rule ouer man: neither is it possible to be brought to
passe, by the wit of one alone. Wherfore those wise men are worthely praised, who
in former age, and at this day, haue had this care, to haue guided kings, by the light
of their wholsome counsels. For wherein could they possibly do better seruice to
mankind?[27]

This emphasis on the prince's need to heed wise counsel and the reciprocal
obligation of the intellectual to offer his learning and wisdom in the service
of the state had long been a central theme of humanist political philosophy,
and indeed of practice, with More providing the leading English example of
both.[28] Jonson, dramatizing what could reasonably be presented as the best
classical example of poets playing such a role (Virgil and Horace did at least
have access to Augustus), distorts the historical account in order to make it
clear that even the wise Augustus needed the restraint of their counsel
to stop him killing his daughter in a fit of rage (4.6.12–15). Having
learnt his lesson, Augustus goes further, accepting a sharp rebuke from
Horace – 'Thanks Horace for thy free and wholsome sharpness /
Which pleaseth Caesar more than servile fawns' (5.1.94–5) – and seating
Virgil above himself to read a passage from his new *Aeneid*. Augustus justifies this elevation with a striking modification of a line of Juvenal:
'Virtue without presumption place may take / Above best kings, whom
only she should make'. Juvenal wrote that '*nobilitas* sola est atque unica
virtus' (8.20, 'Virtue is the sole and single nobility'). Jonson's modification
of *nobilitas* to 'best kings' has obvious implications for a hereditary monarchy. The idea that the only true nobility lay in virtue, and that such virtue

constituted the only valid claim to rule, was a humanist commonplace, but its subversive implications had usually been contained by the convenient discovery that the ruling classes had a special access to such virtue.[29] That Jonson should make the statement so absolute is significant. It smacks more of classical republicanism than Collinson's balanced monarchical republic, and it is a concept to which Jonson returns in *Catiline*.

Whereas *Poetaster* shows the evils of conspiracy and calumny being averted in a monarchical republic through the power delegated by the wise prince to honest counsellors, *Sejanus* presents an almost inverted scenario: here power is delegated by a vicious and hypocritical prince to a corrupt, ambitious favourite who conspires to usurp his patron. Jonson first thought of exploring the dangers presented by a cynically intelligent tyrant through the English example of Richard III. But Richard's career did not give any opportunity to explore the consequences of the delegation of power to a favourite. On the other hand, Machiavelli, whom Jonson appears to have been reading at this time, had singled out Sejanus as an example of the dangers a favourite who is granted 'too many benefits' presents to the prince who has promoted him (*Discourses*, 3.6). Favouritism, factionalism, corruption, and too much power in the hands of the Cecils, father and son, were widely perceived as besetting problems through the 1590s, and, as has been said, a major part of Jonson's purpose in dramatizing the career of Sejanus was to throw light on the contemporary political situation. In this respect it is interesting to compare *Sejanus* with Robert Graves' otherwise similarly scholarly recreation of the same period in *I, Claudius* (1934). There is little sense of Graves commenting on the state of Europe in the early 1930s, whereas in *Sejanus* the reader of the 1605 quarto was made aware of such 'application' from the beginning, partly by the commendatory poems, but even more by the emphatic paragraph which ends 'The Argument', and which was probably inserted late in the printing process, in the immediate aftermath of the Gunpowder Plot:

This do we advance as a mark of terror to all traitors and treasons, to show how just the heavens are in pouring and thundering down a weighty vengeance on their unnatural intents, even to the worst princes; much more to those for guard of whose piety and virtue the angels are in continual watch, and God himself miraculously working.[30]

For the audience in the Globe in 1603 it would have been the opening exchanges between Silius and Sabinus about Tiberius' court that first alerted them to modern English parallels. Sabinus' first speech (1.4–20) is applicable to courts in general, but Silius' reply, as he describes the informers

Pinnius and Natta, becomes specific in a way that, though accurate to
Jonson's sources, also describes the role of informers in England:

> These can lie,
> Flatter, and swear, forswear, deprave, inform,
> Smile, and betray; make guilty men, then beg
> The forfeit lives to get the livings; cut
> Men's throats with whisp'rings.
>
> (1.27–31)

In both England and Rome, informers were rewarded by a substantial
portion of the fines or estates of those who were convicted through their
information. In England they usually reported (or alternatively, black-
mailed) those breaking economic statutes, but frequently betrayed recusants
also. Their unpopularity was at its height when Jonson was writing and
revising *Sejanus*: in 1604 the judges decided unanimously in the *Case of
the Penal Statutes* that the rewards they received (up to a half of fines or
forfeited estates) were 'utterly against the law'. Informers were regularly
attacked in parliament, but they were useful agents to a government with
no police force, and no action was taken to reform the system until 1616.[31]

Although the scene unfolds subsequently in a way that is more specifically
Roman, with denunciation of the loss of republican freedom – 'We that
within these fourscore years were born / Free, equal lords of the triumphèd
world' – further obvious parallels could be seen in the clumsy use of censorship, the faction and intrigue of the court, and the capricious use of power
by the monarch and his or her favourites. It is worth stressing here that the
humanist concept of the use of history to illuminate contemporary events in
this way differed from the manipulation of history to present a covert treatment of such events, what B. N. De Luna called, in her study of *Catiline*, a
'parallelograph'.[32] In that example, she read *Catiline* as a study of the
Gunpowder Plot of 1605, giving a list of twelve characters with specific
1605 counterparts.[33] Here, Catiline is a disguised version of Catesby, and
Cicero of Cecil, while Jonson is unconvincingly identified with the informer and failed rapist Quintus Curius. Such exact parallels are certainly
found in several characters in *Poetaster*, where Crispinus, for example, is
clearly a mocking version of John Marston; and Middleton's *A Game at
Chess* is an extended example of a satirical political 'parallelograph'.
Representation of recognizable contemporaries was in fact more widely
employed on the early modern stage than is usually recognized.[34]
But such 'personation' seems to have belonged exclusively to comedy or
satire. In historical tragedy the parallels between ancient and modern

worlds depend for their significance on the very fact that they are discrete, presenting similar scenarios in societies separated in time. This is as true of drama as it is of such 'politic' histories as Hayward's *Henry IIII* and Cotton's *Henry the Third*, both written with a view to influencing contemporary politics. De Luna is right to argue that Jonson's audience would have expected to find parallels between the Roman conspiracy and the recent English one, but those who interpreted the play as a *pièce à clef* as she does would have been joining the company of what one of the poems that introduced *Sejanus* called 'these simple elves' who were too quick to spy 'Where later times are in some speech enweaved'. In another of the commendatory poems, Hugh Holland makes a clear distinction between historical parallels and 'parallelographs': 'The men are not, some faults may be these times'; / He acts those men, and they did act these crimes'.[35] In neither *Sejanus* nor *Catiline* is Jonson presenting the 'men' of his time disguised as Romans; he is dramatizing two episodes of Roman history in which 'crimes' dominated the state, in order that his contemporaries, some of whom harbour similar 'faults', may learn the dangers that threaten their commonwealth. Humanist history, on stage or page, is interested in the recognition of recurring situations, recurring political types – tyrants, informers, flatterers, favourites, conspirators, but also virtuous princes, honest counsellors. It seeks to show contemporaries how, as Lipsius put it, 'to auoyd, that which is dishonest either to be begunne or ended. In which regard, it is most necessarie in this part of Ciuill life, neither did Polybius without good cause affirme, histories to be the truest doctrine, to practise vs in the managing of Ciuill affaires. And most necessarie they are in matter of publicke counsell, the memorie of things past being most profitable, in common consultations'.[36]

Jonson's treatment of the 'old liberties' of the Roman Republic in *Sejanus* is in line with his advocacy of a monarchical republic in *Poetaster*. Although Arruntius is introduced lamenting the lost spirit of the old Republic, (1.86–104), neither he nor the other Germanicans explicitly advocate its return. Indeed, they agree implicitly with Silius' statement that liberty and monarchy are compatible:

> Men are deceived who think there can be thrall
> Beneath a virtuous prince. Wished liberty
> Ne'er lovelier looks than under such a crown.

> (1.407–9)

This is a translation of a passage from Claudian's *De consulatu Stilichonis*: 'He is deceived who thinks it servitude beneath a noble prince. Liberty

never looks more attractive than under a good king' (3.113–15). The
passage is both underlined and marked in the margin in Jonson's copy of
Claudian, and it probably represents his own position. It may also have
been in Milton's mind in 1649 when he wrote 'look how great a good
and happiness a just king is, so great a mischief is a tyrant'.[37] Milton
wrote this in the confusion of an acephalous republic, completing it just
after Charles I's execution, but his argument is not far removed from
that of Silius. Like him, Milton was arguing against tyranny. Like him, he
accepted the virtuous prince, ruling within the law, advised by 'Counselors
and Parlaments, not to be onely at his beck'.[38] Like Milton, and like almost
any pre-1649 English 'republican', Silius is contrasting the virtuous prince
with the tyrant. Tiberius is a particularly dangerous tyrant because he
appears in public to be just such a virtuous ruler, rejecting the servile
appellation of 'mighty lord' from a flattering counsellor, and presenting
himself as Jonson's (or Milton's) ideal prince:

> We must make up our ears 'gainst these assaults
> Of charming tongues; we pray you use no more
> These contumelies to us; style not us
> Or 'lord', or 'mighty', who profess ourself
> The servant of the Senate, and are proud
> T'enjoy them our good, just, and favouring lords.
>
>   (1.389–94)

'Prince-like, to the life', comments Arruntius, recognizing the hypocrisy.
Silius emphasizes the ideal behind the dissimulation, almost as if he
is refuting the anti-monarchic arguments of such Italian republicans
as Machiavelli or Patrizi, who insist that a 'Republic is preferable to a
principality':[39]

>   If this man
> Had but a mind allied unto his words,
> How blest a fate were it to us, and Rome!
> We could not think that state for which to change,
> Although the aim were our old liberty;
> The ghosts of those that fell for that would grieve
> Their bodies lived not now, again to serve.
>
>   (1.400–6)

Such a virtuous prince was the one proposed by Lipsius, More, and
many other, particularly North European, humanist historians and

theorists, for whom it had become commonplace to prefer monarchy as the best form of government. Such a prince was the Augustus of *Poetaster*, and such, it was possible to hope in 1603–4, James would prove to be. Tiberius, by contrast, is 'dead to virtue', defined in terms of his private lust for flattery, which Jonson, typically conflating the psychological appetite and the physical, links both to tyranny and to Tiberius' notorious sexual corruption:

> But when his grace is merely but lip-good,
> And that no longer than he airs himself
> Abroad in public, there to seem to shun
> The strokes and stripes of flatterers, which within
> Are lechery unto him, and so feed
> His brutish sense with their afflicting sound,
> As, dead to virtue, he permits himself
> Be carried like a pitcher, by the ears,
> To every act of vice: this is a case
> Deserves our fear, and doth presage the nigh
> And close approach of blood and tyranny.
> Flattery is midwife unto princes' rage
> And nothing sooner doth help forth a tyrant
> Than that, and whisperers' grace, who have the time,
> The place, the power to make all men offenders.
>
> (1.410–24)

The innocent 'offenders' include those who should have filled the role of honest counsellors. Here their stoic Roman virtue makes them helpless, the 'slaves to one man's lusts' (1.63). In a similar way Jonson saw Henry VIII's parliaments giving the Tudor tyrant 'a licence to impetuous lust', and, alongside the commonplace that corrupt governments marginalize the virtuous, one of the less obvious parallels he may have wanted to make is that between the destructive socio-political effects of Tiberius' lechery and hunger for flattery, and the corrupted origins of English Protestant power and wealth. Such great houses as Woburn Abbey and Wilton were literally built on the ruins of buried churches, abbeys which became 'the pander's bowers' granted to Henry's clients. Ironically, these two prominent examples were the homes of Jonson's principal patrons, the Russells and the Herberts; in their ability to square such circles lay the secret of survival for many early modern writers.

The favourite who administered 'the strokes and stripes' of flattery, and came thus to carry his master (or mistress) 'like a pitcher, by the ears', was a frequent concomitant of tyranny in Renaissance theory and practice.

Machiavelli had warned of the dangerous dynamics of the relationship in a passage which Jonson versified for his Machiavellian prince, Tiberius:

> Those are the dreadful enemies we raise
> With favours, and make dangerous with praise.
> The injured by us may have will alike,
> But 'tis the favourite hath the power to strike;
> And fury ever boils more high and strong,
> Heat' with ambition, than revenge of wrong.
>
> (3.–637–42)[40]

Machiavelli had cited Sejanus as his prime example. Some in Jonson's audience would inevitably have paralleled him with Essex, and indeed at much the same date, Jonson's close friend, Sir John Roe, had used Machiavelli's dictum explicitly of Essex in his subversive satire 'To Sir Nicholas Smith'.[41] But the clichéd modern picture of Elizabeth's court, which prioritizes her romantic favourites over the more astute, if less attractive political ones, did not hold sway in 1603, and many would have thought also of Burghley, who had used his unprecedented influence over Elizabeth throughout the 1590s to further his own position, and that of his son, who in the last two years of Elizabeth's life enjoyed even more complete hegemony than his father. The readers of the 1605 quarto might have added the Earl of Northampton's name to that of the younger Cecil in these 'applications'. And this is how Jonson would have wished his audience to apply the lessons of his Roman history, not by identifying exclusive representations of contemporary political actors, but through a recognition of how the dynamics of power and ambition could be discerned in a range of contemporaries.

A wider political issue Jonson explores in *Sejanus* is the role of language in the commonwealth. It was axiomatic that histories made the most honest counsellors because they were not affected (in the present at least) by self-interest: the good historian 'dares not write things false, nor hide things true'. Almost as good are living counsellors who will not 'hide things true' from the prince. Lipsius emphasizes the importance of freedom of speech for them, 'that they may with a stout courage, & without feare, vtter their opinion: & not frame their speech, rather with the fortune of the Prince, then with the Prince him selfe'.[42] For Jonson such freedom is the first essential of a healthy state. The usual meaning of 'liberty' or 'freedom' for him is frankness of speech, a freedom important not just for counsellors, but for all the good prince's subjects: 'Hee needs no Emissaries, Spies, Intelligencers, to intrap true Subjects. Hee fears no Libels, no

Treasons. His people speake, what they thinke, and talke openly, what they
doe in secret. They have nothing in their brests, that they need a Cipher
for'.[43] An exactly opposite state of affairs pertains in Tiberian Rome, and
this is another area in which he and many of his audience would have
noted the parallels with late Elizabethan England. Arruntius' bitter attack
on the suffocating atmosphere of fear in Rome would have found an
echo in the experience of many English Catholics like Jonson:

> May I think,
> And not be racked? What danger is't to dream?
> Talk in one's sleep? Or cough? Who knows the law?
> May'I shake my head, without a comment?
>
> (4.304–7)

Earlier, Silius has made a similar point, relating the fear to the informers
whose Elizabethan equivalents Jonson attacks elsewhere:[44]

> Every minist'ring spy
> That will accuse and swear is lord of you,
> Of me, of all, our fortunes, and our lives.
> Our looks are called to question, and our words,
> How innocent soever, are made crimes;
> We shall not shortly dare to tell our dreams,
> Or think, but 'twill be treason.
>
> (1.64–9)

In 1592 Bacon had tried to allay such fears, writing that Elizabeth did not
wish 'to make windows into men's hearts and secret thoughts',[45] but
treason, being a matter of intention almost as much as action, was
'proved' by circumstantial evidence or by confession obtained under
torture, especially during the later years of her reign and that of James.
Ralegh complained at his trial of being convicted by circumstantial evidence
over his intentions, and English Catholics like Jonson at this date were
always at risk from similar interpretation of their motives.[46]

Set against the fears attendant on even the most guarded speech or
thought is the cynical 'mercenary speech' of Sejanus and his agents, and
the dissembling, ambiguous speech of Tiberius, of which the 'long letter'
which destroys Sejanus is a written extension. The discourse of power in
the play is almost always dishonest (exceptions are in the Machiavellian conversations between Sejanus and Tiberius at 2.165–330, 3.488–585, and in
soliloquies by each man). The interpretation of the words heard or read
by the powerful is always destructive. Jonson gives an almost palpably

physical dimension to the way Tiberius and Sejanus distort the sentiments of their enemies through 'malicious and manifold applying, / Foul wresting, and impossible construction' (3.228–9) which will make innocent writings 'speak / What they will have, to fit their tyrannous wreak' (4.134–5). Because Jonson is writing as a historian, it is appropriate that he makes the historian Cremutius Cordus the prime victim of such interpretative malice, condemned not for any deed ('fact') but for 'words' (3.407–10). Cordus' trial is a serious parody of the scene in *Poetaster* in which Horace is accused of 'dangerous, seditious libel' (5.3.43–4). His history threatens the corrupt regime of Sejanus and Tiberius by implicit comparison with the late republic. Sejanus, for all his contempt for the 'writing fellow', perceives the threat the historian can present to a tyranny, describing Cordus as being employed:

> To gather notes of the precedent times,
> And make them into annals – a most tart
> And bitter spirit, I hear, who, under colour
> Of praising those, doth tax the present state,
> Censures the men, the actions, leaves no trick,
> No practice unexamined, parallels
> The times, the governments; a professed champion
> For the old liberty.
>
> (2.304–12)

Auditors and readers of the play know that Sejanus' fears are justified, that Cordus does 'parallel' contemporaries with figures from history, for he has earlier said that he had thought 'T'have paralleled him [Germanicus] with great Alexander' (1.139). For his harking back to 'the old liberty' of the republic Cordus is tried and condemned. Jonson thought his defence important enough to render the whole of Tacitus' version of it in blank verse (3.407–60), a decision that was unwise dramatically, but which reinforces the extent to which he saw *Sejanus* as a play about freedom of speech and the responsibilities of the historian to the state. Unlike Horace, Cordus cannot make his accusers vomit up their words, and unlike Cicero he cannot combine his eloquence with effective action; but in one of the few positive statements in the play Arruntius and Sabinus elaborate on Tacitus' scorn (*Annales* 4.35) at the 'brainless diligence' of those who believe they can, by burning books, destroy the power of words and 'extinguish / The memory of all succeeding times' (3.471–80). The burning of Hayward's *Henry IIII* in 1599, along with books by Marlowe, Marston, and others, was fresh enough in the memory for one contemporary application of this scene to be obvious. But Jonson was himself a historian in this play, and Cordus' speech, though following Tacitus closely, echoes his own frequent complaints against the 'application' of his and others' work (see e.g. *Poetaster*, 'Induction', 22–6, and *Volpone*, 'Epistle', 60–6). The Elizabethan regime had always been sensitive to the written or spoken word; in the years preceding *Sejanus* Jonson had been imprisoned over *The Isle of Dogs*, censured in some way over *Poetaster*, and was to be imprisoned again in 1605 for his part in *Eastward Ho!* D. F. Mackenzie was right to call *Sejanus* 'Jonson's *Areopagitica*'.[47] Nowhere does Tiberius' hypocrisy seem more cynical than in his ringing endorsement of the ideal:

Nor do we desire their authors, though found, be censured, since in a free state (as ours) all men ought to enjoy both their minds and tongues free. (5.551–3)

Jonson did not return to tragedy for another eight years, when *Catiline* was performed, again by the King's Men, with Burbage probably this time playing Cicero. *Catiline* returns to Roman history, and to explicitly political issues by again following the career of an unscrupulous and ambitious opportunist and his conspiracy to seize power. For Jonson's audience in 1611 conspiracy was a highly topical issue. The Gunpowder Plot of 5 November 1605 was still recent enough to come immediately to mind as a parallel to Catiline's plot. Curiously, De Luna believes that 'In all likelihood, for the ordinary playgoer viewing *Catiline*, the Powder Plot never entered his mind'.[48] But the impact of the plot on Londoners was still vivid enough for it to enter the minds of even a fairly young audience,[49] and only the deaf or drunk in the Globe could have failed to notice the parallel between the plot of 5 November 1605 to blow up king and parliament, and Catiline's plot 'on the fifth (the calends of November) / T'have slaughtered this whole order' of the Senate (4.246–7). Many, however, would have applied the parallels with contemporary conspiracies more widely. Some would have been old enough to recall, and many more would have heard of, a succession of conspiracies against Elizabeth, starting with the Ridolfi plot of 1570–1 and culminating in Essex's abortive coup attempt in 1601. Most, too, would have known of the recent (May 1610) assassination of Henri IV in Paris, an event which threatened to plunge France back into the terrible wars of religion which Henri had ended. A similar future seemed, in 1610–11, to threaten England. In a poem that may have been written in the same year as *Catiline*, 'The New Cry', Jonson linked the two recent plots as subjects of common political gossip: 'And of the Powder Plot they will talk yet. / At naming of the French king, their

heads they shake' (lines 32–3).[50] Henri's death was seen in England as part
of a wider Catholic conspiracy. James issued a series of proclamations,
insisting he was a target, and demanding that all Catholics take the Oath
of Allegiance which parliament had first required in the aftermath of the
Gunpowder Plot.[51] It was true that all of these conspiracies, other than
Essex's, were inspired in one way or another by Roman Catholicism,
and even Essex had the backing of many Catholics, including Catesby.
Recent Catholic political philosophy had condoned, even encouraged, the
assassination of heretical rulers, joining Calvinists in their view that, in
respect of religion at least, even the hereditary monarch's position was contractual. It may be no coincidence that Jonson ceased to be a Catholic at
around the time of Henri IV's death, and that he returned to political
tragedy in the context of fears, which he shared, of renewed instability
contingent on Henri's assassination. The situation may well have seemed
to him strikingly similar to that described by Cicero in his first speech
Against Catiline:

> Truly, conscript fathers, for a long time we have lived with these dangers and stra-
> tagems of conspiracy, but, I don't know how, the maturation of all these crimes and
> long-standing madness and audacity has come about during my consulship.[52]

It is no surprise, therefore, that it was to this most famous of rebellions
against the Roman Republic that Jonson turned. As De Luna shows, it
had become commonplace to parallel modern conspiracies, especially
Catholic ones, with Catiline's plot.[53] For Jonson, however, it also involved
an admiring recreation of the Roman Republic in its last period, this time
based on Sallust and Cicero rather than Tacitus. This was a time when the
consular system, in the hands of the wisest and most eloquent of statesmen,
Cicero, was able to preserve those 'old liberties' whose destruction is
mourned in *Sejanus*. If in this respect *Catiline* is less bleak than *Sejanus*,
it is nevertheless a dark play. Rome's future always looms over its present,
and the city itself is portrayed as sick, sleeping, or lost in darkness, with Catiline's conspiracy a 'punishment' for her 'errors . . . crimes . . . faults' (3.873–
5). Jonson shows the Republic defending itself in spite of itself – the sickness
of the state being the root cause of the conspiracy – through the agency of
one or two wise rulers, prepared to use almost any means to do so. He often
represents England in his political poetry as subject to the same kind of corruption, and needing the same virtuous and watchful guardians to save her
from descending into chaos.[54]

   One of the less palatable lessons that Jonson the historian has to offer his
contemporaries is that the successful governor, whether elected consul or

virtuous prince, may have to use secret and often dubious means to defend the common good. The argument over *arcana imperii*, the implementation of policy hidden from parliamentary or legal scrutiny, and its close relative 'reasons of state', was a topical one. Donne had argued, the year before *Catiline*, that

it is impossible, that any Prince should proceede in all causes & occurrences, by a downright Execution of his Lawes ... And therefore these disguisings, and averting of others from discerning them, are so necessarie, that though ... they seeme to be within the compasse of deceite and falshood, yet the end, which is, maintenance of lawfull Authoritie, for the publike good, justifies them.[55]

Lipsius was especially forthright in his belief that 'all things are honest that do conserue authoritie', and that 'if wee can not arriue at the hauen by the right Course, that wee turne sayle, and alter our Nauigation to attaine thereunto'.[56] Jonson uses the same analogy, making Cato advise Cicero that the pilot of the ship of state must know

> His tides, his currents; how to shift his sailes;
> What shee will beare in foule, what in faire weathers.
>
> (3.67–8)

Cotton similarly admires Henry III's 'arte of incomparable wisdom ... to sute himself to the necessitye of the tyme'.[57] These 'arts' are put into effect in Cicero's handling of Fulvia, whom he praises lavishly – 'Here is a lady that hath got the start, / In pietie of us all' (3.341–2), but whom he sees in reality as a 'common strumpet, worthlesse to be nam'd / A haire, or part of [Rome]' (3.451–2). In a similar vein, he calculates that his unreliable fellow consul Antonius must be neutralized by bribery:

> I must with offices, and patience win him;
> Make him, by art, that which he is not borne,
> A friend vnto the publique ...
> . . . .
> 'Tis well, if some men will doe well, for price:
> So few are vertuous, when the reward's away.
>
> (3.474–80)

Although Jonson does not openly laud such amoral policy in the English statesmen he addresses, his praise of Burleigh follows Lipsius and Cato in characterizing him as a helmsman: 'The only faithfull Watchman for the Realme, / That in all tempests, never quit the helme' (*Underwood* 30, lines 9–10). Similarly, Henry Savile is praised, and associated with Sallust, the politician turned historian, as one who would have made a good pilot of the state:

> Whose knowledge claymeth at the helme to stand;
>   But, wisely, thrusts not forth a forward hand,
> No more than Salust in the Romane State!
>
> (Epigrams, 95, lines 21–3)

Though for most of the play Jonson accepts Cicero's own evaluation of himself as such a skilful helmsman, the 'new man' who saves the republic through both his eloquence and his actions, there is one crucial area in which he suggests Cicero miscalculates how 'to shift his sailes'. This is in his treatment of Julius Caesar. One clear indication of Jonson's positive attitude to republicanism in the play is his hostile presentation of its future destroyer. Through Caesar, he reminds his audience (if they needed reminding), the Republic is doomed. Cato intimates as much when, near the end of the play, he warns the Senate that they should fear Caesar (5.541), who is presented throughout as complicit in the conspiracy, using it for his own ends, but skilfully surviving its failure. This is a much more critical version of him than Sallust's, which presents him as falsely accused.[58] It is more hostile, too, than most contemporary English assessments, including the equivocal one that had been offered by Shakespeare in Julius Caesar. Though the suggestion for Caesar's duplicity comes from Cicero himself, and is found in one of Jonson's main sources (the De Coniuratione Catilinae Liber of 1518 by Constanzo Felici), the Caesar of Catiline is represented by Jonson as Italian republican theorists had presented him, 'as the pivot around whose career the liberty of the Roman Republic swings into the tyranny of the Empire'.[59] Jonson accepts Machiavelli's denunciation of him as 'Rome's first tyrant', as corrupt as Catiline, but far more dangerous:

Nor should anyone be deceived by Caesar's renown when he finds writers extolling him before others, for those who praise him have either been corrupted by his fortune or overawed by the long continuance of the empire which, since it was ruled under that name, did not permit writers to speak freely of him. If, however, anyone desires to know what writers would have said, had they been free, he has but to look at what they say of Catiline. For Caesar is the more blameworthy of the two, in that he who has done wrong is more blameworthy than he who has but desired to do wrong.[60]

Cicero's unwillingness to act or speak against Caesar and Crassus, even though he suspects them, is a fatal mistake in the longer perspective. Cicero excuses it as political realism: though they may be 'ill men' they are also 'mightie ones' (4.530–1), and, Cicero insists, 'Ile make / My selfe no enemies, nor the state no traytors'. He therefore ignores his brother's warnings about Caesar, demanding proof of his guilt (5.86–93), even though he has already been told that Caesar was among the conspirators (3.773); and when further proof is produced, in the form of evidence from Catiline's supporters, he dismisses it (5.340–66). Blair Worden has defended the Cicero of the play in this respect, noting that Lipsius counsels princes to move 'warily and slowly' against conspirators, and, if they are 'great personages, whom thou canst not presently punish with safetie', to 'Keepe the matter secret'. In context, however, it is clear that 'presently' is the key word here; this is merely a strategic delay 'before thou take reuenge', which Cicero never seems to contemplate.[61] Much of this is historical, and could be read as a clumsy attempt to reconcile Sallust's account with Cicero's, were it not that Jonson goes out of his way to emphasize the misguidedness of Cicero's inaction by placing the scene in which he refuses to move against Caesar without proof immediately after that in which Caesar and Crassus have a conversation which stresses both their guilt and their political cunning (5.68–85).

This approach may be coloured by Machiavelli's condemnation of Cicero's later attempt to play off Caesar's nephew, Octavius, against Mark Antony, only to see them join forces and defeat the Republicans:

This might easily have been foreseen. The senate ought not to have given credence to Tullius's [Cicero's] arguments, but should have borne ever in mind that name which had so gloriously wiped out its enemies and acquired the princedom of Rome. Nor should they have expected to be able to do anything consistent with the name of liberty with the help of his relatives and his supporters.[62]

It is a miscalculation similar in scale, though a sin of omission rather than commission, that in *Catiline* leads Cicero to turn a blind eye to Caesar's treachery, and by so doing ensure that, beyond the confines of the play, lay civil war and the destruction of the Republic.

Despite the ironies provided by this perspective, however, and despite Rome's endemic sickness, *Catiline* remains a play which celebrates the classical republic as warmly as the monarchical one had been celebrated and then mourned in *Poetaster* and *Sejanus*. Whereas the latter had ended utterly without hope, with Macro and Caligula in the ascendant, and Rome facing a more terrible future than even the Tiberian present, *Catiline* ends on a positive republican note that is more poignant because of what lies ahead, with Petreius exhorting his men to fight 'for your owne republique' (5.14), a significant addition of Jonson's to the little that Sallust records of Petreius' speech, and with Cicero giving 'Thanks to the immortall gods' for helping him save Rome (5.693). Earlier the Chorus at the end of Act 2 presents one of Jonson's most impassioned political statements, celebrating the virtues of those Romans who had selflessly defended the Republic, and praying for 'a free, and worthy choice' of Consuls by 'the publique voice' (2.372–3). Throughout the play it is the 'Commonwealth', 'the Republic', or just 'Rome' which is at stake. The only references to kingship in the play are to the 'stupid' aspirations of Lentulus, while the Roman nobility, with few exceptions, are vicious, foolish, or effete. Kingship is irrelevant: there is no hint that a 'virtuous prince' would have managed the state better than Cicero, the 'new man' who has become Consul through his own 'virtue', not through his blood. This is a treatment of classical republicanism which must at least qualify the characterization of Jonson as an ardent monarchist, an authoritarian in politics as in his attitude to his literary output. As a humanist historian who dares 'not write things false, nor hide things true', he takes a larger view.

NOTES

1. *Wits Common Wealth. The second part*, 2nd edn (London: William Stansby for Richard Royston, 1634), Part 2, 626. Meres' book was first entered in the Stationers' Register in September 1598, and his dedicatory epistle is dated October.
2. E. A. J. Honigmann, *John Weever* (Manchester University Press, 1987), 91.
3. John Weever, *Epigrammes in the Oldest Cut, and Newest Fashion* (London: V[alentine] S[immes] for Thomas Bushell, 1599), sig. F8b. Ironically in view of their future reputations and relations, Weever brackets Jonson with Marston, who is praised for his Horatian manner.
4. Philip Henslowe, *Henslowe's Diary*, ed R. A. Foakes and R. T. Rickert (Cambridge University Press, 1961); in 1597 Henslowe had advanced £1 to Jonson for a play of unknown genre of which he had 'showed the plotte vnto the company' and agreed to finish for Christmas (*Henslowe's Diary*, 73). As David Riggs suggests, this may have been the 'tragedie of bengemens plotte' which Chapman took over in October 1598; see Riggs, *Ben Jonson: A Life* (Cambridge, MA: Harvard University Press, 1989), 53.
5. Milton, 'L'Allegro', line 132.
6. Though it's worth noting that Chettle and Wilson were paid for 'Cattelanes consperesy' in 1598 (*Henslowe's Diary*, 97).
7. For a useful summary of the Westminster curriculum see W. David Kay, *Ben Jonson: A Literary Life* (Basingstoke: Macmillan, 1995), 3–4.
8. The edition of Dio's *Romanorum Historiarum* used for *Sejanus* is a parallel text Greek–Latin one, with Latin translation by Xylander (Geneva: Henricus Stephanus, 1592). There are signs in *Sejanus* that Jonson relied on the Latin

version: see my forthcoming edition in the *Cambridge Works of Ben Jonson* (Cambridge University Press).

9. Lipsius, *Politicorum, sive civilis doctrinae libri sex* was translated as *Sixe bookes of politickes or ciuil doctrine* by William Jones (London: Richard Field for William Ponsonby, 1594).

10. Kevin Sharpe, *Sir Robert Cotton 1586–1631: History and Politics in Early Modern England* (Oxford University Press, 1979), 85–6, 106.

11. References to *Sejanus* are to the edition by Philip J. Ayres (Manchester University Press, 1990). Jonson asks Cotton for a book clarifying the 'distance betwixt Bauli . . . and Villa Augusta'. This will be Letter 2 in the forthcoming *Cambridge Works of Ben Jonson*. There is no evidence for Simpson's assumption that it was 'written in his latest years after the attack of the palsy' (Herford and Simpson, *Ben Jonson*, I, 215). See also Mark Bland, 'Jonson, Biathanotos and the Interpretation of Manuscript Evidence', *Studies in Bibliography* 51 (1998): 154–82, 163–70. Another acknowledgement of Cotton's 'succour' is in 'An Execration upon Vulcan', lines 99–100.

12. For Savile, see Jonson's 'To Sir Henry Savile', *Epigrams*, 95. This can hardly, as Annabel Patterson suggests, have been written on the publication of Savile's translation of Tacitus' *The Ende of Nero and Beginning of Galba. Fower bookes of the Histories of Cornelius Tacitus. The Life of Agricola* (Oxford: Joseph Barnes for Richard Wright, 1591). Jonson was then only eighteen or nineteen, and it was not a 'dedicatory poem for it'. It could date from the publication of the second edition, along with Greneway's translation of the *Annals*, in 1598. See Patterson, '"Roman-Cast Similitude": Ben Jonson and the English Use of Roman History', in *Rome in the Renaissance: The City and the Myth*, ed. P. A. Ramsey (Binghamton, NY: Center for Medieval and Early Renaissance Studies, 1982), 381–94, 385. Jonson's use of Greneway's translation in *Sejanus*, despite his avowed disdain for it, suggests that his Latin was still not quite fluent enough to read Tacitus with ease. Hayward's association with Camden and Cotton is only documented from slightly later, but it is highly probable that he was associated with them during the later 1590s: see *The First and Second Parts of John Hayward's 'The Life and Reign of King Henrie IIII'*, ed. John J. Manning, Camden Fourth Series 42 (London: Royal Historical Society, 1991), 15–16.

13. Cf. Blair Worden's two essays on Jonson's relationship to contemporary and classical historians, 'Ben Jonson Among the Historians', in *Culture and Politics in Early Stuart England*, ed. K. Sharpe and P. Lake (Basingstoke: Macmillan, 1994), 67–90, and 'Politics in *Catiline*: Jonson and His Sources', in *Re-Presenting Ben Jonson: Text, History, Performance*, ed. Martin Butler (Basingstoke: Macmillan, 1999), 152–73.

14. Herford and Simpson, *Ben Jonson*, I, 179. For Cotton's membership of this group, see Sharpe, *Sir Robert Cotton*, 205–7.

15. *Henslowe's Diary*, 182, 203.

16. His marked copy is thoroughly analysed by Robert C. Evans, *Habits of Mind: Evidence and Effects of Ben Jonson's Reading* (Lewisburg, PA: Bucknell University Press, 1995), 160–217.

17. Apart from *Britannia*, Camden wrote *Annales rerum Anglicarum, et Hibernicarum, regnante Elizabetha* (1615), while around 1614 Cotton wrote a tendentiously 'politic' *Short View of the Long Life and Reign of King Henry the Third* (published 1627).

18. Niccolò Machiavelli, *The Discourses*, ed. Bernard Crick, trans. Leslie J. Walker, with revisions by Brian Richardson (London: Penguin Books, 1998), Preface, 99; Cf. Vives, *On Education*, trans. and ed. Foster Watson (Cambridge University Press, 1913), 226–33.

19. For this suggestion, see Julie Sanders, *Ben Jonson's Theatrical Republics* (Basingstoke: Macmillan, 1998), 6–7.

20. Henry Chettle, *England's Mourning Garment* (London: V. S. for Thomas Millington, 1603), sig. D2v.

21. *A Speach Delivered to the Kings Most Excellent Majesty . . . By Maister Richard Martin of the Middle Temple* (London: Thomas Thorppe [sic] for William Aspley, 1603), sig. A4v. Martin's speech was reprinted without alteration in 1642. Hugh Holland, *Pancharis* (1603), sig. D5v; Fuller recorded that Holland when 'in Italy (conceiving himself without ear-reach of the English) let flie freely against the Credit of Queen Elizabeth' (quoted by Colin Burrow, 'Hugh Holland', *Oxford Dictionary of National Biography* (Oxford, 2005)). Donne shared this view of Elizabeth's later years, using the same metaphor of an 'ague' afflicting the state. He tells Wotton that the disease will not be cured 'till we get above the moone whose motions as some have ingeniously [av]erred do make us variable'. See Evelyn M. Simpson, *A Study of the Prose Works of John Donne* (Oxford University Press, 1924), 308. Elizabeth was commonly associated with Cynthia/Diana, the moon goddess.

22. For a similar recognition of the implications of such language, see Sanders, *Ben Jonson's Theatrical Republics*, 4–7. Andrew Hadfield has recently made a convincing case for Shakespeare's close interest in republicanism: see *Shakespeare and Republicanism* (Cambridge University Press, 2005).

23. For a good summary of the debate over Jonson's relationship to authority, see James Loxley, *The Complete Critical Guide to Ben Jonson* (London: Routledge, 2002), 155–75.

24. Patrick Collinson, 'De Republica Anglorum: Or, History with the Politics Put Back' and 'The Monarchical Republic of Queen Elizabeth I', in *Elizabethan Essays* (London: Hambledon Press, 1994), 1–29, 31–57. See also Markku Peltonen, *Classical Humanism and Republicanism in English Political Thought 1570–1640* (Cambridge University Press, 1995), passim, esp. 3–7, 132–4, and Annabel Patterson, *Reading Between the Lines* (London: Routledge, 1993), 210–44.

25. Simpson, *Prose Works*, 308, contractions expanded.

26. *Poetaster*, ed. Tom Cain (Manchester University Press, 1995), 'Induction', lines 33–4.

27. Lipsius, *Six Bookes of Politickes*, sig. A4v. Cf. Donne 'the State is the happier, where businesses are carried by more counsels, then can be in one breast, how large soever'. Donne, 'Meditation 7', in *Devotions upon Emergent Occasions*, ed. Anthony Raspa (Oxford University Press, 1987), 35.

28. The first book of More's *Utopia* discusses the matter of humanist counsellors at some length. For the role of such advisers in the Elizabethan court where 'an almost even balance was struck with the monarch in terms of reciprocal obligations to seek counsel and to give it', see Collinson, 'De Republica Anglorum', 20–1. Collinson cites J. G. A. Pocock, otherwise in disagreement over the extent to which an Elizabethan republicanism can be seen emerging, as finding the embryonic citizen of the republic in 'the humanist turned statesman'; see Pocock, *The Machiavellian Moment: Florentine Political Thought and the Atlantic Republican Tradition* (Princeton University Press, 1975): 'An impressive literature of recent historiography indicates that English humanism developed its civil awareness by projecting the image of the humanist as counselor to his prince' (338). In fact Pocock goes further, accepting that it was possible in Jacobean England to do what I am suggesting Jonson did, to 'incorporate elements of civic and even Machiavellian thought with the dominant paradigm of monarchy' (354).

29. See Quentin Skinner, *The Foundations of Modern Political Thought*, 2 vols. (Cambridge University Press, 1978), I, 81–2, 236–8.

30. The type used suggests that this was a late addition, made after copy had been cast off.

31. M. W. Beresford, 'The Common Informer, the Penal Statutes and Economic Regulation', *Economic History Review* 2nd series 10 (1957–8): 221–38.

32. B. N. De Luna, *Jonson's Romish Plot: A Study of 'Catiline' and its Historical Context* (Oxford: Clarendon Press, 1967), 32.

33. *Ibid.*, 179.

34. See my '"Comparisons and Wounding Flouts": *Love's Labour's Lost* and the Tradition of Personal Satire', in *Shakespearean Continuities: Essays in Honour of E. A. J. Honigmann*, ed. John Batchelor, Tom Cain, and Claire Lamont (Basingstoke: Macmillan, 1997), 193–205.

35. Hugh Holland, 'To Him that Hath So Excelled on This Excellent Subject', lines 10–12; 'For His Worthy Friend, the Author', line 13.

36. Lipsius, *Six Bookes of Politickes*, 14.

37. Cl. Claudianus, *Theod. Pulmanni . . . évetustis codicibus restitutus* (Antwerp, 1585), 226. The book is charred, suggesting it is a rare survival of the fire of 1623. It passed to Selden, and is now Bodleian 80 c 90 Art. Sel. For Milton, see *Tenure of Kings and Magistrates*, in *Complete Prose Works of John Milton*, vol. III, ed. Merrit Y. Hughes (New Haven and London: Yale University Press, 1962), 212.

38. Milton, *Tenure of Kings and Magistrates*, 200.

39. Francesco Patrizi, *De Institutione Reipublicae* (Paris, 1585), quoted in Skinner, *Foundations*, I, 158.

40. Machiavelli, *Discourses*, 3.6, (404): 'A prince . . . who wants to guard against conspiracies, should fear those on whom he has conferred excessive favours more than those to whom he has done excessive injury. For the latter lack opportunity, whereas the former abound in it, and the desire is the same in both cases; for the desire to rule is as great as, or greater than, is the desire for vengeance. Consequently princes should confer on their friends an authority of such magnitude that between it and that of the prince there remains a certain interval, and between the two a something else to be desired. Otherwise it will be a strange thing if that does not happen to them which happened to the princes we have been talking about'.

41. *Poems of John Donne*, ed. Herbert Grierson, 2 vols. (Oxford University Press, 1912), I, 405. Roe's poem was attributed to Donne in early editions and in many MSS.

42. Lipsius, *Six Bookes of Politickes*, 3.5, (47).

43. Jonson, *Discoveries*, 1191–6.

44. See e.g. *Discoveries*, 1612–35; *Underwood* 15, lines 163–5; *Epigrams* 59.

45. Bacon, *Certain Observations Made upon a Libel*, in *Works*, ed. J. Spedding, Robert Leslie Ellis, and Douglas Dennon Heath (London: Longmans, 1861), VIII, 178.

46. It has been suggested that Silius' trial is intended to 'parallel' that of Ralegh in November 1603, to which it does bear some interesting resemblances; but even if my suggested dating of the first performances in May 1603 is wrong, it is hard to believe that the King's Men would, later in 1603, and before the royal court, have performed a scene within a few weeks of the trial that could be interpreted as presenting James as Tiberius and Ralegh as Silius. For the argument in favour, see Philip J. Ayres, 'Jonson, Northampton, and the "Treason" in *Sejanus*', *Modern Philology* 80 (1983): 356–63.

47. Unpublished lecture, 1988, 27.

48. De Luna, *Jonson's Romish Plot*, 34.

49. See Antonia Fraser, *The Gunpowder Plot* (London: Phoenix, 2002), 207, citing Stowe, *Annales, or, A General Chronicle of England* (1631 edn), 879, 881.

50. *Epigrams*, 92. The dating is F. G. Fleay's, based on a perceived reference to Carr's peerage of 1611. See *A Biographical Chronicle of English Drama, 1559–1642*, 2 vols. (London: Reeves and Turner, 1891), I, 319.

51. Riggs, *Ben Jonson*, 175–6.

52. *Contra Catlininam* 1.31, my translation.

53. De Luna, *Jonson's Romish Plot*, 110–12.

54. For such poems, see Worden, 'Politics in *Catiline*', 153–7.

55. Donne, *Pseudo-Martyr*, ed. Anthony Raspa (Montreal and Kingston: McGill-Queens University Press, 1993), 57.

56. *Six Bookes of Politickes*, 113–14. Lipsius is implicitly challenging Erasmus as unworldly for arguing that justice must never be compromised, however damaging the consequences; see Erasmus, *The Education of a Christian Prince*, trans. Lester K. Born (New York: Columbia University Press, 1936), 155.

57. Quoted in Sharpe, *Sir Robert Cotton*, 238.
58. *Bellum Catilinae*, 49.
59. Skinner, *Foundations*, I, 83; cf 1.55.
60. *Discourses* 1.10 (135–6); cf. 158, 203.
61. *Sixe Bookes of Politickes*, 89–90. For a good discussion of the debate over Jonson's attitude to Cicero in the play, see Richard Dutton, *Ben Jonson: To the First Folio* (Cambridge University Press, 1983), 124–32.
62. *Discourses*, 1.52 (238).

CHAPTER 8

A generic prompt in Jonson's Timber, or Discoveries

Eugene D. Hill

Students of Jonson's *Timber* have long found themselves drawn in opposite directions. On the one hand, they are chary of making any large claim for the work's merit, ever mindful of the derivative nature of much of the text. In 1907 Percy Simpson wrote of the *Discoveries*, 'I doubt if they contain a single original remark.'[1] The year before in a thesis at Paris Maurice Castelain went so far as to contend 'that the Discoveries might be, without any serious objection, left out of the Jonsonian canon; that, practically, the book is not his; or, at least, the merit and interest of it are for the most part attributable to other men'.[2]

Identification of new sources has proceeded apace in the past century, as with Margaret Clayton's identification of John of Salisbury as the source for Jonson's treatment of flattery.[3] The temptation is to leave the text to its own second-handedness and talk about other things – or to use it for source material (that's what Timber means here, initially) but never study the piece on its own: to look through it but not at it. On the other hand, readers of Jonson find something attractive and compelling in the *Discoveries*, though what they find differs vastly from reader to reader. George Parfitt has given a strong portrait of the authorial voice in *Timber* as that of a melancholy sage.[4] Jennifer Brady in a fine article offers a thoroughly different version of the man: he is a 'progenitor ... capable of identifying with his heirs' need to convert humanist legacies to their own use. *Discoveries* encourages its readers to assimilate, to emulate, and to dissent.'[5] Unlike Parfitt's sad sage, Brady's figure is a Whitman-like solicitor of the future, who might say (to cite two verses from 'Crossing Brooklyn Ferry'): 'I am with you, you men and women of a generation, or ever so many generations, hence'; and 'What thought you have of me now, I had as much of you – I laid in my stores in advance.'

Brady has given the most effective treatment to date precisely in that she recognizes that the problems we have with *Timber* were anticipated by its author/compiler; he was there before us. Ian Donaldson, editor of the

Oxford Authors Jonson (1985) from which the present essay draws its citations, expresses a similar intuition: 'Castelain [did not] notice that throughout ... Jonson returns to the very problem that Castelain himself was attempting to describe: the problem of distinguishing between literary imitation and literary plagiarism' (xiv). This is well said; but I want to argue that Donaldson, like Brady, leaves undiscovered a vital dimension of Jonson's little text. The cue here – as so often with Ben Jonson, who decidedly does abide our questions, if we know which ones to ask – lies ready at hand. Here is the full title (521):

TIMBER,

OR,

DISCOVERIES,

Made upon men and matter, as they have flowed out
of his daily readings, or had their reflux
to his peculiar notion of the times,
By
Ben Jonson
Tecum habita, ut noris quam sit tibi curta supellex.
Pers[ius], *Sat.* iv.

At best most of us will puzzle out the tag of verse. Schelling's edition of *Timber* (1892) gives the old rendering by Gifford of the Persius: 'To your own breast in quest of worth repair, / And blush to find how poor a stock is there.' Donaldson provides the crisper Loeb translation of Ramsay: 'live in your own house, and recognize how poorly it is furnished'. This seems clear enough and of scant interest: know yourself, it enjoins. A commonplace – indeed, to begin to twist some meanings here, a commonplace commonplace.

But what if Jonson expected us to do a little work, to seek out, if we don't already have a sense of what this verse of the Latin poet could have meant in directing our attention to its source, the fourth satire of Persius? And here a simple trip to the Loeb, even to the verso Latin therein, may not suffice. For Jonson would expect us, it is a reasonable guess, to consult the brilliant edition in which and in light of which he would have read this poet.

That of course would be the excellent volume by Isaac Casaubon, which was and is recognized as a landmark of classical scholarship; the Loeb editor Ramsay writes that '[o]f the numerous editions of Persius the most famous is the great Classical Edition of Isaac Casaubon (Paris, 1605)'.[6] The commentary here on the six short poems that make up the Persian corpus runs to well over five hundred pages, exceeding the verse text by a factor of better than ten to one. And the Casaubonian explanations by no means prove excessive; indeed in its own day Scaliger remarked that in the book 'la sauce vaut mieux que le poisson'. Jonson himself inscribed a copy of the 1605 tome to his friend Sir John Rowe, commending 'doctissimum PERSIUM cum doctissimo commentario' (Herford and Simpson, *Ben Jonson*, VIII, 663).

So to discover what Jonson might have been up to we want to look at Persius IV, first acquainting ourselves with the poem as it is given in the twentieth-century English versions, then seeing what Jonson following Casaubon would have made of it. I begin with G. G. Ramsay's Loeb volume *Juvenal and Persius* (1961; first published 1918); and W. S. Merwin's *The Satires of Persius* (1961), with introduction and commentary by William S. Anderson. Both the briefest and (as Anderson notes) 'the most obscene' of his six satires, 4 shows 'Persius find[ing] his inspiration for an opening in one of the lesser Platonic dialogues, *Alcibiades I*. But where Plato represented the discussion between Alcibiades and his revered master Socrates as a serious inquiry into the possibilities of directing the destiny of a city-state without training, Persius assumes our familiarity with the situation and immediately focuses attention on the self-deception of Alcibiades'.[7] The poem opens with an abrupt and scornful query:

> 'Rem populi tractas?' barbatum haec crede magistrum
>   dicere, sorbitio tollit quem dira cicutae
>   quo fretus? dic hoc, magni pupille Pericli.

Ramsay translates:

> 'WHAT? Are you busying yourself with affairs of state?'
> Imagine these to be the words of the bearded sage who was
> carried off by that deadly draught of hemlock. Tell me, you
>   ward of the mighty Pericles, what are your qualifications?

The speaker goes on to berate the youth for his lack of self-knowledge. Ramsay paraphrases: 'he has no higher ideals than an old woman who hawks vegetables in the street'. Indeed, '[n]ot one of us has any knowledge of himself', the paraphrase continues. Adulation and flattery deceive us; the best one can do is (the Loeb version concludes): 'Cast off everything that is not yourself; let the mob take back what they have given you; live in your own house, and recognise how poorly it is furnished.'

Prose paraphrase and translation cannot begin to capture the energy and quirkily difficult turns of the Latin; readers of the present volume might think of the opening of *The Alchemist*. A couple of passages in Merwin's rendering gives some idea of the original's velocity and force:

> What's the highest good, to your way of thinking? Rich dishes
> Everlastingly, and nothing to trouble your sunbaths?
> You'll find this hag has the same ideas. Then blow your horn:
> 'I'm Dinomache's son,' (that's the way) 'I'm a dazzler' –
> You, as high-minded as the rag-propping crone
> Screeching, 'Buy my cabbages,' to slatternly house-slaves.

And later in the poem, still Merwin's verse:

> But suppose
> You're lolling oiled and naked in the sun; still some
> Total stranger, knocking your elbow, will spit
> Savagely at you, 'Some habits: plucking your crotch
> To make public its secrets – penis and shrivelled testes!
> You pamper a perfumed beard on your jaws, why then
> Must your cock emerge from an unwhiskered groin? When even
> If five wrestlers hauled on the hairs there, attacking
> Your flabby buttocks with tweezers shaped for the job,
> Still that fern-patch would not be plowed as it should be.'

A far cry indeed from the sententiousness of the Latin tag in isolation. Indeed it's as if we're watching a berating at the opening of a Jonsonian comedy. But more is suggested by the citation of Persius, far more, if we read the fourth satire, not with Ramsay or Merwin, but with Jonson's contemporary, Isaac Casaubon.

In the *Prolegomena* to his edition of the satires, most usefully translated by Peter E. Medine in *English Literary Renaissance* (1976), Casaubon explains that 'the soul of this poetry [satire], its "definition of being" so to speak, is the persecution of vice and exhortation to virtue, to the achieving of which ends it uses humor and jesting like a weapon'. As to this author's difficulty, that is partly to be attributed 'to the genius of the poet, which, since it was great, attacked great things' – and these require the force of strong Longinian figuration. Casaubon writes: 'I shall not deny that there are certain very obscure parts in the fourth and also in the first satires. But I easily forgive the poet when I reflect that he poured in some ink of cuttlefish on purpose, out of fear of that most cruel and bloodthirsty of tyrants against whom they [his satires] were [written]; nor do I doubt that that very wise preceptor Cornutus supported such writings, who as an old man repeatedly whispered to him the words, "be obscure".'[8]

As Anderson remarks, 'Persius must have begun writing his satires near the end of Nero's first five years, around 58 or 59, by which time the spell of youthful brilliance had worn thin and the true perversity of Nero showed through', though 'Nero had not yet reached his nadir when Persius died of a stomach ailment in 62.'[9] But our twentieth-century editions do not offer the explicit identification to be found in Casaubon's commentary on Satire 4: the story of Alcibiades and Socrates represents a defensive ploy on the author's part, his real subject being the incumbent ruler Nero. Even a casual reader will gather as much from the first words of commentary 'AD SATIRAM QVARTAM': 'Nerone principe, quanta fuerit bonorum ciuium indignatio, quantus moeror, cùm viderent perditissimum iuuenem imperio Ro. illudere, facilè cuiuis aestimare est.' ['When Nero became ruler, it can easily be guessed how great was the indignation of the honest citizens, how vast their grief, when they saw this most wretched youth make a mockery of the Roman state.'] The unprepared youth who is now handling public affairs is Nero: 'Remp. suscepit gubernandam, tanto oneri prorsus impar.' ['He assumed power in the state, altogether unequal to such a burden.'] But the poet cannot say this directly and must assail him covertly ('tectè' is the Latin adverb). Indeed this was a dangerous undertaking for the satirist: 'Probè verò norat Persius, cùm ad hanc satiram scribendam se accingeret, quantam rem & quam periculosam moliretur, quamobrem consilio prudentissimo hoc argumentum Platonis imitatione sibi tractandum censuit.' ['Rightly indeed did Persius recognize, when he prepared himself to write this satire, how great and how dangerous a task he was undertaking, wherefore with utmost discretion he deemed it best to handle the subject by way of a Platonic imitation.'] This indirection would provide an excuse with which to defend himself ('suum defendere').[10] Even thus early in his reign Nero was an apt subject of moral reprobation – not yet the (rightly or wrongly) proverbial monster of his later years but already an ideal type of emergent moral corruption.

Even Maurice Castelain, who attributes almost nothing to Jonson, grants that the motto from Persius 'was of his choice'.[11] But no critic seems to have thought through that choice on Jonson's part. And Jonson, the great jailbird among Elizabethan and Jacobean playwrights, was certainly aware of the risks as well as the rewards of topical political satire. Indeed the cue of the Persian tag directs us to an uncanvassed function of the *Discoveries*. Scholars have offered various possibilities: notes for a series of lectures on rhetoric, raw material for future verse compositions, for example. But

what if, like Persius, Ben had in mind an assemblage of applicable commonplaces for political writing? Scholars have devoted so much attention to
Timber as a commonplace book in the *OED*'s third definition of commonplace ('A striking or notable passage, noted . . . in a book of commonplaces')
that they have neglected the first *OED* definition ('A passage of general
application, such as may serve as the basis of argument'). A commonplace
book works as a recycling zone, a site of 'refluxes', to recall the word in
Jonson's title. The book stands as a perpetual invitation to topical appropriation. Kingship, adulation, virtue, decorum: the text positions its
readers at the fruitful fraught intersection of the literary and the political.
And it is we as readers who make the lovely commonplace – the Dol
Common, that famous *res publica* – a Dol particular, a Dol topical.

As to the widespread presence of explicitly political stuff in *Timber*,
Summers and Pebworth rightly observe that 'overtly political statements
are scattered throughout'.[12] Castelain himself found that the political
remarks 'look like the "materials" of a letter to the king on the attributes
and duties of a regal function'. Castelain adds: 'As they particularly insist
on the necessity of clemency, I have sometimes thought that the letter, if
ever written, was meant to implore Charles's mercy on behalf of one of
the poet's friends', perhaps (he proposes) 'John Selden, who remained in
prison from March 1629 to May 1631'.[13] One could do worse than take
the *Discoveries* as a guide to political epistolography, a work that draws
together comments on flattery from sources as different as Persius 4 and
John of Salisbury's *Policraticus, or the Statesman's Handbook*.

But the political material need not be explicit. So when our editor
Donaldson cites (xiii) a portion from the *Discoveries* beginning 'I have
known a man vehement on both sides', he observes 'that the passage is
borrowed from the elder Seneca, describing the habits of his friend the rhe-
torician Porcius Latro'. Donaldson comments: 'Possibly Jonson saw a
resemblance between his own working habits and those of Porcius Latro;
possibly he had an actual acquaintance in mind; possibly he was just following Seneca. We simply cannot tell.' To these intelligent remarks I wish to
add the option of topical applicability: Jonson would have known, in the
politically turbulent late years of his life (when, as scholars agree, *Timber*
was prepared), many a man proved effusively vehement on both sides of dis-
puted questions. We know many such today. If the cap fits . . . ; that's how
satire does its insidious moral work. The present chapter, not itself a reading
of *Timber*, proposes rather an approach to future readings, applications.
Jonson intended just such applications, for us, his progeny, in our own
contested common place: the *res publica*.

By way of conclusion, a return to the initial point. Castelain's researches seemed to render the *Discoveries* a nugatory tissue of borrowings. Perhaps some readers would accept John Palmer's apologia of 1934: 'The words had slept in his ear, with a prodigious company of others, just for this apt occasion. They fall from him as naturally as native wood notes. Jonson wrote quite naturally and involuntarily in quotations.'[14] But few students could buy the notion of Unconscious Ben, so more sophisticated apologiae were constructed, drawing upon the humanist identification with past masters. Jonson would have welcomed these approaches and been familiar with an excellent statement about such procedures in Casaubon's 1605 Persius. In a concluding essay on Persius' imitations of Horace, Jonson would have read these words: 'Et tamen ea arte eo iudicio in hoc parte usus est poèta ingeniosissimus, ut qui adeo multa non sua usurpat, suus tamen ubique sit, nec alieni beneficii setè quicquam, verum propria omnia habere videatur.'[15] ['And yet this cleverest of poets employed such art and such judgment in this regard, that he was like one who takes possession of so many things not his own, in order that he may be himself everywhere; and he may appear to have nothing borrowed greedily from another but all things exclusively his own.'] The Latin original here is tricky, densely elliptical in its Tacitean play of off-kilter reciprocities; but the basic point is clear: the poet appropriates ('usurpat') in such a way that he makes the many borrowings ('multa non sua') altogether his own ('verum propria omnia').

The present chapter suggests that Jonson was not only identifying with the great known masters of the past, but providing stuff for the unknown readers of the future who would find themselves inclined *rem populi tractare*. To them, to us, he passes forward his *Timber*, his *curta supellex*. This last word indicates a supply – but it also referred to the material on which an operation or experiment is performed, the raw material for alchemy. Jonson's early readers could have recognized that, for all its borrowing – indeed, precisely in all its transforming appropriation – *Timber, or Discoveries* bore Jonson's mark on every page. The text speaks in Ben's voice: it manifests his sound, his *timbre*.[16]

Far from meriting exclusion from the Jonsonian corpus, the little book can be read as exemplary of Ben's achievement. It is indeed a *Timbre* in one of the key senses given by Cotgrave in his French dictionary of 1611: 'the creast, or cognizance, that is borne upon the helmet of a coat of Armes'. Cotgrave also reports the phrase 'Cerveau mal timbré. An idle, ignorant, or ill-furnished braine; a wit that wanteth fit or due ornaments.' That would be someone like Persius' Alcibiades or Nero or ... Candidates abound; the central generic rule of satire comes into play here: if the cap fits··· Himself a *cerveau très bien timbré*, Jonson lets us in on, invites our participation in, the arcana of discovery – a word in which the old and the new, the wondrous and the scandalous, delightfully converge.

NOTES

1. Percy Simpson, '"Tanquam Explorator": Jonson's Method in the "Discoveries"', *Modern Language Review* 2.3 (April 1907): 201–10, 202.
2. Maurice Castelain, *'Discoveries': A Critical Edition* (Paris: Hachette, 1906), vii.
3. Margaret Clayton, 'Ben Jonson, "In Travaile with Expression of Another": His Use of John of Salisbury's *Policraticus* in *Timber*', *Review of English Studies* n.s. 30 (1979): 397–408.
4. George Parfitt, *Ben Jonson: Public Poet and Private Man* (London: Dent, 1976), 21–35.
5. Jennifer Brady, 'Progenitors and Other Sons in Ben Jonson's *Discoveries*', in *New Perspectives on Ben Jonson*, ed. James Hirsch (Madison, NJ: Fairleigh Dickinson University Press, 1997), 16–34, 30.
6. G. G. Ramsay, ed., *Juvenal and Persius*, Loeb Classic (Cambridge, MA: Harvard University Press, 1961), xi.
7. *The Satires of Persius*, trans. W. S. Merwin, introduction and notes by William S. Anderson (Bloomington: Indiana University Press, 1961), 29–30.
8. Peter E. Medine, 'Isaac Casaubon's *Prolegomena* to the *Satires* of Persius: An Introduction, Text and Translation', *English Literary Renaissance* 6 (1976): 271–98, 288, 297, 296.
9. Anderson's introduction to Merwin's translation of *The Satires of Persius*, 13–14.
10. *Auli Persi Flacci Satirarum Liber*, ed. Isaac Casaubon (Paris: Droyat, 1605). Commentary on number 4 runs from 315 to 357. I cite and paraphrase the introductory pages, 315–19, the spelling silently regularized, as with the elimination of the long s. A word of thanks is due the scholarly librarians at the Ruth Mortimer Rare Book Room at Smith College, who facilitated my work with their lovely copy of this book.
11. Castelain, *Discoveries*, viii.
12. Claude J. Summers and Ted-Larry Pebworth, *Ben Jonson Revised* (New York: Twayne, 1999), 231.
13. Castelain, *Discoveries*, xxi.
14. John Palmer, *Ben Jonson* (London: Routledge, 1934), 132.
15. Casaubon, ed., *Satirarum* (1605), 523. The 'Persiana Horatii Imitatio' runs from 523 to 558.
16. 'Timbre' did not bear the meaning of quality of sound in early modern English. But it did in seventeenth-century French. See *Le Grand Robert de la Langue Française*, 2001 edn, s.v. 'timbre.'

Bibliography

Ames-Lewis, Francis and Anka Bednarek, eds. *Decorum in Renaissance Narrative Art: Papers Delivered at the Annual Conference of the Association of Art Historians, London, April 1991*. London: Birkbeck College, 1992.

Aquinas, Thomas. *Summa Theologica*. Trans. Fathers of the English Dominican Province. New York: Benziger Bros, 1947.

Athenaeus. *The Deipnosophists*. Trans. Charles Burton Gulick. Loeb Classical Library. London: Heinemann; Cambridge, MA: Harvard University Press, 1961.

Ayres, Philip J. 'Jonson, Northampton, and the "Treason" in *Sejanus*.' *Modern Philology* 80 (1983): 356–63.

Bacon, Francis. *Certain Observations Made upon a Libel*. In *Works*. Ed. J. Spedding, Robert Leslie Ellis, and Douglas Dennon Heath. 9 vols. London: Longman, 1861. Vol. VII.

'Of Masques and Triumphs.' In *Francis Bacon: The Major Works*. Ed. Brian Vickers. Oxford University Press, 2002.

Bakhtin, Mikhail. *Problems of Dostoevsky's Poetics*. Ed. and trans. Caryl Emerson. Manchester University Press, 1984.

Speech Genres and Other Late Essays. Trans. Vern W. McGee. Ed. Caryl Emerson and Michael Holquist (1986). Austin: University of Texas, 1987.

Bakhtin, Mikhail and P. N. Medvedev. *The Formal Method in Literary Scholarship: A Critical Introduction to Sociological Poetics*. Trans. Albert J. Wehrle (1978). Cambridge, MA: Harvard University Press, 1985.

Barish, Jonas A. *The Anti-Theatrical Prejudice*. Berkeley: University of California Press, 1984.

Ben Jonson and the Language of Prose Comedy. Cambridge, MA: Harvard University Press, 1960.

Barker, J. R. 'A Pendant to Drummond of Hawthornden's Conversations.' *Review of English Studies* n.s. 16 (1965): 284–8.

Barrell, John. *Poetry, Language and Politics*. Manchester and New York: Saint Martin's Press, 1988.

Barroll, Leeds. 'The Court of the First Stuart Queen.' In *The Mental World of the Jacobean Court*. Ed. Linda Levy Peck. Cambridge University Press, 1991. 191–208.

Barton, Anne. *Ben Jonson, Dramatist*. Cambridge University Press, 1984.

Batchelor, John, Tom Cain, and Claire Lamont, eds. *Shakespearean Continuities: Essays in Honour of E. A. J. Honigmann.* Basingstoke: Macmillan, 1997.

Baumlin, James S. 'Ciceronian Decorum and the Temporalities of Renaissance Rhetoric.' In *Rhetoric and Kairos: Essays in History, Theory, and Praxis.* Ed. Phillip Sipiora and James S. Baumlin. Albany: State University Press of New York, 2002. 138–64.

Beal, Peter, comp. *Index of English Literary Manuscripts.* 4 vols. London and New York: Mansell, 1980. Vol. I.

Benedikt, Amélie Frost. 'On Doing the Right Thing at the Right Time: Toward an Ethics of *Kairos*.' In *Rhetoric and Kairos: Essays in History, Theory, and Praxis.* Ed. Phillip Sipiora and James S. Baumlin. Albany: State University Press of New York, 2002. 226–36.

Beresford, M. W. 'The Common Informer, the Penal Statutes and Economic Regulation.' *Economic History Review* 2nd series 10 (1957–8): 221–38.

Bevington, David and Peter Holbrook, eds. *The Politics of the Stuart Court Masque.* Cambridge University Press, 1998.

Bidpai. *The Fables of Bidpai.* Trans. Thomas North. Ed. Joseph Jacobs. London, 1888.

Bishop, Tom. 'The Gingerbread Host: Tradition and Novelty in the Jacobean Masque.' In *The Politics of the Stuart Court Masque.* Ed. David Bevington and Peter Holbrook. Cambridge University Press, 1998. 88–120.

Blackley, Brian M. 'The Generic Play and Spenserian Parody of John Donne's "Metempsychosis".' Diss. University of Kentucky, 1994.

Bland, Mark. 'Jonson, Biathanatos and the Interpretation of Manuscript Evidence.' *Studies in Bibliography* 51 (1998): 154–82.

Blissett, William. 'Roman Ben Jonson.' In *Ben Jonson's 1616 Folio.* Ed. Jennifer Brady and W. H. Herendeen. Newark: University of Delaware Press; London/Toronto: Associated University Presses, 1991. 90–110.

Boehrer, Bruce. *The Fury of Men's Gullet: Ben Jonson and the Digestive Canal.* Philadelphia: University of Pennsylvania, 1997.

 'The Poet of Labour: Authorship and Property in the Work of Ben Jonson.' *Philological Quarterly* 72 (1993): 289–312.

Boughner, Daniel C. 'Lewkenor and *Volpone*.' *Notes and Queries* n.s. 9 (1962): 124–30.

Brady, Jennifer. 'Progenitors and Other Sons in Ben Jonson's *Discoveries*.' In *New Perspectives on Ben Jonson.* Ed. James Hirsch. Madison, NJ: Fairleigh Dickinson University Press, 1997. 16–34.

Brady, Jennifer and W. H. Herendeen, eds. *Ben Jonson's 1616 Folio.* Newark: University of Delaware Press; London/Toronto: Associated University Presses, 1991.

Brennan, Michael G. 'Creating Female Authorship in the Early Seventeenth Century: Ben Jonson and Lady Mary Wroth.' In *Women's Writing and the Circulation of Ideas: Manuscript Publication in England 1550–1800.* Ed. George L. Justice and Nathan Tinker. Cambridge University Press, 2002. 73–93.

Briggs, William Dinsmore. 'Ben Jonson: Notes on "Underwoods XXX" and on the "New Inn".' *Modern Philology* 10 (1913): 573–85.

Burdett, John and Jonathan Wright. 'Ben Jonson in Recent General Scholarship, 1972–1996.' *Ben Jonson Journal* 4 (1997): 151–79.

Burrow, Colin. 'Hugh Holland.' *Oxford Dictionary of National Biography*. Oxford University Press, 2005.

Burt, Richard. *Licensed by Authority: Ben Jonson and the Discourses of Censorship*. Ithaca, NY: Cornell University Press, 1993.

Butler, Martin. 'Courtly Negotiations.' In *The Politics of the Stuart Court Masque*. Ed. David Bevington and Peter Holbrook. Cambridge University Press, 1998. 20–40.

'"Servant But Not Slave": Ben Jonson at the Jacobean Court.' *Proceedings of the British Academy* 90 (1996): 65–93.

Butler, Martin, ed. *Re-Presenting Ben Jonson: Text, History, Performance*. Basingstoke: Macmillan, 1999.

Cain, Tom. '"Comparisons and Wounding Flouts": *Love's Labour's Lost* and the Tradition of Personal Satire.' In *Shakespearean Continuities: Essays in Honour of E. A. J. Honigmann*. Ed. John Batchelor, Tom Cain, and Claire Lamont. Basingstoke: Macmillan, 1997. 193–205.

Chedgzoy, Kate, Melanie Hansen, and Suzanne Trill, eds. *Voicing Women: Gender and Sexuality in Early Modern Writing*. Keele, Staffordshire: Keele University Press, 1996.

Chettle, Henry. *England's Mourning Garment*. London: V. S. for Thomas Millington, 1603.

Cicero. *De Inventione, De Optimo Genere Oratorum, Topica*. Ed. and trans. H. M. Hubbell. Loeb Classical Library (1949). Cambridge, MA: Harvard University Press, 1968.

De Officiis. Trans. Walter Miller. Loeb Classical Library (1913). London: Heinemann; Cambridge, MA: Harvard University Press, 1968.

'De Oratore', 'Brutus' and 'Orator'. Trans. G. L. Hendrickson and H. M. Hubbell. London: William Heinemann; Cambridge, MA: Harvard University Press, 1939.

Clayton, Margaret. 'Ben Jonson, "In Travaile with Expression of Another": His Use of John of Salisbury's *Policraticus* in *Timber*.' *Review of English Studies* n.s. 30 (1979): 397–408.

Colie, Rosalie L. *The Resources of Kind: Genre-Theory in the Renaissance*. Berkeley: University of California Press, 1973.

Collinson, Patrick. *Elizabethan Essays*. London: Hambledon Press, 1994.

Corthell, Ronald J. 'Donne's "Metempsychosis": An "Alarum to Truth."' *Studies in English Literature* 21 (1981): 97–110.

Cousins, A. D. *Shakespeare's Sonnets and Narrative Poems*. Harlow: Longman, 2000.

Cousins, A. D. and Damian Grace, eds. *Donne and the Resources of Kind*. Madison: Fairleigh Dickinson University Press, 2002.

Cousins, A. D. and R. J. Webb. 'Appropriating and Attributing the Supernatural in the Early Modern Country House Poem.' *Early Modern Literary Studies* 11 (2005): 1–26.

Craig, Hugh. 'Jonson, the Antimasque and the "Rules of Flattery".' In *The Politics of the Stuart Court Masque*. Ed. David Bevington and Peter Holbrook. Cambridge University Press, 1998. 176–96.

Croft, Pauline. 'The Religion of Robert Cecil.' *Historical Journal* 34 (1991): 773–96.

———. 'The Reputation of Robert Cecil: Libels, Political Opinion and Popular Awareness in the Early Seventeenth Century.' *Transactions of the Royal Historical Society* 1 (1991): 43–68.

Croft, Pauline, ed. *Patronage, Culture and Power: The Early Cecils*. Studies in British Art 8. New Haven: Yale Center for British Art and Yale University Press; London: Paul Mellon Centre for Studies in British Art, 2002.

Cruickshanks, Eveline, ed. *The Stuart Courts*. Stroud: Sutton Publishing, 2000.

Cubeta, Paul M. 'A Jonsonian Ideal: "To Penshurst".' *Philological Quarterly* 42 (1963): 14–24.

Davies, Sir John. *The Poems of Sir John Davies*. Ed. Robert Krueger. Oxford: Clarendon Press, 1975.

De Luna, B. N. *Jonson's Romish Plot: A Study of 'Catiline' and its Historical Context*. Oxford: Clarendon Press, 1967.

Dollimore, Jonathan and Alan Sinfield, eds. *Political Shakespeare: New Essays in Cultural Materialism*. Ithaca, NY: Cornell University Press, 1985.

Donaldson, Ian. *Jonson's Magic Houses: Essays in Interpretation*. Oxford: Clarendon Press, 1997.

———. 'Jonson's Poetry.' In *The Cambridge Companion to Ben Jonson*. Ed. Richard Harp and Stanley Stewart. Cambridge University Press, 2000. 119–39.

Doni, Anton Francesco. *Moral Philosophy*. Trans. Sir Thomas North. London, 1570.

Donne, John. *Devotions upon Emergent Occasions*. Ed. Anthony Raspa. Oxford University Press, 1987.

———. *John Donne's Poetry*. Ed. Donald R. Dickson. New York and London: Norton, 2007.

———. *The Poems of John Donne*. Ed. Herbert Grierson. 2 vols. Oxford University Press, 1912.

———. *Pseudo-Martyr*. Ed. Anthony Raspa. Montreal and Kingston: McGill-Queens University Press, 1993.

Dryden, John. *Of Dramatick Poesie: An Essay by John Dryden Esq*. London, 1668.

Dubrow, Heather. *A Happier Eden*. Ithaca, NY: Cornell University Press, 1990.

———. 'The Country-House Poem: A Study in Generic Development.' *Genre* 12 (1979): 153–79.

Duckworth, Alistair M. 'Raymond Williams and Literary History.' *Papers on Language and Literature* 11 (1975): 420–41.

Dundas, Judith. 'A Pattern of the Mind: The Country House Poem Revisited.' *Connotations* 8.1 (1998–9): 22–47.

Dutton, Richard. *Ben Jonson: Authority: Criticism*. Basingstoke: Macmillan, 1996.

Ben Jonson: To the First Folio. Cambridge University Press, 1983.

'Jonson, Shakespeare, and the Exorcists.' *Shakespeare Survey* 58 (2005): 15–22.

'Jonson's Satiric Styles.' In *The Cambridge Companion to Ben Jonson*. Ed. Richard Harp and Stanley Stewart. Cambridge University Press, 2000. 58–71.

'The Lone Wolf: Jonson's Epistle to *Volpone*.' In *Refashioning Ben Jonson: Gender, Politics and the Jonsonian Canon*. Ed. Julie Sanders with Kate Chedgzoy and Susan Wiseman. Basingstoke: Macmillan, 1998. 114–33.

Mastering the Revels: The Regulation and Censorship of Early Modern Drama. Iowa City: University of Iowa Press, 1991.

'Venice in London, London in Venice.' In *Mighty Europe 1400–1700: Writing an Early Modern Continent*. Ed. Andrew Hiscock. Oxford: Peter Lang, 2007. 133–51.

'*Volpone* and Beast Fable: Early Modern Analogic Reading.' *Huntington Library Quarterly* 67 (2004): 347–70.

Elsky, Martin. 'Ben Jonson's Poems of Place and the Culture of Land: From the Military to the Domestic.' *English Literary Renaissance* 31 (2001): 392–411.

'Microhistory and Cultural Geography: Ben Jonson's "To Sir Robert Wroth" and the Absorption of Local Community in the Commonwealth.' *Renaissance Quarterly* 53. 2 (2000): 500–28.

'The Mixed Genre of Ben Jonson's "To Penshurst" and the Perilous Springs of Netherlandish Landscape.' *Ben Jonson Journal* 9 (2002): 1–35.

Erasmus, Desiderius. *The Education of a Christian Prince*. Trans. Lester K. Born. New York: Columbia University Press, 1936.

Evans, Robert C. *Ben Jonson and the Poetics of Patronage*. Lewisburg, PA: Bucknell University Press; London: Associated University Presses, 1989.

Habits of Mind: Evidence and Effects of Ben Jonson's Reading. Lewisburg, PA: Bucknell University Press, 1995.

Jonson, Lipsius and the Politics of Renaissance Stoicism. Durango, CO: Longwood, 1992.

Falco, Raphael. *Conceived Presences: Literary Genealogy in Renaissance England*. Amherst: University of Massachusetts Press, 1994.

Fermor, Sharon. 'Decorum in Figural Movement: The Dance as Measure and Metaphor.' In *Decorum in Renaissance Narrative Art: Papers delivered at the Annual Conference of the Association of Art Historians, London, April 1991*. Ed. Francis Ames-Lewis and Anka Bednarek. London: Birkbeck College, 1992. 78–88.

Ficino, Marsilio. *The 'Philebus' Commentary*. Ed. and trans. Michael J. B. Allen. Berkeley: University of California Press, 1975.

Fish, Stanley. 'Authors-Readers: Jonson's Community of the Same.' *Representations* 7 (1984): 26–58.

Fleay, F. G. *A Biographical Chronicle of English Drama, 1559–1642*. 2 vols. London: Reeves and Turner, 1891.

Flynn, Dennis. 'Donne's "*Amicissimo, et Meritissimo Ben: Jonson*" and the Daring of *Volpone*.' *The Literary Imagination* 6 (2004): 368–89.

'Donne's *Ignatius His Conclave* and Other Libels on Sir Robert Cecil.' *John Donne Journal* 6 (1987): 163–83.

John Donne and the Ancient Catholic Nobility. Bloomington and Indianapolis: Indiana University Press, 1995.

Fowler, Alastair. 'The Beginnings of English Georgic.' In *Renaissance Genres: Essays on Theory, History and Interpretation*. Ed. Barbara Kiefer Lewalski. Cambridge, MA: Harvard University Press, 1986. 105–25.

'The "Better Marks" of Jonson's "To Penshurst".' *Review of English Studies* n.s. 24 (1973): 266–82.

The Country House Poem: A Cabinet of Seventeenth-Century Estate Poems and Related Items. Edinburgh University Press, 1994.

'Country House Poems: The Politics of a Genre.' *The Seventeenth Century* 1 (1986): 1–14.

'Georgic and Pastoral: Laws of Genre in the Seventeenth Century.' In *Culture and Cultivation in Early Modern England: Writing and the Land*. Ed. Michael Leslie and Timothy Raylor. Leicester: Leicester University Press, 1992. 81–8.

Kinds of Literature: An Introduction to the Theory of Genres and Modes. 1982. Oxford: Clarendon Press, 1985.

'The Silva Tradition in Jonson's *The Forrest*.' In *Poetic Traditions of the English Renaissance*. Ed. Maynard Mack and George deForest Lord. New Haven: Yale University Press, 1982. 163–80.

Fraser, Antonia. *The Gunpowder Plot*. London: Phoenix, 2002.

Frye, Northrop. *An Anatomy of Criticism*. Princeton University Press, 1957.

Fulgentii, Fabii Planciadis. *Opera*. Ed. Rudolfus Helm. Lipsiae: Teubneri, 1898.

Fumerton, Patricia. *Cultural Aesthetics: Renaissance Literature and the Practice of Social Ornament*. Chicago University Press, 1991.

Gaggero, Christopher. 'Civic Humanism and Gender Politics in Jonson's *Catiline*.' *Studies in English Literature* 45.2 (2005): 401–24.

Gianakaras, G. J. 'Jonson's Use of "Avocatori" in *Volpone*.' *English Language Notes* 12 (1974): 8–14.

Goffman, Erving. *The Presentation of Self in Everyday Life*. 1959. Rev. edn New York: Doubleday, n.d.

Stigma: Notes on the Management of Spoiled Identity. 1963. Harmondsworth: Penguin, 1973.

Goldberg, Jonathan. *James I and the Politics of Literature*. Baltimore: Johns Hopkins University Press, 1983.

Greenblatt, Stephen J. 'The False Ending in *Volpone*.' *Journal of English and Germanic Philology* 75 (1976): 90–104.

Greene, Thomas M. 'Ben Jonson and the Centred Self.' *Studies in English Literature, 1500–1900* 10 (1970): 325–48.

The Light in Troy: Imitation and Discovery in Renaissance Poetry. New Haven: Yale University Press, 1982.

Gross, Kenneth. 'John Donne's Lyric Skepticism: In Strange Way.' *Modern Philology* 101 (2004): 371–99.

Guibbory, Achsah. *The Map of Time: Seventeenth-Century English Literature and Ideas of Pattern in History*. Urbana: University of Illinois Press, 1986.

Hackett, Helen. *Women and Romance Fiction in the English Renaissance*. Cambridge University Press, 2000.

Hadfield, Andrew. *Shakespeare and Republicanism*. Cambridge University Press, 2005.

Harp, Richard. 'Jonson's "To Penshurst": The Country House as Church.' *John Donne Journal* 7.1 (1985): 73–89.

Harp, Richard and Stanley Stewart, eds. *The Cambridge Companion to Ben Jonson*. Cambridge University Press, 2000.

Harvey, Elizabeth D. and Katharine Eisaman Maus, eds. *Soliciting Interpretation: Literary Theory and Seventeenth-Century English Poetry*. University of Chicago Press, 1990.

Haynes, Jonathan. *The Social Relations of Jonson's Theatre*. Cambridge University Press, 1992.

Hayward, John. *The First and Second Parts of John Hayward's 'The Life and Reign of King Henrie IIII.'* Ed. John J. Manning, Camden Fourth Series 42. London: Offices of the Royal Historical Society, University College, London, 1991.

Helgerson, Richard. *Self-Crowned Laureates: Spenser, Jonson, Milton and the Literary System*. Berkeley: University of California Press, 1983.

Henslowe, Philip. *Henslowe's Diary*. Ed. R. A. Foakes and R. T. Rickert. Cambridge University Press, 1961.

Herford, C. H., Percy Simpson, and Evelyn Simpson, eds. *Ben Jonson*, 11 vols. Oxford: Clarendon Press, 1925–52. Rpt 1965–70.

Hibbard, G. R. 'The Country House Poem of the Seventeenth Century.' *Journal of the Warburg and Courtauld Institutes* 19.1–2 (1956): 159–74.

Hirsch, James, ed. *New Perspectives on Ben Jonson*. Madison, NJ: Fairleigh Dickinson University Press, 1997.

Honigmann, E. A. J. *John Weever: A Biography of a Literary Associate of Shakespeare and Jonson together with a facsimile of Weever's 'Epigrammes' (1599)*. Manchester University Press, 1987.

Hyland, Peter. *Disguise and Role-Playing in Ben Jonson's Drama*. Salzburg: Institute for English Speech and Drama, 1977.

Inwood, Brad, ed. *The Cambridge Companion to the Stoics*. Cambridge University Press, 2000.

Jackson-Stops, Gervase, Gordon J. Schochet, Lena Cowen Orlin, and Elisabeth Blair MacDougall, eds. *The Fashioning and Functioning of the British Country House*. Washington, DC: National Gallery of Art, 1989.

Jacobs, Joseph, ed. *The Fables of Bidpai*. London, 1888.

Jenkins, Hugh. *Feigned Commonwealths: The Country-House Poem and the Fashioning of the Ideal Community*. Pittsburgh, PA: Duquesne University Press, 1998.

Jonson, Ben. *Ben Jonson*. Ed. C. H. Herford, Percy Simpson, and Evelyn Simpson. 11 vols. Oxford: Clarendon Press, 1925–52. Rpt 1965–70.

Ben Jonson. Ed. Ian Donaldson. The Oxford Authors. Oxford University Press, 1985.

Ben Jonson: The Complete Poems. Ed. George Parfitt. Harmondsworth: Penguin, 1975; rpt New Haven: Yale University Press, 1982.

Ben Jonson: Poems. Ed. Ian Donaldson. Oxford University Press, 1975.

The Complete Masques. Ed. Stephen Orgel. New Haven: Yale University Press, 1969.

'Discoveries': A Critical Edition. Ed. Maurice Castelain. Paris: Hachette, 1906.

Epicene, or The Silent Woman. Ed. Richard Dutton. Revels Plays. Manchester University Press, 2003.

Poetaster. Ed. Tom Cain. Revels Plays. Manchester University Press, 1995.

Sejanus. Ed. Philip J. Ayres. Revels Plays. Manchester University Press, 1990.

Sejanus. Ed. Tom Cain. *The Cambridge Edition of the Works of Ben Jonson*. Cambridge University Press, forthcoming.

Selected Masques. Ed. Stephen Orgel (1970). New Haven: Yale University Press, 1975.

Volpone, or The Fox. Ed. R. B. Parker (1983). Revels Plays. Rev. edn. Manchester University Press, 1999.

Jonson, Ben, George Chapman, and John Marston. *Eastward Ho!* Ed. R. W. Van Fossen. Revels Plays. Manchester University Press, 1979.

Justice, George L. and Nathan Tinker, eds. *Women's Writing and the Circulation of Ideas: Manuscript Publication in England 1550–1800*. Cambridge University Press, 2002.

Kahn, Victoria. *Rhetoric, Prudence, and Skepticism in the Renaissance*. Ithaca, NY: Cornell University Press, 1985.

Kastner, L. E., ed. *The Poetical Works of William Drummond of Hawthornden*. 2 vols. Manchester University Press, 1913.

Kay, W. David. *Ben Jonson: A Literary Life*. Basingstoke: Macmillan, 1995.

Kinneavy, James L. 'Kairos in Classical and Modern Rhetorical Theory.' In *Rhetoric and Kairos: Essays in History, Theory, and Praxis*. Ed. Phillip Sipiora and James S. Baumlin. Albany: State University of New York Press, 2002. 343–59.

Kinney, Clare R. 'Mary Wroth's Guilty "secrett art": The Poetics of Jealousy in *Pamphilia to Amphilanthus*.' In *Write or Be Written: Early Modern Women Poets and Cultural Constraints*. Ed. Barbara Smith and Ursula Appelt. Aldershot: Ashgate, 2001. 69–85.

Klause, John. 'The Montaigneity of Donne's "Metempsychosis".' In *Renaissance Genres: Essays on Theory, History and Interpretation*. Ed. Barbara Lewalski. Cambridge, MA: Harvard University Press, 1986. 418–43.

Knowles, James. '"To raise a house of better frame": Jonson's Cecilian Entertainments.' In *Patronage, Culture and Power: The Early Cecils*. Ed. Pauline Croft. Studies in British Art 8. New Haven: Yale Centre for British Art and Yale University Press; London: Paul Mellon Centre for Studies in British Art, 2002. 181–95.

Lane, M. S. *Method and Politics in Plato's Statesman*. Cambridge University Press, 1998.

Lanham, Richard A. *A Handlist of Rhetorical Terms*. Berkeley: University of California Press, 1991.

Leinwand, Theodore B. 'Negotiation and New Historicism.' *PMLA* 105.3 (1990): 477–90.

Leslie, Michael and Timothy Raylor. *Culture and Cultivation in Early Modern England: Writing and the Land*. Leicester University Press, 1992.

Levin, Harry. 'Jonson's Metempsychosis.' *Philological Quarterly* 22 (1943): 231–9.

Lewalski, Barbara Kiefer. 'The Lady of the Country-House Poem.' In *The Fashioning and Functioning of the British Country House*. Ed. Gervase Jackson-Stops, Gordon J. Schochet, Lena Cowen Orlin, and Elisabeth Blair MacDougall. Washington, DC: National Gallery of Art, 1989. 261–75.

Writing Women in Jacobean England. Cambridge, MA: Harvard University Press, 1994.

Lewalski, Barbara Kiefer, ed. *Renaissance Genres: Essays on Theory, History and Interpretation*. Cambridge, MA: Harvard University Press, 1986.

Lindley, David. 'Courtly Play: The Politics of Chapman's *The Memorable Masque*.' In *The Stuart Courts*. Ed. Eveline Cruickshanks. Stroud: Sutton Publishing, 2000. 43–58.

'Embarrassing Ben: Masques for Frances Howard.' *English Literary Renaissance* 16 (1986): 343–59.

Lipking, Lawrence. *Life of the Poet: Beginning and Ending Poetic Careers*. University of Chicago Press, 1981.

Lipsius, Justus. *Sixe Bookes of Politickes or Civil Doctrine*. Trans. William Jones. London: Richard Field for William Ponsonby, 1594.

Two Bookes of Constancie. Trans. Sir John Stradling. Ed. Rudolf Kirk. Annot. Clayton Morris Hall. New Brunswick: Rutgers University Press, 1939.

Little, Geoffrey, ed. *Apprehensions: Essays in Honour of G. A. Wilkes*. Sydney: Challis Press, 1996.

Loewenstein, Joseph. *Ben Jonson and Possessive Authorship*. Cambridge University Press, 2002.

'The Script in the Marketplace.' *Representations* 12 (1985): 101–14.

Long, A. A. *Hellenistic Philosophy: Stoics, Epicureans, Sceptics* (1974). 2nd edn. Berkeley: University of California Press, 1986.

Loxley, James. *The Complete Critical Guide to Ben Jonson*. London: Routledge, 2002.

McBride, Kari Boyd. *Country House Discourse in Early Modern England: A Cultural Study of Landscape and Legitimacy*. Aldershot: Ashgate, 2001.

McCanles, Michael. *Jonsonian Discriminations: The Humanist Poet and the Praise of True Nobility*. University of Toronto Press, 1992.

McClung, William A. 'The Country-House Arcadia.' In *The Fashioning and Functioning of the British Country House*. Ed. Gervase Jackson-Stops, Gordon J. Schochet, Lena Cowen Orlin, and Elisabeth Blair MacDougall. Washington, DC: National Gallery of Art, 1989. 277–87.

The Country House in English Renaissance Poetry. Berkeley: University of California Press, 1977.

McComiskey, Bruce. *'Gorgias' and the New Sophistic Rhetoric*. Carbondale: Southern Illinois University Press, 2002.

McCrae, Adriana. *Constant Minds: Political Virtue and the Lipsian Paradigm in England, 1584–1650*. University of Toronto Press, 1997.

McGuire, Mary Ann C. 'The Cavalier Country-House Poem: Mutations on a Jonsonian Tradition.' *Studies in English Literature* 19 (1979): 93–108.

Maclean, Ian. *The Renaissance Notion of Woman: A Study in the Fortunes of Scholasticism and Medical Science in European Intellectual Life*. 1983. Rpt Cambridge University Press, 1992.

McMullan, Gordon, ed. *Renaissance Configurations: Voices/Bodies/Spaces 1580–1690*. London: Macmillan, 1998.

McPherson, David. *Shakespeare, Jonson and the Myth of Venice*. Newark: University of Delaware Press, 1991.

McRae, Andrew. *God Speed the Plough: The Representation of Agrarian England, 1500–1660*. Cambridge University Press, 1996.

Machiavelli, Niccolò. *The Discourses*. Ed. Bernard Crick. Trans. Leslie J. Walker SJ with revisions by Brian Richardson. London: Penguin Books, 1998.

The Prince. Intro. Max Lerner. New York: The Modern Library, 1950.

Mack, Maynard and George deForest Lord, eds. *Poetic Traditions of the English Renaissance*. New Haven: Yale University Press, 1982.

Macrobius. *Commentarii in Somnium Scipionis*. Ed. Jacobus Willis. Leipzig: Teubner Verlagsgesellschaft, 1970.

Marcus, Leah S. *The Politics of Mirth: Jonson, Herrick, Milton, Marvell and the Defense of Old Holiday Pastimes*. University of Chicago Press, 1986.

Marotti, Arthur F. *John Donne, Coterie Poet*. Madison: University of Wisconsin Press, 1986.

Martial. *Epigrams*. Ed. and trans. Walter C. A. Ker (1919). Loeb Classical Library. 2 vols. Cambridge, MA: Harvard University Press, 1990.

Martin, Richard. *A Speach Delivered to the Kings Most Excellent Majesty . . . By Maister Richard Martin of the Middle Temple*. London: Thomas Thorppe [sic] for William Aspley, 1603.

Maus, Katharine Eisaman. *Ben Jonson and the Roman Frame of Mind*. Princeton University Press, 1984.

'Facts of the Matter: Satiric and Ideal Economies in the Jonsonian Imagination.' In *Ben Jonson's 1616 Folio*. Ed. Jennifer Brady and W. H. Herendeen. Newark: University of Delaware Press; London/Toronto: Associated University Presses, 1991. 64–89.

Mears, Francis. *Wits Common Wealth: The Second Part*. 2nd edn. London: William Stansby for Richard Royston, 1634.

Medine, Peter E. 'Isaac Casaubon's *Prolegomena* to the *Satires* of Persius: An Introduction, Text and Translation.' *English Literary Renaissance* 6 (1976): 271–98.

Mentz, Steve. *Romance for Sale in Early Modern England*. Aldershot: Ashgate, 2006.

Mickel, Lesley. *Ben Jonson's Antimasques: A History of Growth and Decline*. Aldershot: Ashgate, 1999.

Miles, Rosalind. *Ben Jonson: His Craft and Art*. London: Routledge, 1990.

Miller, Naomi J. and Gary Waller, eds. *Reading Mary Wroth: Representing Alternatives in Early Modern England*. Knoxville: University of Tennessee Press, 1991.

Milton, John. *The Tenure of Magistrates and Kings*. Ed. Merritt Y. Hughes. In *The Complete Prose Works of John Milton*. Gen. ed. Don M. Wolfe. 8 vols. New Haven and London: Yale University Press, 1962. Vol. III.

Mitchell, Marea and Dianne Osland. *Representing Women and Female Desire*. New York: Palgrave, 2005.

Molesworth, Charles. 'Property and Virtue: The Genre of the Country-House Poem in the Seventeenth Century.' *Genre* 1 (1968): 141–57.

Monsarrat, Giles D. *Light from the Porch: Stoicism and English Renaissance Literature*. Paris: Didier-Erudition, 1984.

Montaigne, Michel de. 'Of Drunkennesse.' In *The Essayes of Montaigne*. Trans. John Florio. New York: Random House, n.d.

Morford, Mark. *Stoics and Neostoics: Rubens and the Circle of Lipsius*. Princeton University Press, 1991.

Mortimer, Anthony. 'The Feigned Commonwealth in the Poetry of Ben Jonson.' *Studies in English Literature* 13.1 (1973): 69–79.

Mueller, Janel M. 'Donne's Epic Venture in "Metempsychosis".' *Modern Philology* 70 (1972): 109–37.

Mulryan, John. 'Jonson's Classicism.' In *The Cambridge Companion to Ben Jonson*. Ed. Richard Harp and Stanley Stewart. Cambridge University Press, 2000. 163–74.

Mulryne, J. R. and Margaret Shewring. *Theatre and Government under the Early Stuarts*. Cambridge University Press, 1993.

Mulryne, J. R. and Margaret Shewring, eds. *Theatre of the English and Italian Renaissance*. Basingstoke: Macmillan, 1991.

Murray, W. A. 'What Was the Soul of the Apple?' *Review of English Studies* 38 (1959): 141–55.

Niccols, Richard. *The Beggars Ape*. Post. Brice Harris. New York: Scholars' Facsimiles and Reprints, 1936.

Nietzsche, Friedrich. 'The Birth of Tragedy.' In *The Birth of Tragedy and The Case of Wagner*. Trans. Walter Kaufmann. New York: Vintage, 1967.

Norbrook, David. *Poetry and Politics in the English Renaissance*. Oxford University Press, 2002.

Oestreich, Gerhard. *Neostoicism and the Early Modern State*. Ed. Brigitta Oestreich and H. G. Koenigsberger. Trans. David McLintock. Cambridge University Press, 1982.

Orgel, Stephen, *The Illusion of Power*. Berkeley: University of California Press, 1975.

'Jonson and the Amazons.' In *Soliciting Interpretation: Literary Theory and Seventeenth-Century English Poetry*. Ed. Elizabeth D. Harvey and Katharine Eisaman Maus. Chicago: University of Chicago Press, 1990. 119–42.

The Jonsonian Masque. Cambridge, MA: Harvard University Press, 1967.

'Marginal Jonson.' In *The Politics of the Stuart Court Masque*. Ed. David Bevington and Peter Holbrook. Cambridge University Press, 1998. 144–75.

Ostovich, Helen. 'Hell for Lovers: Shades of Adultery in *The Devil is an Ass*.' In *Refashioning Ben Jonson: Gender, Politics and the Jonsonian Canon*. Ed. Julie Sanders with Kate Chedgzoy and Susan Wiseman. Basingstoke: Macmillan, 1998. 155–82.

Pachecho, Anita, ed. *Early Women Writers 1600–1720*. London: Longman, 1998.

Paglia, Camille. *Sexual Personae: Art and Decadence from Nefertiti to Emily Dickinson*. London: Penguin, 1991.

Palmer, John. *Ben Jonson*. London: Routledge, 1934.

Parfitt, George. *Ben Jonson: Public Poet and Private Man*. London: Dent, 1976.

Parker, R. B. 'Jonson's Venice.' In *Theatre of the English and Italian Renaissance*. Ed. J. R. Mulryne and M. Shewring. Basingstoke: Macmillan, 1991. 95–112.

'*Volpone* and *Reynard the Fox*.' *Renaissance Drama* 7 (1976): 3–42.

Parry, Graham. 'The Politics of the Jacobean Masque.' In *Theatre and Government under the Early Stuarts*. Ed. J. R. Mulryne and Margaret Shewring. Cambridge University Press, 1993. 87–117.

Partridge, E. B. *The Broken Compass*. London: Chatto and Windus, 1958.

Patterson, Annabel. *Reading Between the Lines*. London: Routledge, 1993.

'"Roman-cast Similitude": Ben Jonson and the English Use of Roman History.' In *Rome in the Renaissance: The City and the Myth*. Ed. P. A. Ramsey. Binghamton, NY: Center for Medieval and Early Renaissance Studies, 1982. 381–94.

Payne, Alina. *The Architectural Treatise in the Italian Renaissance: Architectural Invention, Ornament, and Literary Culture*. Cambridge University Press, 1999.

Peck, Linda Levy, ed. *The Mental World of the Jacobean Court*. Cambridge University Press, 1991.

Peltonen, Markku. *Classical Humanism and Republicanism in English Political Thought 1570–1640*. Cambridge University Press, 1995.

Perkinson, Richard M. '*Volpone* and the Reputation of Venetian Justice.' *Modern Language Review* 35 (1940): 11–18.

Persius Flaccus, Aulus. *Auli Persi Flacci Satirarum Liber*. Ed. Isaac Casaubon. Paris: Droyat, 1605.

The Satires of Persius. Trans. W. S. Merwin. Introduction and notes by William S. Anderson. Bloomington: Indiana University Press, 1961.

Peterson, Richard S. *Imitation and Praise in the Poems of Ben Jonson*. New Haven: Yale University Press, 1981.

'Laurel Crown and Ape's Tail: New Light on Spenser's Career from Sir Thomas Tresham.' *Spenser Studies* 12 (1998): 1–31.

Plato. *Gorgias*. Trans. W. R. M. Lamb. Loeb Classical Library (1925). London: Heinemann; Cambridge, MA: Harvard University Press, 1967.

The Republic. Trans. Robin Waterfield. Oxford University Press, 1998.

Plutarch. *Moralia*. Trans. Harold Cherniss and William C. Helmbold (1957). London: William Heinemann; Cambridge, MA: Harvard University Press, 1968.

    The Training of Children. Trans. R. C. Trench. In *The Essays and Miscellanies*. 3 vols. New York: Crowell, 1909.

Pocock, J. G. A. *The Machiavellian Moment: Florentine Political Thought and the Atlantic Republican Tradition*. Princeton University Press, 1975.

    'Texts as Events: Reflections on the History of Political Thought.' In *Politics of Discourse: The Literature and History of Seventeenth-Century England*. Ed. Kevin Sharpe and Steven Zwicker. Berkeley: University of California Press, 1987. 21–34.

Quilligan, Maureen. 'The Constant Subject: Instability and Female Authority in Wroth's *Urania* Poems.' In *Soliciting Interpretation: Literary Theory and Seventeenth-Century English Poetry*. Ed. Elizabeth D. Harvey and Katharine Eisaman Maus. University of Chicago Press, 1990. 307–35.

Quintilian. *Institutio Oratoria*. Trans. H. E. Butler. Loeb Classical Library. 4 vols. London: Heinemann; Cambridge, MA: Harvard University Press, 1961.

Ramsay, G. G., ed. *Juvenal and Persius*. Loeb Classics. Cambridge, MA: Harvard University Press, 1961.

Ramsay, P. A., ed. *Rome in the Renaissance: The City and the Myth*. Binghamton, NY: Center for Medieval and Early Renaissance Studies, 1982.

Raspa, Anthony, ed. *Devotions upon Emergent Occasions*. By John Donne. Oxford University Press, 1987.

Rathmell, J. C. A. 'Jonson, Lord Lisle, and Penshurst.' *English Literary Renaissance* 1 (1971): 250–60.

Rebhorn, Wayne. *The Emperor of Men's Minds: Literature and the Renaissance Discourse of Rhetoric*. Ithaca, NY: Cornell University Press, 1985.

Redwine Jr, James D. *Ben Jonson's Literary Criticism*. Lincoln: University of Nebraska Press, 1971.

Revard, Stella P. 'Classicism and Neo-Classicism in Jonson's *Epigrammes* and *The Forrest*.' In *Ben Jonson's 1616 Folio*. Ed. Jennifer Brady and W. H. Herendeen. Newark: University of Delaware Press; London/Toronto: Associated University Presses, 1991. 138–67.

Riddell, James A. and Stanley Stewart. *Jonson's Spenser: Evidence and Historical Criticism*. Pittsburgh: Duquesne University Press, 1995.

Riggs, David. *Ben Jonson: A Life*. Cambridge, MA: Harvard University Press, 1989.

Rist, J. M. *Stoic Philosophy*. 1969. Cambridge University Press, 1977.

Rivers, Isabel. *The Poetry of Conservatism, 1600–1745: A Study of Poets and Public Affairs from Jonson to Pope*. Cambridge: Rivers Press, 1973.

Roberts, George, ed. *The Diary of Walter Yonge, Esq*. Camden Society 41. London, 1848.

Roberts, Josephine A., ed. *The First Part of the Countess of Montgomery's 'Urania'*. Medieval and Renaissance Texts and Studies. Binghamton, NY: Center for Medieval and Early Renaissance Studies, 1995.

The Poems of Lady Mary Wroth. Baton Rouge: Louisiana State University Press, 1983.

Sanders, Julie. *Ben Jonson's Theatrical Republics*. Basingstoke: Macmillan, 1998.

Sanders, Julie, ed., with Kate Chedgzoy and Susan Wiseman. *Refashioning Ben Jonson: Gender, Politics and the Jonsonian Canon*. Basingstoke: Macmillan, 1998.

Sanford, Rhonda Lemke. *Maps and Memory in Early Modern England: A Sense of Place*. New York: Palgrave, 2002.

Scaliger, Julius Caesar. *Poetices Libri Septem*. Lyon, 1561.

Schoenfeldt, Michael C. '"The Mysteries of Manners, Armes, and Arts": "Inviting a Friend to Supper" and "To Penshurst".' In *'The Muses Commonweale': Poetry and Politics in the Seventeenth Century*. Ed. Claude J. Summers and Ted-Larry Pebworth. Columbia: University of Missouri Press, 1988. 62–79.

Schofield, Malcolm. 'Stoic Ethics.' In *The Cambridge Companion to the Stoics*. Ed. Brad Inwood. Cambridge University Press, 2003. 233–56.

Scott, Alison V. *Selfish Gifts: The Politics of Exchange and English Courtly Literature, 1580–1628*. Madison: Fairleigh Dickinson University Press, 2006.

Seneca. *Ad Lucilium Epistulae Morales*. Ed. and trans. R. M. Gummere (1917–25). Loeb Classical Library. 3 vols. Cambridge, MA: Harvard University Press, 1967–71.

Moral Essays. Ed. and trans. John W. Basore (1928–35). Loeb Classical Library. Cambridge, MA: Harvard University Press, 1963–70.

Sharpe, Kevin. *Sir Robert Cotton 1586–1631: History and Politics in Early Modern England*. Oxford University Press, 1979.

Sharpe, Kevin and Peter Lake, eds. *Culture and Politics in Early Stuart England*. Basingstoke: Macmillan, 1994.

Sharpe, Kevin and Steven Zwicker. *Politics of Discourse: The Literature and History of Seventeenth-Century England*. Berkeley: University of California Press, 1987.

Sidney, Philip. *An Apology for Poetry*. Ed. R. W. Maslen. 3rd rev. edn. Manchester University Press, 2002.

Arcadia. Ed. Maurice Evans. Harmondsworth: Penguin, 1977.

The Poems of Sir Philip Sidney. Ed. William A. Ringler, Jr. Oxford: Clarendon Press, 1962.

Sidney, Robert. *The Poems of Robert Sidney edited from the Poet's Autograph Notebook*. Ed. P. J. Croft. Oxford: Clarendon Press, 1984.

Simpson, Evelyn M. *A Study of the Prose Works of John Donne*. Oxford University Press, 1924.

Simpson, Percy. '"Tanquam Explorator": Jonson's Method in the "Discoveries".' *Modern Language Review* 2.3 (1907): 201–10.

Sipiora, Phillip and James S. Baumlin, eds. *Rhetoric and Kairos: Essays in History, Theory, and Praxis*. Albany: State University of New York Press, 2002.

Skinner, Quentin. *The Foundations of Modern Political Thought*. 2 vols. Cambridge University Press, 1978.

Regarding Method. Cambridge University Press, 2002.

Smith, Barbara. *The Women of Ben Jonson's Poetry: Female Representations in the Non-Dramatic Verse*. Aldershot: Scolar Press, 1995.

Smith, Barbara and Ursula Appelt, eds. *Write or Be Written: Early Modern Poets and Cultural Constraints*. Aldershot: Ashgate, 2001.

Smith, James M. 'Effaced History: Facing the Colonial Contexts of Ben Jonson's *Irish Masque at Court*.' *English Literary History* 65.2 (1998): 297–321.

Smith, M. van Wyk. 'John Donne's "Metempsychosis".' *Review of English Studies* 24 (1973): 17–25, 141–52.

Spenser, Edmund. *The Yale Edition of the Shorter Poems of Edmund Spenser*. Ed. William Oram, Einar Bjorvand, and Ronald Bond. New Haven: Yale University Press, 1989.

Strong, Roy. *Henry Prince of Wales and England's Lost Renaissance*. London: Thames and Hudson, 1986.

Summers, Claude J. and Ted-Larry Pebworth. *Ben Jonson Revised*. New York: Twayne, 1999.

Thomson, Elizabeth McClure, ed. *The Chamberlain Letters*. New York: G. P. Putnam's Sons, 1965.

Tuck, Richard. *Philosophy and Government 1572–1651*. Cambridge University Press, 1993.

Tulip, James. 'Comedy as Equivocation: An Approach to the Reference of *Volpone*.' *Southern Review* 5 (1972): 91–101.

   'The Contexts of *Volpone*.' In *Imperfect Apprehensions: Essays in English Literature in Honour of G. A. Wilkes*. Ed. Geoffrey Little. Sydney: Challis Press, 1996. 74–87.

Van den Berg, Sara. *The Action of Ben Jonson's Poetry*. Newark: University of Delaware Press, 1987.

   'Ben Jonson and the Ideology of Authorship.' In *Ben Jonson's 1616 Folio*. Ed. Jennifer Brady and W. H. Herendeen. Newark: University of Delaware Press; London/Toronto: Associated University Presses, 1991. 111–37.

Verstegen, Richard. *A declaration of the true cause of the great troubles, presupposed to be intended against the realme of England*. Antwerp, 1592.

Virgil. *Aeneid*. Trans. H. R. Fairclough. 1918. Rev. edn. Loeb Classical Library. London: Heinemann; Cambridge, MA: Harvard University Press, 2000.

Vitruvius. *The Ten Books of Architecture*. Trans. Morris Hicky Morgan. New York: Dover Publications, 1960.

Vives, Juan Luis. *On Education*. Ed. and trans. Foster Watson. Cambridge University Press, 1913.

Wall, Wendy. *The Imprint of Gender: Authorship and Publication in the English Renaissance*. Ithaca, NY: Cornell University Press, 1993.

Wayne, Dom E. *Penshurst: The Semiotics of Place and the Poetics of History*. Madison: University of Wisconsin Press, 1984.

Weever, John. *Epigrammes in the Oldest Cut, and Newest Fashion*. London: V.S. for Thomas Bushell, 1599.

Wells, Robin Headlam. '"Manhood and Chevalrie": *Corialanus*, Prince Henry, and the Chivalric Revival.' *Review of English Studies* n.s. 51 (2000): 395–422.

Wentersdorf, Karl P. 'Symbol and Meaning in Donne's "Metempsychosis or the Progresse of the Soule".' *Studies in English Literature* 22 (1982): 69–90.

White, Eric Charles. *Kaironomia: On the Will to Invent*. Ithaca, NY: Cornell University Press, 1987.

Wilcox, Helen, ed. *Women and Literature in Britain 1500–1700*. Cambridge University Press, 1996.

Williams, Raymond. *The Country and the City*. New York: Oxford University Press, 1973.

Wilson, Gayle Edward. 'Jonson's Use of the Bible and the Great Chain of Being in "To Penshurst".' *Studies in English Literature* 8 (1968): 77–89.

Wiltenburg, Robert. *Ben Jonson and Self-Love: The Subtlest Maze of All*. Columbia: University of Missouri Press, 1990.

Wind, Edgar. *Pagan Mysteries in the Renaissance*. Rev. edn. Harmondsworth: Penguin, 1967.

Worden, Blair. 'Ben Jonson Among the Historians.' In *Culture and Politics in Early Stuart England*. Ed. K. Sharpe and P. Lake. Basingstoke: Macmillan, 1994. 67–90.

'Politics in *Catiline*: Jonson and His Sources.' In *Re-Presenting Ben Jonson: Text, History, Performance*. Ed. Martin Butler. Basingstoke: Macmillan, 1999. 152–73.

Zunder, William and Suzanne Trills, eds. *Writing and the English Renaissance*. London: Longman, 1996.

Index